yt8
27.7.05

Remediation

The MIT Press   Cambridge, Massachusetts   London, England

Jay David Bolter and Richard Grusin

Remediation

Understanding New Media

First MIT Press paperback edition, 2000
© 1999 Jay David Bolter and Richard Grusin

This book was set in Garamond 3, ITC Goudy Sans, Snell Roundhand, DIN, Stone Sans bold by Graphic Composition, Inc. and was printed and bound in the United States of America.

Library of Congress Cataloging-in-Publication Data

Bolter, J. David, 1951–
    Remediation / Jay David Bolter and Richard Grusin.
        p.   cm.
    Includes bibliographical references and index.
    ISBN 0-262-02452-7 (hardcover : alk. paper), 0-262-52279-9 (pb)
        1. Mass media—Technological innovations.
    I. Grusin, Richard. II. Title.
    P96.T42B59   1998
    302.2223—dc21   98-25672
                                                                                    CIP

10 9 8 7 6

To our families

Christine and David
Ann, Sarah, and Sam

Contents

Like remediation itself, this book has its own genealogy. And like the genealogy of remediation, our book's genealogy is one of historical affiliations or resonances, not of origins. In examining these affiliations, we would begin by noticing "the myriad events through which—thanks to which, against which—they were formed" (Foucault 1977, 146). Indeed, the initial affiliation was our own, which began on the January evening in 1991 when President George Bush ordered the bombing campaign for what has been characterized as the first totally mediated war.

We could also trace the book's descent to the resonances set in motion in September 1994, when one of us (JDB) decided to sit in on the graduate seminar the other (RG) was offering: "The Visual Genealogy of Multimedia." Each of us brought to that course the conception of one of the three genealogical traits that our book traces: JDB the trait of immediacy, which he was beginning to outline in a project whose earliest manifestation appeared on the Internet under the name of "Degrees of Freedom"; RG the trait of hypermediacy, which (operating under the name of multimediacy) provided the organizing logic of the seminar. Remediation itself was our third trait.

We might more precisely trace the book's beginnings to May 1996, when we were completing our first truly collaborative venture, a team-taught version of the original genealogy seminar, in which the contradiction between immediacy and multimediacy formed the organizing principle of the course. It was in May 1996, in a meeting in his office with Sandra Beaudin, that RG was reported to have coined the term *remediation* as a way to complicate the notion of "repurposing" that Beaudin was working with for her class project. But, as most origin stories go, it was not until well after the fact, when Beaudin reported the coinage to JDB, who later reminded RG that he had coined the term, that the concept of "remediation" could be said to have emerged. Indeed although the term *remediation* was coined in RG's office, neither of us really knew what it meant until we had worked out together the double logic of immediacy and hypermediacy.

If *remediation* can be traced to that fateful day in May, the book itself, as a jointly authored collaboration, has its own lineage. The idea of collaborating on an essay was set in play in 1994, during the first genealogy seminar (which ended up being more or less team-taught itself). Almost from the first class meeting, we realized that between us we had grasped something exponentially more powerful than what either of us brought to the table. For more than eighteen months, we took turns telling each other that we should collaborate on an essay. We passed each other in the hall; we sat in one another's office; we chatted in the faculty lounge or before and after department meetings and lectures. But our daily obligations prevented us from seriously undertaking the project that would eventually become this book. Indeed it was not until the Olympic summer of 1996, when RG was about to embark on a trip to Oxford, to teach in a Georgia Tech summer-abroad program, that the decision to collaborate on an essay was finally made.

It is hardly accidental to the thesis of this book that it was only when we found ourselves on either side of the Atlantic Ocean, communicating with each other through the medium of email, that we were able finally to undertake the collaboration we had been discussing for more than a year. In what was in many senses a reversal of roles, RG found himself traveling through Europe, thinking through the histories of Western art from the medieval period to the present; while JDB was at home in Atlanta, watching the Olympics on TV, thinking through the relations among contemporary media, sports, and the culture of entertainment.

The genealogy of the book is well documented through that summer's emails: as multimediacy evolved into hypermediacy; as the initial idea for an essay (which was published in the fall 1996 issue of *Configurations*) evolved into our plan for a book; and as we began to work through the way in which the concept of remediation helped to make sense of the apparent contradiction between our two logics of mediation. What is also well documented in those emails is the evolution of a mutual friendship and trust, a growing respect and admiration between two very different (indeed in many basic senses opposite) individuals. If we are right in characterizing remediation as reform, then it would be fair to say that among those things that *Remediation* reformed were ourselves.

We wish to acknowledge here the encouragement and thoughtful critiques that we received from colleagues and friends.

Those with whom we have shared our ideas include Gregory Abowd, Amy Bruckman, Matthew Causey, Sandra Corse, Stuart Culver, Mark Guzdial, N. Katherine Hayles, Henry Jenkins, John Johnston, Dalia Judovitz, Alan Kay, Wendy Kellogg, Irene Klaver, Ken Knoespel, George Landow, Candace Lang, Elissa Marder, Robert Markley, Pete McGuire, Rebecca Merrens, Jacob Nielsen, Greg Nobles, Claire Nouvet, Cíaran O'Faoláin, David Porush, Ashwin Ram, Alan Rauch,

William Ribarsky, Ben Schneiderman, Ian Smith, Ellen Strain, Laura Sullivan, Jay Telotte, Bruce Tognazzini, John Tolva, and Greg VanHoosier-Carey.

Those who commented on various portions of the manuscript, and from whose counsel we benefited, include Phil Auslander, Hugh Crawford, Terry Harpold, Howard Horwitz, Michael Joyce, Richard Lanham, Blake Leland, and Anne Wysocki.

Jim Bono and Kathy Onofrio worked with us on the original essay, "Remediation," which appeared in *Configurations* 3 (Fall 1996): 311–358. We thank them and the journal for allowing us to refashion (if not remediate) material in chapters 1 through 3 of this book.

We thank Lance Strate, Ron Jacobson, and Stephanie Gibson, and the Hampton Press for allowing us to reuse in chapters 15 and 16 of this book material from JDB's "Virtual Reality and the Redefinition of Self" originally published in 1996 in *Communication and Cyberspace: Social Interaction in an Electronic Environment.*

We wish to thank Robert Prior of The MIT Press for his indispensable advice and support. Thanks also to Managing Editor Michael Sims and to those at The MIT Press who put their expertise and enthusiasm into the editing, design, production, and marketing of this book: Julie Grimaldi, Yasuyo Iguchi, Vicki Jennings, Ori Kometani, Terry Lamoureux, Thomas McCorkle, Gita Manaktala, Bev Miller, and Sandra Minkkinen.

Like all other teachers, we have learned much from our students, in particular, those in the graduate program in Information Design and Technology of the School of Literature, Communication, and Culture here at Georgia Tech. Since 1994 we have offered three graduate seminars in the genealogy of new media. In each case, the students in these courses have helped us define and refine our ideas. Also during this period, Kelly Balcom, Rhonda Nelson, Aida Najarian, and Vicky Pickens served as intelligent and enthuasistic research assistants and made a real contribution to the research and production of this book. Our students Michael Koetter, Debbi Faye Levin, and Ian Seymour produced the first *Remediation* video.

David Joseph Bolter provided helpful information on the remediating strategies of animated film. Sarah and Sam Grusin offered important lessons on the inseparability of mediation and reality.

We cannot exaggerate the contribution made by Lori Levy, who took on the important task of helping us locate, interpret, and present the various graphic images that appear in this book. To this task, she brought her fine graphic and computer skills, as well as her aesthetic and critical judgment and her extraordinary energy and dedication. Without her, this book would not have the visual documentation that it needs and would certainly not have been published on schedule.

Our colleague and friend Anne Balsamo proved to be our most dedicated reader. She devoted many hours to a patient and yet critical analysis of portions of the manuscript—in particular, those sections in which we deal with the gender implications of remediation. As a result of her insightful suggestions, these sections have been vastly improved. If our text remains in some ways insensitive or incomplete in its treatment of these issues, the failings are in part due to our inability fully to appreciate and respond to her critique.

Atlanta, Georgia
February 1, 1998

Introduction: The Double Logic of Remediation

"This is not like TV only better," says Lenny Nero in the futuristic film *Strange Days*. "This is life. It's a piece of somebody's life. Pure and uncut, straight from the cerebral cortex. You're there. You're doing it, seeing it, hearing it . . . feeling it." Lenny is touting to a potential customer a technological wonder called "the wire." When the user places the device over her head, its sensors make contact with the perceptual centers in her brain. In its recording mode, the wire captures the sense perceptions of the wearer; in its playback mode, it delivers these recorded perceptions to the wearer. If the ultimate purpose of media is indeed to transfer sense experiences from one person to another, the wire threatens to make all media obsolete. Lenny mentions television, but the same critique would seem to apply to books, paintings, photographs, film, and so on. The wire bypasses all forms of mediation and transmits directly from one consciousness to another.

The film *Strange Days* is less enthusiastic about the wire than Lenny and his customers. Although the wire embodies the desire to get beyond mediation, *Strange Days* offers us a world fascinated by the power and ubiquity of media technologies. Los Angeles in the last two days of 1999, on the eve of "2K," is saturated with cellular phones, voice- and text-based telephone answering systems, radios, and bill-board–sized television screens that constitute public media spaces. In this media-filled world, the wire itself is the ultimate mediating technology, despite—or indeed because of—the fact that the wire is designed to efface itself, to disappear from the user's consciousness. When Lenny coaches the "actors" who will appear in a pornographic recording, it becomes clear that the experience the wire offers can be as contrived as a traditional film. Although Lenny insists that the wire is

Figure I.1 A virtual reality head-mounted display. Courtesy of Professor Larry Hodges, GVU Center, Georgia Institute of Technology.

"not TV only better," the film ends up representing the wire as "film only better." When Lenny himself puts on the wire and closes his eyes, he experiences the world in a continuous, first-person point-of-view shot, which in film criticism is called the "subjective camera."

Strange Days captures the ambivalent and contradictory ways in which new digital media function for our culture today. The film projects our own cultural moment a few years into the future in order to examine that moment with greater clarity. The wire is just a fanciful extrapolation of contemporary virtual reality, with its goal of unmediated visual experience. The contemporary head-mounted display of virtual reality is considerably less comfortable and fashionable (fig. I.1), and the visual world it generates is far less compelling. Still, contemporary virtual reality is, like the wire in *Strange Days*, an experiment in cinematic point of view. Meanwhile, the proliferation of media in 2K L.A. is only a slight exaggeration of our current media-rich environment, in which digital technologies are proliferating faster than our cultural, legal, or educational institutions can keep up with them. In addressing our culture's contradictory imperatives for immediacy and hypermediacy, this film demonstrates what we call a double logic of *remediation.* Our culture wants both to multiply its media and to erase all traces of mediation: ideally, it wants to erase its media in the very act of multiplying them.

In this last decade of the twentieth century, we are in an unusual position to appreciate remediation, because of the rapid development of new digital media and the nearly as rapid response by traditional media. Older electronic and print media are seeking to reaffirm their status within our culture as digital media challenge that status. Both new and old media are invoking the twin logics of immediacy and hypermediacy in their efforts to remake themselves and each other. To fulfill our apparently insatiable desire for immediacy, "live" point-of-view television programs show viewers what it is like to accompany a police officer on a dangerous raid or to be a skydiver or a race car driver hurtling through space. Filmmakers routinely spend tens of millions of dollars to film on location or to recreate period costumes and places in order to make their viewers feel as if they were "really" there. "Webcams" on the Internet pretend to locate us in various natural environments—from a backyard bird feeder in Indianapolis (Fig. I.2) to a panorama in the Canadian Rockies (Fig. I.3). In all these cases, the logic

Figure I.2 Bird feeder webcam: the view is updated every three minutes. http://www.wbu.com/feedercam_home.htm January 24, 1998.
© 1997, Wild Birds Unlimited. All rights reserved. Used by permission.

Figure I.3 Sulphur Mountain web-cam, providing a repeatedly updated view of a mountain in the Canadian Rockies in Banff, Alberta. http://www.banffgondola.com/ January 24, 1998. © 1998, Sulphur Mountain Gondola. All rights reserved. Used by permission.

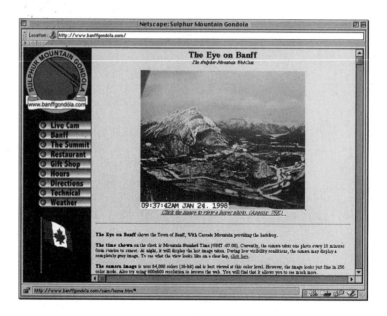

of immediacy dictates that the medium itself should disappear and leave us in the presence of the thing represented: sitting in the race car or standing on a mountaintop.

Yet these same old and new media often refuse to leave us alone. Many web sites are riots of diverse media forms—graphics, digitized photographs, animation, and video—all set up in pages whose graphic design principles recall the psychedelic 1960s or dada in the 1910s and 1920s (Fig. I.4; Fig. I.5). Hollywood films, such as *Natural Born Killers* and *Strange Days*, mix media and styles unabashedly. Televised news programs feature multiple video streams, split-screen displays, composites of graphics and text—a welter of media that is somehow meant to make the news more perspicuous. Even webcams, which operate under the logic of immediacy, can be embedded in a hypermediated web site (Fig. I.6), where the user can select from a "jukebox" of webcam images to generate her own paneled display.

As the webcam jukebox shows, our two seemingly contradictory logics not only coexist in digital media today but are mutually dependent. Immediacy depends on hypermediacy. In the effort to create a seamless moving image, filmmakers combine live-action footage with computer compositing and two- and three-dimensional computer graphics. In the effort to be up to the minute and complete, television

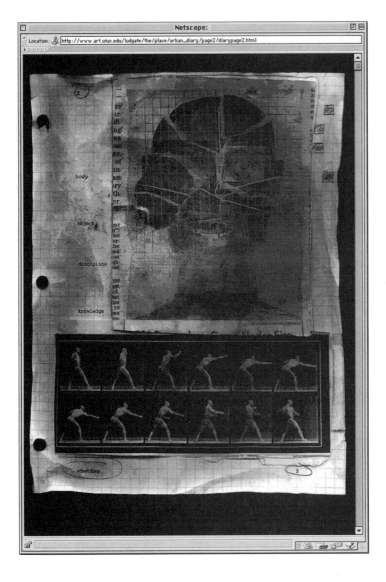

Figure I.4 A page from Joseph Squire's *Urban Diary.* http://gertrude.art.uiuc.edu/ludgate/the/place/urban_diary/intro.html January 24, 1998. © 1995 Urban Desires. Used by permission.

Figure I.5 An image from the RGB Gallery at the Hotwired web site: a collection of digital art. http://www.hotwired.com/rgb/opp/ +++++++++++++++++++++ January 24, 1998. © 1994–1998 Wired Digital, Inc. All rights reserved.

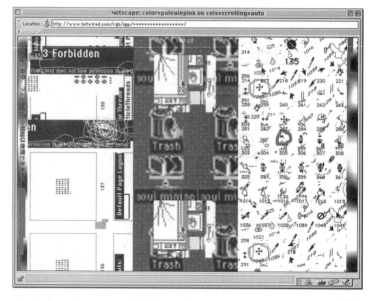

Figure I.6 This webcam jukebox allows the user to combine three individual webcams of her choosing. http://wct.images.com/jukebox January 29, 1998. © 1998, Kamal A. Mostafa. All rights reserved. Used by permission.

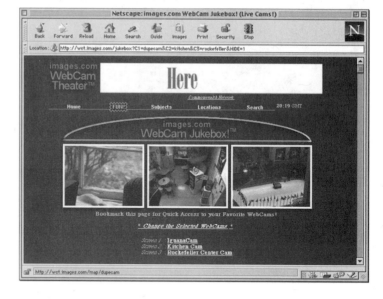

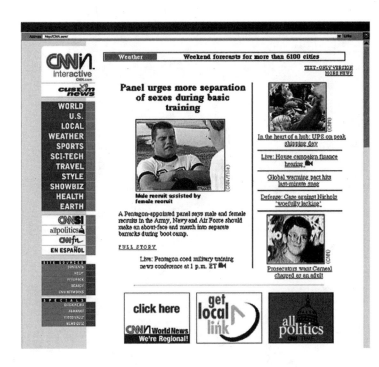

news producers assemble on the screen ribbons of text, photographs, graphics, and even audio without a video signal when necessary (as was the case during the Persian Gulf War). At the same time, even the most hypermediated productions strive for their own brand of immediacy. Directors of music videos rely on multiple media and elaborate editing to create an immediate and apparently spontaneous style; they take great pains to achieve the sense of "liveness" that characterizes rock music. The desire for immediacy leads digital media to borrow avidly from each other as well as from their analog predecessors such as film, television, and photography. Whenever one medium seems to have convinced viewers of its immediacy, other media try to appropriate that conviction. The CNN site is hypermediated—arranging text, graphics, and video in multiple panes and windows and joining them with numerous hyperlinks; yet the web site borrows its sense of immediacy from the televised CNN newscasts. At the same time televised newcasts are coming to resemble web pages in their hypermediacy (fig. I.7 and I.8). The team of web editors and designers, working in the same building in Atlanta from which the television news networks are also administered, clearly want their technology to be "television only better." Similarly,

Figure I.8 CNN Headline News.
© 1997 Cable News Network, Inc.
All rights reserved.

Figure I.9 Photorealistic Piper Sen-
eca III Module: the interface for a
flight simulator. © 1998 Initiative
Computing AG, Switzerland. Reprinted with permission.

Figure I.10 Saenredam, Pieter Jansz. "S. Bavo in Haarlem" 1631. The John G. Johnson Collection, Philadelphia Museum of Art. Used by permission.

one of the most popular genres of computer games is the flight simulator (fig. I.9). The action unfolds in real time, as the player is required to monitor the instruments and fly the plane. The game promises to show the player "what it is like to be" a pilot, and yet in what does the immediacy of the experience consist? As in a real plane, the simulated cockpit is full of dials to read and switches to flip. As in a real plane, the experience of the game is that of working an interface, so that the immediacy of this experience is pure hypermediacy.

Remediation did not begin with the introduction of digital media. We can identify the same process throughout the last several hundred years of Western visual representation. A painting by the seventeenth-century artist Pieter Saenredam, a photograph by Edward Weston, and a computer system for virtual reality are different in many important ways, but they are all attempts to achieve immediacy by ignoring or denying the presence of the medium and the act of mediation. All of them seek to put the viewer in the same space as the objects viewed. The illusionistic painter employs linear perspective and "realistic" lighting (fig. I.10), while the computer graphics specialist mathematizes linear perspective and creates "models" of shading and illumination (fig. I.11; plate 1). Furthermore, the goal of the computer graphics specialists is to do as well as, and eventually better than, the painter or even the photographer.

Figure I.11 A photorealistic computer graphic: the nave of Chartres Cathedral, by John Wallace and John Lin. © 1989, Hewlett-Packard Co. Used by permission.

Like immediacy, hypermediacy also has its history. A medieval illuminated manuscript, a seventeenth-century painting by David Bailly, and a buttoned and windowed multimedia application are all expressions of a fascination with media. In medieval manuscripts, the large initial capital letters may be elaborately decorated, but they still constitute part of the text itself, and we are challenged to appreciate the integration of text and image (fig. I.12; plate 2). In many multimedia applications, icons and graphics perform the same dual role (as in figure I.13; plate 3), in which the images peek out at us through the word ARKANSAS. This dual role has a history in popular graphic design, as a

Figure I.12 A page from a Book of Hours, circa 1450. © Robert W. Woodruff Library, Emory University. Used by permission.

Figure I.13 Arkansas: the splash (opening) screen for a multimedia celebration of the state.

Figure I.14 A Coney Island post-card from the 1910s. http://naid.sppsr.ucla.edu/coneyisland/histart.htm January 24, 1998.

postcard of Coney Island from the early twentieth-century shows (fig. I.14). Today as in the past, designers of hypermediated forms ask us to take pleasure in the act of mediation, and even our popular culture does take pleasure. Some hypermediated art has been and remains an elite taste, but the elaborate stage productions of many rock stars are among many examples of hypermediated events that appeal to millions.

In the chapters that follow, we examine the process of remediation in contemporary media. In part I, we place the concept of remediation within the traditions of recent literary and cultural theory. Readers who are less interested in theory may want to turn directly to part II, which illustrates the work of remediation in such media as computer graphics, film, television, the World Wide Web, and virtual reality. These illustrative chapters should make sense even without the fuller explanations of transparent immediacy, hypermediacy, and remediation provided in part I. In part III, which is again more theoretical, we consider how new digital media are participating in our culture's redefinition of self. Because readers may choose not to read the book in linear order, we have provided references—the printed equivalent of hyperlinks—to connect points made in the theoretical chapters with examples in the illustrative chapters, as well as some references from each illustrative chapter to others. This link directs the reader to part II. ⊙ **p. 85**

Our primary concern will be with visual technologies, such as computer graphics and the World Wide Web. We will argue that these new media are doing exactly what their predecessors have done: presenting themselves as refashioned and improved versions of other media. Digital visual media can best be understood through the ways in which they honor, rival, and revise linear-perspective painting, photography, film, television, and print. No medium today, and certainly no single media event, seems to do its cultural work in isolation from other media, any more than it works in isolation from other social and economic forces. What is new about new media comes from the particular ways in which they refashion older media and the ways in which older media refashion themselves to answer the challenges of new media.

In part I we explain in greater detail the theory and history of remediation. Like other media since the Renaissance—in particular, perspective painting, photography, film, and television—new digital media oscillate between immediacy and hypermediacy, between transparency and opacity. This oscillation is the key to understanding how a medium refashions its predecessors and other contemporary media. Although each medium promises to reform its predecessors by offering a more immediate or authentic experience, the promise of reform inevitably leads us to become aware of the new medium as a medium. Thus, immediacy leads to hypermediacy. The process of remediation makes us aware that all media are at one level a "play of signs," which is a lesson that we take from poststructuralist literary theory. At the same time, this process insists on the real, effective presence of media in our culture. Media have the same claim to reality as more tangible cultural artifacts; photographs, films, and computer applications are as real as airplanes and buildings.

Futhermore, media technologies constitute networks or hybrids that can be expressed in physical, social, aesthetic, and economic terms. Introducing a new media technology does not mean simply inventing new hardware and software, but rather fashioning (or refashioning) such a network. The World Wide Web is not merely a software protocol and text and data files. It is also the sum of the uses to which this protocol is now being put: for marketing and advertising, scholarship, personal expression, and so on. These uses are as much a part of the technology as the software itself. For this reason, we can say that media technologies are agents in our culture without falling into the trap of technological determinism. New digital media are not external agents that come to disrupt an unsuspecting culture. They emerge from within cultural contexts, and they refashion other media, which are embedded in the same or similar contexts.

The two logics of remediation have a long history, for their interplay defines a genealogy that dates back at least to the Renaissance and the invention of linear perspective. We do not claim that immediacy, hypermediacy, and remediation are universal aesthetic truths; rather, we regard them as practices of specific groups in specific times.[1] Although the logic of immediacy has manifested itself from the Renaissance to the present day, each manifestation in each age may be significantly different, and immediacy may mean one thing to theorists, another to practicing artists or designers, and a third to viewers. The diversity is even greater for hypermediacy, which seems always to offer a number of different reactions to the contemporary logic of immediacy. Remediation always operates under the current cultural assumptions about immediacy and hypermediacy.

We cannot hope to explore the genealogy of remediation in detail. What concerns us is remediation in our current media in North America, and here we can analyze specific images, texts, and uses. The historical resonances (to Renaissance painting, nineteenth-century photography, twentieth-century film, and so on) will be offered to help explain the contemporary situation. At the same time, the practices of contemporary media constitute a lens through which we can view the history of remediation. What we wish to highlight from the past is what resonates with the twin preoccupations of contemporary media: the transparent presentation of the real and the enjoyment of the opacity of media themselves.

THE LOGIC OF TRANSPARENT IMMEDIACY

Virtual reality is immersive, which means that it is a medium whose purpose is to disappear. This disappearing act, however, is made diffi-

1. Our notion of genealogy is indebted to Foucault's, for we too are looking for historical affiliations or resonances and not for origins. Foucault (1977) characterized genealogy as "an examination of descent," which "permits the discovery, under the unique aspect of a trait or a concept, of the myriad events through which—thanks to which, against which—they were formed" (146). Our genealogical traits will be immediacy, hypermediacy, and remediation; however, where Foucault was concerned with relations of power, our proposed genealogy is defined by the formal relations within and among media as well as by relations of cultural power and prestige.

cult by the apparatus that virtual reality requires. In *Strange Days*, users of the wire had only to put on a slender skullcap, but in today's virtual reality systems, the viewer must wear a bulky head-mounted display, a helmet with eyepieces for each eye (fig. I.1). In other systems known as "caves," the walls (and sometimes the floor and ceiling) are themselves giant computer screens. Although less subtle than the wire, current virtual reality systems also surround the viewer with a computer-generated image. With the head-mounted display in particular, virtual reality is literally "in the viewer's face." The viewer is given a first-person point of view, as she gazes on a graphic world from a station point that is always the visual center of that world. As computer scientists themselves put it, the goal of virtual reality is to foster in the viewer a sense of presence: the viewer should forget that she is in fact wearing a computer interface and accept the graphic image that it offers as her own visual world (Hodges et al. 1994).

In order to create a sense of presence, virtual reality should come as close as possible to our daily visual experience. Its graphic space should be continuous and full of objects and should fill the viewer's field of vision without rupture. But today's technology still contains many ruptures: slow frame rates, jagged graphics, bright colors, bland lighting, and system crashes. Some of these ruptures are apparent even in the single static images that we see, for example, in figures 9.1, 9.2, and 9.3. We notice immediately the cartoon-like simplicity of the scene, which no user could confuse with the world that greets her when she takes off the helmet. For the enthusiasts of virtual reality, however, today's technological limitations simply point to its great potential, which for them lies in a future not much further removed than *Strange Days*. In fact, Lenny Nero's words could almost have been written by these enthusiasts. In his book on virtual reality, Howard Rheingold (1991) claims that "at the heart of VR [virtual reality] is an experience—the experience of being in a virtual world or remote location" (46). Jaron Lanier, a developer of one of the first commercial virtual reality systems, suggests that in virtual reality "you can visit the world of the dinosaur, then become a Tyrannosaurus. Not only can you see DNA, you can experience what it's like to be a molecule" (quoted in Ditlea 1989, 97). Meredith Bricken (1991), an interface designer, writes that in a virtual environment, "You can be the mad hatter or you can be the teapot; you can move back and forth to the rhythm of a song. You can be a tiny droplet in the rain or in the river" (372). All of these enthusiasts promise us transparent, perceptual immediacy, experience without mediation, for they expect virtual reality to diminish and ultimately to deny the mediating presence of the computer and its interface. Bricken's work is, in fact, entitled "Virtual Worlds: No Interface to Design."

The logic of transparent immediacy is also at work in nonimmersive digital graphics—that is, in two- and three-dimensional images projected on to traditional computer, film, or television screens. Digital graphics have become tremendously popular and lucrative and in fact are leading to a new cultural definition of the computer. If even ten years ago we thought of computers exclusively as numerical engines and word processors, we now think of them also as devices for generating images, reworking photographs, holding videoconferences, and providing animation and special effects for film and television. With these new applications, the desire for immediacy is apparent in claims that digital images are more exciting, lively, and realistic than mere text on a computer screen and that a videoconference will lead to more effective communication than a telephone call. The desire for immediacy is apparent in the increasing popularity of the digital compositing of film and in Hollywood's interest in replacing stunt men and eventually even actors with computer animations. And it is apparent in the triumph of the graphical user interface (GUI) for personal computers. The desktop metaphor, which has replaced the wholly textual command-line interface, is supposed to assimilate the computer to the physical desktop and to the materials (file folders, sheets of paper, inbox, trash basket, etc.) familiar to office workers. The mouse and the pen-based interface allow the user the immediacy of touching, dragging, and manipulating visually attractive ideograms. Immediacy is supposed to make this computer interface "natural" rather than arbitrary. And although the standard desktop interface has been two-dimensional, designers are experimenting with three-dimensional versions—virtual spaces in which the user can move in, around, and through information (Card, Robertson, and Macinlay 1991). These three-dimensional views are meant to lend even greater immediacy to the experience of computing. What designers often say they want is an "interfaceless" interface, in which there will be no recognizable electronic tools—no buttons, windows, scroll bars, or even icons as such. Instead the user will move through the space interacting with the objects "naturally," as she does in the physical world. Virtual reality, three-dimensional graphics, and graphical interface design are all seeking to make digital technology "transparent." In this sense, a transparent interface would be one that erases itself, so that the user is no longer aware of confronting a medium, but instead stands in an immediate relationship to the contents of that medium.

The transparent interface is one more manifestation of the need to deny the mediated character of digital technology altogether. To believe that with digital technology we have passed beyond mediation is also to assert the uniqueness of our present technological moment. For many virtual reality enthusiasts, the computer so far surpasses other technologies in its power to make the world present that the history of earlier media has little relevance. Even those, like Rheingold, who do acknowledge technological precursors (particularly film and television) still emphasize the novelty of virtual reality. Their view is that virtual reality (or digital technology in general) completes and overcomes the history of media. In *Strange Days,* the wire is the last and most powerful technology created before the end of the millennium. However, the desire for immediacy itself has a history that is not easily overcome. At least since the Renaissance, it has been a defining feature of Western visual (and for that matter verbal) representation. To understand immediacy in computer graphics, it is important to keep in mind the ways in which painting, photography, film, and television have sought to satisfy this same desire. These earlier media sought immediacy through the interplay of the aesthetic value of transparency with techniques of linear perspective, erasure, and automaticity, all of which are strategies also at work in digital technology.

As Albrecht Dürer noted, and as Panofsky (1991) reminded us in *Perspective as Symbolic Form* (27), *perspective* means a "seeing through," and, like the interface designers of today, students of linear perspective promised immediacy through transparency. They trusted in linear perspective to achieve transparency because by mathematizing space, it used the "right" technique to measure the world. Martin Jay and others have argued for a close connection between Albertian perspective and Descartes's spatial mathematics. For Jay (1988), "Cartesian perspectivalism" constituted a peculiar way of seeing that dominated Western culture from the seventeenth century to the early twentieth by allowing the Cartesian subject to control space from a single vantage point.[2] By using projective geometry to represent the space beyond the canvas, linear perspective could be regarded as the technique that effaced itself as technique. As Alberti (1972) expressed it in his treatise *On Painting,* "On the surface on which I am going to paint, I draw a rectangle of whatever size I want, which I regard as an open window through which

2. See also Martin Jay (1993, 69–82). Unlike Jay, Samuel Edgerton (1975) not only documents a connection between the mathematization of space and linear perspective, but seems to accept it as true. Bruno Latour (1990) also remarks on the significance of perspectivalism. Building on William Ivins's study, *On the Rationalization of Sight* (1973), Latour argues that by mathematizing space, linear perspective enabled visual representations to be transported from one context to another without being altered or distorted. By manipulating these "immutable mobiles," practitioners of linear perspective could in effect manipulate the world itself, because the mathematization of space makes the context or medium transparent and provides immediate access to the world. See Latour (1987, chap. 6, 1990).

the subject to be painted is seen"(55). If executed properly, the surface of the painting dissolved and presented to the viewer the scene beyond. To achieve transparency, however, linear perspective was regarded as necessary but not sufficient, for the artist must also work the surface to erase his brush strokes. Norman Bryson (1983) has argued that "through much of the Western tradition oil paint is treated primarily as an *erasive* medium. What it must first erase is the surface of the picture-plane" (92). Erasing the surface in this way concealed and denied the process of painting in favor of the perfected product. Although effacement is by no means universal in Western painting, even before the nineteenth century, it was one important technique for making the space of the picture continuous with the viewer's space. This continuity between depicted and "real" space was particularly apparent in trompe l'oeil art—for example, in ceilings where the painting continues the architecture of the building itself (Kemp 1990). The irony is that it was hard work to make the surface disappear in this fashion, and in fact the artist's success at effacing his process, and thereby himself, became for trained viewers a mark of his skill and therefore his presence.

A third strategy for achieving transparency has been to automate the technique of linear perspective. This quality of automaticity has been ascribed to the technology of the camera obscura and subsequently to photography, film, and television. In the most familiar story of the development of Western representation, the invention of photography represented the perfection of linear perspective. (For a revisionist view, see Crary 1990.) A photograph could be regarded as a perfect Albertian window. André Bazin (1980) expressed this view with untroubled certainty: "The decisive moment [in Western painting] undoubtedly came with the discovery of the first scientific and already, in a sense, mechanical systems of reproduction, namely, perspective: the camera obscura of da Vinci foreshadowed the camera of Niepce. The artist was now in a position to create the illusion of three-dimensional space within which things appeared to exist as our eyes in reality see them" (239). Photography was a mechanical and chemical process, whose automatic character seemed to many to complete the earlier trend to conceal both the process and the artist. In fact, photography was often regarded as going too far in the direction of concealing the artist by eliminating him altogether. In the nineteenth and early twentieth centuries, this question was extensively debated. Was photography an art? Did it make painting and painters unnecessary? And so on (Trachtenberg 1980, vii–xiii). In examining automatic reproduction and the artist as a creative agent, Stanley Cavell (1979) expanded on and revised Bazin: "Photography overcame subjectivity in a way undreamed of by painting, a way that could not satisfy painting, one which does not so much defeat the act of painting as escape it altogether: by automatism, by removing the human agent from the task of reproduction" (23). For both Bazin and Cavell, photography offered its own route to immediacy. The photograph was transparent and followed the rules of linear perspective; it achieved transparency through automatic reproduction; and it apparently removed the artist as an agent who stood between the viewer and the reality of the image.[3]

Bazin (1980) concluded that "photography and the cinema . . . are discoveries that satisfy, once and for all and in its very essence, our obsession with realism," yet he was certainly wrong. These two visual technologies did not satisfy our culture's desire for immediacy (240). Computer graphics has become the latest expression of that desire, and its strategy for achieving immediacy owes something to several earlier traditions. William J. Mitchell (1994) claims, "The tale of computer image synthesis in the 1970s and 1980s . . . strikingly recapitulates the history of European painting from the miracle of Masaccio's *Trinity* to the birth of photography. . . . Synthesized images can now be virtually point-for-point matches to photographs of actual scenes, and there is experimental evidence that, for certain sorts of scenes, observers cannot distinguish these images from photographs" (161). But even if we cannot always tell synthesized images from photographs, we can distinguish the different strategies that painting and photography have adopted in striving for immediacy, and we can explore how digital graphics borrows and adapts each of these strategies.

Digital graphics extends the tradition of the Albertian window. It creates images in perspective, but it applies to perspective the rigor of contemporary linear algebra and projective geometry (Foley et al. 1996, 229–283). Computer-generated projective images are mathematically perfect, at least within the limits of computational error and the resolution of the pixelated screen. Renaissance perspective was never perfect in this sense, not only because of hand methods, but also because the artists often manipulated the perspective for dramatic or allegorical effect (Elkins 1994; Kemp 1990, 20, 47–49; Hagen 1986). (Of course, digital graphic perspective can be distorted too, but even these distortions are generated mathematically.) Computer graphics also expresses color, illumination, and shading in mathematical terms (Foley et al. 1996, 563–604, 721–814), although so far less success-

3. A similar argument could be made for television, especially for the "live" coverage of news and sporting events, which promise immediacy through their real-time presentation. In "The Fact of Television," Stanley Cavell has described what he calls the "monitoring" function of television. The case for immediacy in film is complicated by the intervention of the director and the editor, but film is still experienced as immediate during the time of its showing—an immediacy that greatly troubled Christian Metz (1977).

fully than perspective. So, as with perspective painting, when computer graphics lays claim to the real or the natural, it seems to be appealing to the Cartesian or Galilean proposition that mathematics is appropriate for describing nature.

Furthermore, to Cartesian geometry computer graphics adds the algorithmic mathematics of John von Neumann and Alan Turing. Computer programs may ultimately be human products, in the sense that they embody algorithms devised by human programmers, but once the program is written and loaded, the machine can operate without human intervention. Programming, then, employs erasure or effacement, much as Norman Bryson defines erasure for Western painting, or as Cavell and others describe the erasure of human agency from the production of photographs.[4] Programmers seek to remove the traces of their presence in order to give the program the greatest possible autonomy. In digital graphics, human programmers may be involved at several levels. The computer operating systems are written by one group of specialists; graphics languages, such as Open GL, are written by others; and applications are programs that exploit the resources offered by languages and operating systems. All of these classes of programmers are simultaneously erased at the moment in which the computer actually generates an image by executing the instructions they have collectively written.

The fact that digital graphics is automatic suggests an affinity to photography. In both cases, the human agent is erased, although the techniques of erasure are rather different. With photography, the automatic process is mechanical and chemical. The shutter opens, and light streams in through the lens and is focused on a chemical film. The process of recording itself is holistic, with no clearly defined parts or steps. For this reason, many in the nineteenth century could regard light or nature itself as the painter. Talbot did so in his book *The Pencil of Nature* (1969), and Niepce did as well, when he wrote that "the Daguerrotype is not merely an instrument which serves to draw Nature; on the contrary it is a chemical and physical process which gives her the power to reproduce herself" (Trachtenberg 1980, 13; see also Jussim 1983, 50). In digital graphics, however, it is not easy to regard the program as a natural product, except in the sense that nature steers the electrons inside the computer chips. Digital graphic images are the work of humans, whose agency, however, is often deferred so far from the act of drawing that it seems to disappear. This deferral is especially important in real-time animation and virtual reality, where the computer is draw-

4. Computer graphics, representational painting, and traditional photography efface the visible signs of agency; an American abstract artist like Rauschenberg, however, seeks to efface the act of erasure itself. (See Fisher 1991, 98–99.)

ing ten or twenty frames per second, all without the programmer's intervention. The automatic or deferred quality of computer programming promotes in the viewer a sense of immediate contact with the image.

Experts on computer graphics often say that they are striving to achieve "photorealism"—in other words, to make their synthetic images indistinguishable from photographs. ⊘ **p. 119** This comparison may take the explicit form of putting a photograph side by side with a synthetic digital image. In such cases the computer is imitating not an external reality but rather another medium. (We argue later that this is all *any* new technology could do: define itself in relationship to earlier technologies of representation.) To achieve photorealism, the synthetic digital image adopts the criteria of the photograph. It offers a single station point, a monocular point of view, and a photographic sense of appropriate composition. Computer graphics experts do not in general imitate "poor" or "distorted" photographs (exotic camera angles or lighting effects), precisely because these distorted photographs, which make the viewer conscious of the photographic process, are themselves not regarded as realistic or immediate. Thus, photographs and synthetic images achieve the same effect of erasure through different means. The photograph erases the human subject through the mechanics and chemistry of lens, shutter, and film. Digital graphics erases the subject algorithmically through the mathematics of perspective and shading embodied in a program. So-called digital photography is a hybrid that combines and reconfigures these two kinds of automaticity. ⊘ **p. 104**

Obviously the test of photorealism can apply only to single, static images. The equivalent for computer animation would be "filmic" realism: a sequence of computer images that could not be distinguished from a traditional film, a feat that is technically even more challenging than photorealism. However, the very fact that the images are in motion (in computer animation and virtual reality) suggests new strategies for achieving immediacy. If immediacy is promoted by removing the programmer/creator from the image, it can also be promoted by involving the viewer more intimately in the image. The production of computer animation seems to be automatic, yet the viewing can be interactive, although the interaction may be as simple as the capacity to change one's point of view. In painting and photography, the user's point of view was fixed. In film and television, the point of view was set in motion, but it was the director or editor who controlled

the movement. Now, computer animation can function like film in this respect, for it too can present a sequence of predetermined camera shots. However, the sequence can also be placed under the viewer's control, as it is in animated computer video games or virtual reality.

In virtual reality, the helmet that contains the eyepieces also typically contains a tracking device. As the viewer turns her head, the tracker registers the change in her orientation, and the computer re-draws the image in each eyepiece to match her new perspective. Because she can move her head, the viewer can see that she is immersed—that she has jumped through Alberti's window and is now inside the de-picted space. For virtual reality enthusiasts, the plane defined by the video screen on the outmoded desktop computer is like Alberti's win-dow, and it is this plane that virtual reality now shatters. Rheingold (1991) claims that "in the 1990s, VR technology is taking people be-yond and through the display screen into virtual worlds" (75). As Rheingold implies, in graphics delivered on a conventional video screen, for example, in computer games, the interface is more obtrusive. The viewer must use the mouse or the keyboard to control what she sees. Yet even here, the viewer can manipulate her point of view and may still have a feeling of immersion, especially if she can turn in a full circle. It is remarkable how easily a player can project herself into a computer game like *Myst, Riven,* or *Doom,* despite the relatively low resolution and limited field of view afforded by the screen (fig. 1.1). ▷ **p. 94** It is also a creed among interface designers that interactivity increases the realism and effectiveness of a graphical user interface: the icons become more present to the user if she can reposition them or activate them with a click of the mouse.

Contemporary literary and cultural theorists would deny that linear-perspective painting, photography, film, television, or computer graphics could ever achieve unmediated presentation.[5] For such theorists, the desire for immediacy through visual representation has become a somewhat embarrassing (because undertheorized) tradition.[6] Outside the circles of theory, however, the discourse of the immediate has been and remains culturally compelling. Even within the academic community, among art historians and perceptual psychologists, linear perspective is still regarded as having some claim to being natural. (See, for example, Gombrich 1982; Hagen 1980, 1986.) Meanwhile, computer graphics experts, computer users, and the vast audiences for popular film and television continue to assume that unmediated presentation is the ultimate goal of visual representation and to believe that technological progress toward that goal is being made. When interactivity is combined with automaticity and the five-hundred-year-old perspective method, the result is one account of mediation that millions of viewers today find compelling.

It is important to note that the logic of transparent immediacy does not necessarily commit the viewer to an utterly naive or magical conviction that the representation is the same thing as what it represents. *Immediacy* is our name for a family of beliefs and practices that express themselves differently at various times among various groups, and our quick survey cannot do justice to this variety. The common feature of all these forms is the belief in some necessary contact point between the medium and what it represents. For those who believe in the immediacy of photography, from Talbot to Bazin to Barthes, the contact point is the light that is reflected from the objects on to the film. This light establishes an immediate relationship between the photograph and the object. For theorists of linear-perspective painting and perhaps for some painters, the contact point is the mathematical relationship established between the supposed objects and their projection on the canvas. However, probably at no time or place has the logic of immediacy required that the viewer be completely fooled by the painting or photograph. Trompe l'oeil, which does completely fool the viewer for a moment, has always been an exceptional practice. The film theorist Tom Gunning (1995) has argued that what we are calling the logic of transparent immediacy worked in a subtle way for filmgoers of the earliest films. The audience members knew at one level that the film

5. Theorists in the second half of the twentieth century have consistently denied that an image is a more direct presentation of the world than is written or spoken language. Their approach has generally been to textualize the image and therefore to take it into the discourse of poststructuralism—a strategy apparent in works as diverse as Derrida's *Of Grammatology* (1976) and Nelson Goodman's *Languages of Art* (1968). W. J. T. Mitchell (1994) attempts to break down the dichotomy between words and images by arguing for a hybrid, the "imagetext," but his picture theory finally assimilates images to words more than the reverse. Martin Jay (1993) has shown how almost all the influential French theoreticians of the twentieth century have sought to surround and subdue the image by means of text.

6. In some theorists the embarrassment becomes acute. The "punctum" in Barthes's *Camera Lucida* is precisely that element in photography that threatens to become immediate, to pull the viewer into the photograph itself. Meanwhile, in his analysis of the pernicious reality effect of cinema, Christian Metz (1977) seems appalled at the thought that the "apparatus" of the cinema can lull the viewer into a hypnotic state of apparently unmediated experience.

of a train was not really a train, and yet they marveled at the discrepancy between what they knew and what their eyes told them (114–133). On the other hand, the marveling could not have happened unless the logic of immediacy had had a hold on the viewers. There was a sense in which they believed in the reality of the image, and theorists since the Renaissance have underwritten that belief. This "naive" view of immediacy is the expression of a historical desire, and it is one necessary half of the double logic of remediation.

The Logic of Hypermediacy

Like the desire for transparent immediacy, the fascination with media also has a history as a representational practice and a cultural logic. In digital media today, the practice of hypermediacy is most evident in the heterogeneous "windowed style" of World Wide Web pages, the desktop interface, multimedia programs, and video games. It is a visual style that, in the words of William J. Mitchell (1994), "privileges fragmentation, indeterminacy, and heterogeneity and . . . emphasizes process or performance rather than the finished art object" (8). Interactive applications are often grouped under the rubric of "hypermedia," and hypermedia's "combination of random access with multiple media" has been described with typical hyperbole by Bob Cotten and Richard Oliver (1993) as "an entirely new kind of media experience born from the marriage of TV and computer technologies. Its raw ingredients are images, sound, text, animation and video, which can be brought together in any combination. It is a medium that offers 'random access'; it has no physical beginning, middle, or end" (8). This definition suggests that the logic of hypermediacy had to wait for the invention of the cathode ray tube and the transistor. However, the same logic is at work in the frenetic graphic design of cyberculture magazines like *Wired* and *Mondo 2000,* in the patchwork layout of such mainstream print publications as *USA Today,* and even in the earlier "multimediated" spaces of Dutch painting, medieval cathedrals, and illuminated manuscripts.

When in the 1960s and 1970s Douglas Englebart, Alan Kay, and their colleagues at Xerox PARC and elsewhere invented the graphical user interface and called their resizable, scrollable rectangles "windows," they were implicitly relying on Alberti's metaphor. Their windows opened on to a world of information made visible and almost tangible to the user, and their goal was to make the surface of these windows, the interface itself, transparent. As the windowed style has evolved in the 1980s and 1990s, however, transparency and immediacy have had to compete with other values. In current interfaces, windows multiply on the screen: it is not unusual for sophisticated users to have ten or more overlapping or nested windows open at one time. The multiple representations inside the windows (text, graphics, video) create a heterogeneous space, as they compete for the viewer's attention. Icons, menus, and toolbars add further layers of visual and verbal meaning.

The graphical interface replaced the command-line interface, which was wholly textual. By introducing graphical objects into the representation scheme, designers believed that they were making the interfaces "transparent" and therefore more "natural." Media theorist Simon Penny (1995) points out that for interface designers: "*transparent* means that the computer interface fades into the experiential background and the analogy on which the software is based (typewriter, drawing table, paintbox, etc.) is foregrounded. If the paintbox software is 'intuitive,' it is only intuitive because the paintbox is a culturally familiar object" (55). In fact, the graphical interface referred not only to culturally familiar objects, but specifically to prior media, such as painting, typewriting, and handwriting. In making such references, computer designers were in fact creating a more complex system in which iconic and arbitrary forms of representation interact. We have only to place figure 1.2 beside the virtual environment in figure 9.1 to see that a wholly different visual logic is operating.

Figure 1.2 The windowed style of the desktop interface.

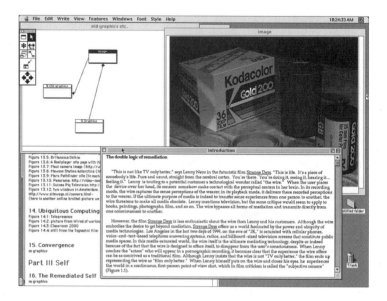

Unlike a perspective painting or three-dimensional computer graphic, this windowed interface does not attempt to unify the space around any one point of view. Instead, each text window defines its own verbal, each graphic window its own visual, point of view. Windows may change scale quickly and radically, expanding to fill the screen or shrinking to the size of an icon. And unlike the painting or computer graphic, the desktop interface does not erase itself. The multiplicity of windows and the heterogeneity of their contents mean that the user is repeatedly brought back into contact with the interface, which she learns to read just as she would read any hypertext. She oscillates between manipulating the windows and examining their contents, just as she oscillates between looking at a hypertext as a texture of links and looking through the links to the textual units as language.

With each return to the interface, the user confronts the fact that the windowed computer is simultaneously automatic and inter-active. We have argued that the automatic character of photography contributes to the photograph's feeling of immediacy, but with the windowed computer, the situation is more complicated. Its interface is automatic in the sense that it consists of layers of programming that are executed with each click of the mouse. Its interface is interactive in the sense that these layers of programming always return control to the user, who then initiates another automated action. Although the programmer is not visible in the interface, the user as a subject is constantly present, clicking on buttons, choosing menu items, and dragging icons and windows. While the apparent autonomy of the machine can contribute to the transparency of the technology, the buttons and menus that provide user interaction can be seen as getting in the way of the transparency. If software designers now characterize the two-dimensional desktop interface as unnatural, they really mean that it is too obviously mediated. They prefer to imagine an "interfaceless" computer offering some brand of virtual reality. Nevertheless, the possibilities of the windowed style have probably not been fully explored and elaborated.

One reason that this style has not been exhausted is that it functions as a cultural counterbalance to the desire for immediacy in digital technology. As a counterbalance hypermediacy is more complicated and various. In digital technology, as often in the earlier history of Western representation, hypermediacy expresses itself as multiplicity. If the logic of immediacy leads one either to erase or to render automatic the act of representation, the logic of hypermediacy acknowledges multiple acts of representation and makes them visible. Where immediacy suggests a unified visual space, contemporary hypermediacy offers a heterogeneous space, in which representation is conceived of not as a window on to the world, but rather as "windowed" itself—with windows that open on to other representations or other media. The logic of hypermediacy multiplies the signs of mediation and in this way tries to reproduce the rich sensorium of human experience. On the other hand, hypermediacy can operate even in a single and apparently unified medium, particularly when the illusion of realistic representation is somehow stretched or altogether ruptured. For example, perspective paintings or computer graphics are often hypermediated, particularly when they offer fantastic scenes that the viewer is not expected to accept as real or even possible. Hypermediacy can also manifest itself in the creation of multimedia spaces in the physical world, such as theme parks or video arcades. ⊘ **p. 173** In every manifestation, hypermediacy makes us aware of the medium or media and (in sometimes subtle and sometimes obvious ways) reminds us of our desire for immediacy.

As a historical counterpart to the desire for transparent immediacy, the fascination with media or mediation can be found in such diverse forms as medieval illuminated manuscripts, Renaissance altarpieces, Dutch painting, baroque cabinets, and modernist collage and photomontage. The logic of immediacy has perhaps been dominant in Western representation, at least from the Renaissance until the coming of modernism, while hypermediacy has often had to content itself with a secondary, if nonetheless important, status. Sometimes hypermediacy has adopted a playful or subversive attitude, both acknowledging and undercutting the desire for immediacy. At other times, the two logics have coexisted, even when the prevailing readings of art history have made it hard to appreciate their coexistence. At the end of the twentieth century, we are in a position to understand hypermediacy as immediacy's opposite number, an alter ego that has never been suppressed fully or for long periods of time.

We cannot hope to explore in detail the complex genealogy of hypermediacy through centuries of Western visual representation; we can only offer a few examples that are particularly resonant with digital hypermediacy today. Some resonances seem obvious. For example, the European cathedral with its stained glass, relief statuary, and inscriptions was a collection of hypermediated spaces, both physical and representational. And within the grand space of the cathedral, altarpieces provided a sophisticated form of hypermediacy, because they not only juxtaposed media but also embodied contradictory spatial logics. As perspectival representation came into painting, it is interesting to see, for example, a Flemish altarpiece by Arnt van Kalker, now in the Musée de Cluny in Paris, with a carved representation of the Passion at the center and painted perspectival scenes on both the inside and the outside of the cabinet doors. The closed doors depict depth in the represented space; when they are opened, they reveal a bas-relief three-dimensional Passion scene that stops at the back of the cabinet. Through this interplay of the real third dimension with its perspectival representation, the Kalker altarpiece connects the older sculptural tradition with the newer tradition of perspectival representation.

Represented and real three-dimensional spaces were also combined in many secular cabinets of the sixteenth and seventeenth centuries, which could have upwards of fifty drawers, doors, and panels, each painted with a perspectival landscape or genre scene. The pictures on the doors and drawers of these cabinets ironically duplicated the three-dimensional space that they concealed. Thus, the two-dimensional pictures on the doors opened on to a fictional space, while the painted doors themselves opened on to a physical one. (For an example, see figure 1.3.) Something similar is happening in digital design today. The windowed style is beginning to play a similar game of hide and seek as two-dimensional text windows and icons conceal and then expose three-dimensional graphic images and digitized video. Even the icons and folders of the conventional desktop metaphor function in two spaces: the pictorial space of the desktop and the informational space of the computer and the Internet.

We are not alone in noting this resemblance. In *Good Looking,* art historian Barbara Stafford has remarked on the parallels between digital media and baroque cabinets—in particular when she describes the so-called *Wunderkammer:*

Turning . . . to the disjunctive jumble stored in an eighteenth-century cabinet or chamber of curiosities, the modern viewer is struck by the intensely interactive demands it places on the visitor. . . . Looking back from the perspective of the computer era, the artifacts in a Wunderkammer seem less physical phenomena and more material links permitting the beholder to retrieve complicated personal and cultural associations. Looking forward from the Enlightenment world of apparently miscellaneous pleasures, we discern that scraps of wood, stone, or metal,

Figure 1.3 An Italian cabinet, circa 1660, made of rosewood, ebony, and tortoise shell with painted glass plaques. Photography courtesy of Victoria and Albert Museum.

religious relics, ancient shards, exotic fetishes, animal remains, miniature portraits, small engravings, pages torn from a sketchbook, are the distant ancestors of today's sophisticated software [e.g., multimedia encyclopedias]. (74–75)

With its multiplicity of forms and its associative links, the Wunderkammer is a fine example of the hypermediacy of the baroque.

We can also identify hypermediacy in oil painting—for example, in the Dutch "art of describing" explored by Svetlana Alpers (1983). With their fascination for mirrors, windows, maps, paintings within paintings, and written and read epistles, such artists as Gabriel

Metsu, David Bailly, and especially Jan Vermeer often represented the world as made up of a multiplicity of representations. Their paintings were not multimedia; rather, they absorbed and captured multiple media and multiple forms in oil. This Dutch art has often been contrasted with the paradigm of Renaissance Italian painting with its representation of a more unified visual space, in which the signs of mediation were meticulously erased. We can in fact find hypermediacy in individual works and individual painters throughout the period in which linear perspective and erasure were ascendant: for example, in Velasquez's *Las Meninas,* discussed by Alpers, Foucault, and, because of Foucault, many others (Alpers 1982, 69–70; Foucault 1971, 3–16) One could argue— and this would simply be a version of a familiar poststructuralist argument—that hypermediacy was the counterpart to transparency in Western painting, an awareness of mediation whose repression almost guaranteed its repeated return.

Hypermediacy can be found even in the mechanical technologies of reproduction of the nineteenth century. Jonathan Crary (1990) has challenged the traditional view that photography is the continuation and perfection of the technique of linear-perspective painting. For Crary, there was a rupture early in the nineteenth century, when the stable observation captured by the old camera obscura and by perspective painting was replaced by a new goal of mobility of observation. Reflecting this goal was a new set of (now archaic) devices: the diorama, the phenakistoscope, and the stereoscope. These devices, characterized by multiple images, moving images, or sometimes moving observers, seem to have operated under both these logics at the same time, as they incorporated transparent immediacy *within* hypermediacy. The phenakistoscope employed a spinning wheel and multiple images to give the impression of movement. The appeal to immediacy here was that a moving picture, say, of a horse, is more realistic than a static image. On the other hand, it was not easy for the user to ignore or forget the contraption of the phenakistoscope itself, when even its name was so contrived. The phenakistoscope made the user aware of the desire for immediacy that it attempted to satisfy. The same was true of the stereoscope, which offered users a three-dimensional image that seemed to float in space. The image was eerie, and the device unwieldy so that the stereoscope (fig. 1.4) too seemed to be a more or less ironic comment on the desire for immediacy. Crary shows us that hypermediacy manifested itself in the nineteenth century alongside and around the transparent

Figure 1.4 A nineteenth-century stereoscope. © 1998 Richard Grusin.

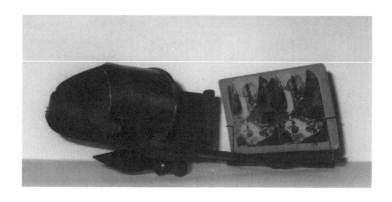

7. As Clement Greenberg (1973) puts it, "Realistic, illusionist art had dissembled the medium, using art to conceal art. Modernism used art to call attention to art. The limitations that constitute the medium of painting—the flat surface, the shape of the support, the properties of pigment—were treated by the Old Masters as negative factors that could be acknowledged only implicitly or indirectly. Modernist painting has come to regard these same limitations as positive factors that are to be acknowledged openly." (68–69).

8. Greenberg (1965, 70–74) sees collage as an expression of the tension between the modernist emphasis on the surface of the painting and the inherited tradition of three-dimensional representation. When Braque and Picasso took to pasting scraps of newspaper and wallpaper on their canvases, they created a hypermediated experience in which the viewer oscillates between seeing the pasted objects as objects and seeing them as part of the painted scene. The viewer is constantly reminded of the materials, the surface, and the mediated character of this space.

9. In making us conscious of the medium, photomontage can be seen

technology of photography. Nevertheless, the logic of transparent immediacy remained dominant. The obvious fact is that the conventional camera survived and flourished, while these other technologies did not.

According to Clement Greenberg's influential formulation, it was not until modernism that the cultural dominance of the paradigm of transparency was effectively challenged.[7] In modernist art, the logic of hypermediacy could express itself both as a fracturing of the space of the picture and as a hyperconscious recognition or acknowledgment of the medium. Collage and photomontage in particular provide evidence of the modernist fascination with the reality of media.[8] Just as collage challenges the immediacy of perspective painting, photomontage challenges the immediacy of the photograph. When photomonteurs cut up and recombine conventional photographs, they discredit the notion that the photograph is drawn by the "pencil of nature," as Talbot (1969) had suggested. Instead, the photographs themselves become elements that human intervention has selected and arranged for artistic purposes. Photographs pasted beside and on top of each other and in the context of other media, such as type, painting, or pencil drawing, create a layered effect that we also find in electronic multimedia. As we look at Richard Hamilton's *Just What Is It That Makes Today's Homes So Different, So Appealing?* (fig. 1.5), its cluttered space makes us aware of the process of construction. We become hyperconscious of the medium in photomontage, precisely because conventional photography is a medium with such loud historical claims to transparency.[9]

Richard Lanham (1993) notes how well Hamilton's piece from the 1950s suits today's "digital rhetoric" and then asks: "Couldn't this—collaged up as it is with clip art and advertising icons—just as well be called: 'Just What Is It That Makes Today's Desktop So Differ-

Figure 1.5 Richard Hamilton, *Just What Is It That Makes Today's Homes So Different, So Appealing?* © 1998 Artists Rights Society (ARS), New York/DACS, London.

ent, So Appealing'?" (40). In collage and photomontage as in hypermedia, to create is to rearrange existing forms. In photomontage the preexisting forms are photographs; in literary hypertext they are paragraphs of prose; and in hypermedia they may be prose, graphics, animations, videos, and sounds. In all cases, the artist is defining a space through the disposition and interplay of forms that have been detached from their original context and then recombined. Like Greenberg, Lanham regards collage as "the central technique of twentieth-century visual art"; Lanham wants to include digital design in the twentieth-century mainstream, which has often created heterogeneous spaces and made viewers conscious of the act of representation (40–41).

In the twentieth century, as indeed earlier, it is not only high art that seeks to combine heterogeneous spaces. Graphic design for print, particularly for magazines and newspapers, is becoming increasingly hypermediated as well. Magazines like *Wired* or *Mondo 2000* owe their conception of hypermediacy less to the World Wide Web than to the both to accept and to challenge the received understanding of photography as transparent. From one point of view, photomontage can be interpreted as a deviation from the essentially transparent and unified nature of photography. On the other hand, photomontage can be seen not as deviating from photography's true nature as a transparent medium but as exemplifying its irreducible hypermediacy. This latter interpretation of the photographic medium has been advanced by W. J. T. Mitchell (1994) in the idea of the "imagetext."

Figure 1.6 The front page of *USA TODAY,* January 23, 1998. © 1998 USA TODAY. Reprinted with permission.

tradition of graphic design that grows out of pop art and ultimately lettrisme, photomontage, and dada. The affiliations of a newspaper like the *USA Today* are more contemporary. Although the paper has been criticized for lowering print journalism to the level of television news, visually the *USA Today* does not draw primarily on television. Its layout resembles a multimedia computer application more than it does a television broadcast; the paper attempts to emulate in print (fig. 1.6) the graphical user interface of a web site (fig. 1.7). For that matter, television news programs also show the influence of the graphical user interface when they divide the screen into two or more frames and place text and numbers over and around the framed video images. ⊘ **p. 189**

In all its various forms, the logic of hypermediacy expresses the tension between regarding a visual space as mediated and as a "real" space that lies beyond mediation. Lanham (1993) calls this the tension between looking *at* and looking *through,* and he sees it as a feature of twentieth-century art in general and now digital representation in particular (3–28, 31–52). A viewer confronting a collage, for example, oscillates between looking at the patches of paper and paint on the surface of the work and looking through to the depicted objects as if they occupied a real space beyond the surface. What characterizes modern art is an insistence that the viewer keep coming back to the surface or, in extreme cases, an attempt to hold the viewer at the surface indefinitely. In the logic of hypermediacy, the artist (or multimedia programmer or web designer) strives to make the viewer acknowledge the medium as a medium and to delight in that acknowledgment. She does so by multiplying spaces and media and by repeatedly redefining the visual and conceptual relationships among mediated spaces—relationships that may range from simple juxtaposition to complete absorption.

For digital artist David Rokeby, the dichotomy between transparency and opacity is precisely what distinguishes the attitude of engineers from that of artists in the new technologies. Rokeby (1995) is clearly adopting a modernist aesthetic when he writes that "while engineers strive to maintain the illusion of transparency in the design and refinement of media technologies, artists explore the meaning of the interface itself, using various transformations of the media as their palette" (133). In fact, since Matisse and Picasso, or perhaps since the impressionists, artists have been "exploring the interface." However, Rokeby may not be doing justice to "modern" engineering. Media theorist Erkki Huhtamo (1995) points out that acknowledgment is characteristic of our culture's attitude to digital technology in general: "Technology is gradually becoming a second nature, a territory both external and internalized, and an object of desire. There is no need to make it transparent any longer, simply because it is not felt to be in contradiction to the 'authenticity' of the experience" (171). And Huhtamo is right to insist that hypermediacy can also provide an "authentic" experience, at least for our current culture; otherwise, we could not account for the tremendous influence of, for example, rock music.

Above, we identified the logic of transparent immediacy in computer games such as *Myst* and *Doom,* but other CD-ROMs operate according to our other logic and seem to revel in their nature as mediated artifacts. It should not be surprising that some of the clearest examples of digital hypermediacy (such as the Residents' *Freak Show,* Peter Gabriel's *Xplora 1,* and the Emergency Broadcast Network's *Telecommunications Breakdown*) come directly or indirectly from the world of rock music production and presentation. Initially, when "liveness" was the signifying mark of the rock sound, early recordings adhered to the logic of transparency and aimed to sound "live." As live performance became hypermediated, so did the recordings—as electric and then digital sampling, rave, ambient music, and other techniques became increasingly popular (cf. Auslander, forthcoming). The evolution of recording techniques also changed the nature of live performance. As early as the late 1960s and 1970s, performers such as Alice Cooper, David Bowie, and Kiss began to create elaborate, consciously artificial productions. The traditional "musical" qualities of these productions,

Figure 1.8 A screen capture from the *Telecommunications Breakdown* CD-ROM by the Emergency Broadcast Network. © 1995 TVT Records. Reprinted with permission.

never very complicated, became progressively less important than the volume and variety of sound and the visual spectacle. Today, the stage presentations of rock bands like U2 are celebrations of media and the act of mediation, while "avant-garde" artists like Laurie Anderson, the Residents, and the Emergency Broadcast Network are creating CD-ROMs that reflect and comment on such stage presentations with their seemingly endless repetition within the medium and multiplication across media. For example, in the number "Electronic Behavior Control System" by the Emergency Broadcast Network, the computer screen can be tiled into numerous small windows with shifting graphics, while a central window displays digitized clips from old films and television shows (fig. 1.8). This visual multiplicity is synchronized to an insistent "techno-rock" soundtrack. At times one or other digitized character will seem to enunciate a corresponding phrase on the soundtrack, as if all these remnants of old media had come together to perform this piece of music. In a similar spirit, the Residents' *Freak Show* both juxtaposes media and replaces one medium with another as it combines music with graphics and animations reminiscent of comic books and other popular forms.

Except for rock music, the World Wide Web is perhaps our culture's most influential expression of hypermediacy. As Michael Joyce (1995) reminds us, replacement is the essence of hypertext, and in a sense the whole World Wide Web is an exercise in replacement: "Print stays itself; electronic text replaces itself" (232). When the user clicks on an underlined phrase or an iconic anchor on a web page, a link is activated that calls up another page. The new material usually appears in the original window and erases the previous text or graphic, although the action of clicking may instead create a separate frame within the same window or a new window laid over the first. The new page wins our attention through the erasure (interpenetration), tiling (juxtaposition), or overlapping (multiplication) of the previous page. And beyond the Web, replacement is the operative strategy of the whole windowed style. In using the standard computer desktop, we pull down menus, click on icons, and drag scroll bars, all of which are devices for replacing the current visual space with another.

Replacement is at its most radical when the new space is of a different medium—for example, when the user clicks on an underlined phrase on a web page and a graphic appears. Hypermedia CD-ROMs and windowed applications replace one medium with another all the time, confronting the user with the problem of multiple representation and challenging her to consider why one medium might offer a more appropriate representation than another. In doing so, they are performing what we characterize as acts of remediation.

REMEDIATION

In the early and mid-1990s, perhaps to a greater extent than at any other time since the 1930s, Hollywood produced numerous filmed versions of classic novels, including Hawthorne, Wharton, and even Henry James. There has been a particular vogue for the novels of Jane Austen (*Sense and Sensibility, Pride and Prejudice,* and *Emma*). Some of the adaptations are quite free, but (except for the odd *Clueless*) the Austen films, whose popularity swept the others aside, are historically accurate in costume and setting and very faithful to the original novels. Yet they do not contain any overt reference to the novels on which they are based; they certainly do not acknowledge that they are adaptations. Acknowledging the novel in the film would disrupt the continuity and the illusion of immediacy that Austen's readers expect, for they want to view the film in the same seamless way in which they read the novels. The content has been borrowed, but the medium has not been appropriated or quoted. This kind of borrowing, extremely common in popular culture today, is also very old. One example with a long pedigree are paintings illustrating stories from the Bible or other literary sources, where apparently only the story content is borrowed. The contemporary entertainment industry calls such borrowing "repurposing": to take a "property" from one medium and reuse it in another. With reuse comes a necessary redefinition, but there may be no conscious interplay between media. The interplay happens, if at all, only for the reader or viewer who happens to know both versions and can compare them.

On the opening page of *Understanding Media* (1964), Marshall McLuhan remarked that "the 'content' of any medium is always another medium. The content of writing is speech, just as the written word is the content of print, and print is the content of the telegraph" (23–24). As his problematic examples suggest, McLuhan was not thinking of simple repurposing, but perhaps of a more complex kind of borrowing in which one medium is itself incorporated or represented in another medium. Dutch painters incorporated maps, globes, inscriptions, letters, and mirrors in their works. In fact, all of our examples of hypermediacy are characterized by this kind of borrowing, as is also ancient and modern *ekphrasis,* the literary description of works of visual art, which W. J. T. Mitchell (1994) defines as "the verbal representation of visual representation" (151–152). Again, we call the representation of one medium in another *remediation,* and we will argue that remediation is a defining characteristic of the new digital media. What might seem at first to be an esoteric practice is so widespread that we can identify a spectrum of different ways in which digital media remediate their predecessors, a spectrum depending on the degree of perceived competition or rivalry between the new media and the old.

At one extreme, an older medium is highlighted and represented in digital form without apparent irony or critique. Examples include CD-ROM (or DVD) picture galleries (digitized paintings or photographs) and collections of literary texts. There are also numerous web sites that offer pictures or texts for users to download. In these cases, the electronic medium is not set in opposition to painting, photography, or printing; instead, the computer is offered as a new means of gaining access to these older materials, as if the content of the older media could simply be poured into the new one. Since the electronic version justifies itself by granting access to the older media, it wants to be transparent. The digital medium wants to erase itself, so that the viewer stands in the same relationship to the content as she would if she were confronting the original medium. Ideally, there should be no difference between the experience of seeing a painting in person and on the computer screen, but this is never so. The computer always intervenes and makes its presence felt in some way, perhaps because the viewer must click on a button or slide a bar to view a whole picture or perhaps because the digital image appears grainy or with untrue colors. Transparency, however, remains the goal.

Creators of other electronic remediations seem to want to emphasize the difference rather than erase it. In these cases, the electronic version is offered as an improvement, although the new is still justified in terms of the old and seeks to remain faithful to the older medium's character. There are various degrees of fidelity. Encyclopedias on CD-ROM, such as Microsoft's *Encarta* and Grolier's *Electronic Encyclopedia,* seek to improve on printed encyclopedias by providing not only text and graphics, but also sound and video, and they feature electronic searching and linking capabilities. Yet because they are presenting discrete, alphabetized articles on technical subjects, they are still recognizably in the tradition of the printed encyclopedia since the eighteenth-century *Encyclopédie* and *Encyclopaedia Britannica.* In the early 1990s, the Voyager Company published series of "Expanded Books" on CD-ROM, an eclectic set of books originally written for printed publication, including *Jurassic Park* and *Brave New World.* The Voyager interface remediated the printed book without doing much to challenge print's assumptions about linearity and closure. Even the name, "Expanded Books," indicated the priority of the older medium. Much of the current World Wide Web also remediates older forms without challenging them. Its point-and-click interface allows the developer to reorganize texts and images taken from books, magazines, film, or television, but the reorganization does not call into question the character of a text or the status of an image. In all these cases, the new medium does not want to efface itself entirely. Microsoft wants the buyer to understand that she has purchased not simply an encyclopedia, but an electronic, and therefore improved, encyclopedia. The borrowing might be said to be translucent rather than transparent.

The digital medium can be more aggressive in its remediation. It can try to refashion the older medium or media entirely, while still marking the presence of the older media and therefore maintaining a sense of multiplicity or hypermediacy. This is particularly clear in the rock CD-ROMs, such as the Emergency Broadcast Network's *Telecommunications Breakdown,* in which the principal refashioned media are music recorded on CD and its live performance on stage. This form of aggressive remediation throws into relief both the source and the target media. In the "Electronic Behavior Control System," old television and movie clips are taken out of context (and therefore out of scale) and inserted absurdly into the techno-music chant (fig. 1.8). This tearing out of context makes us aware of the artificiality of both the digital version and the original clip. The work becomes a mosaic in which we are simultaneously aware of the individual pieces and their new, inappropriate setting. In this kind of remediation, the older media are presented in a space whose discontinuities, like those of collage and photomontage, are clearly visible. In CD-ROM multimedia, the discontinuities are indicated by the window frames themselves and by buttons, sliders, and other controls, that start or end the various media segments. The windowed style of the graphical user interface favors this kind of remediation. Different programs, representing different media, can appear in each window—a word processing document in one, a digital photograph in another, digitized video in a third—while clickable tools activate and control the different programs and media. The graphical user interface acknowledges and controls the discontinuities as the user moves among media.

Finally, the new medium can remediate by trying to absorb the older medium entirely, so that the discontinuities between the two are minimized. The very act of remediation, however, ensures that the older medium cannot be entirely effaced; the new medium remains dependent on the older one in acknowledged or unacknowledged ways. For example, the genre of computer games like *Myst* or *Doom* remediates cinema, and such games are sometimes called "interactive films." ⊘ **p. 94** The idea is that the players become characters in a cinematic narrative. They have some control over both the narrative itself and the stylistic realization of it, in the sense that they can decide where to go and what to do in an effort to dispatch villains (in *Doom*) or solve puzzles (in *Myst*). They can also decide where to look—where to direct their graphically realized points of view—so that in interactive film, the player is often both actor and director. On the World Wide Web, on the other hand, it is television rather than cinema that is remediated. ⊘ **p. 204** Numerous web sites borrow the monitoring function of broadcast television. These sites present a stream of images from digital cameras aimed at various parts of the environment: pets in cages, fish in tanks, a soft drink machine, one's office, a highway, and so on. Although these point-of-view sites monitor the world for the Web, they do not always acknowledge television as the medium that they are refashioning. In fact, television and the World Wide Web are engaged in an unacknowledged competition in which each now seeks to remediate the other. The competition is economic as well as aesthetic; it is a struggle to determine whether broadcast television or the Internet will dominate the American and world markets.

Like television, film is also trying to absorb and repurpose digital technology. As we have mentioned, digital compositing and other special effects are now standard features of Hollywood films, particularly in the action-adventure genre. And in most cases, the goal is to make these electronic interventions transparent. The stunt or special effect should look as "natural" as possible, as if the camera were simply capturing what really happened in the light. Computer graphics processing is rapidly taking over the animated cartoon; indeed, the take-over was already complete in Disney's *Toy Story.* ⊘ **p. 147** And here too the goal is to make the computer disappear: to make the settings, toys, and human characters look as much as possible like live-action film. Hollywood has incorporated computer graphics at least in part in an attempt to hold off the threat that digital media might pose for the traditional, linear film. This attempt shows that remediation operates in both directions: users of older media such as film and television can seek to appropriate and refashion digital graphics, just as digital graphics artists can refashion film and television.

Unlike our other examples of hypermediacy, this form of aggressive remediation does create an apparently seamless space. It conceals its relationship to earlier media in the name of transparency; it promises the user an unmediated experience, whose paradigm again is virtual reality. Games like *Myst* and *Doom* are desktop virtual reality applications, and, like immersive virtual reality, they aim to inspire in the player a feeling of presence. On the other hand, like these computer games, immersive virtual reality also remediates both television and film: it depends on the conventions and associations of the first-person point of view or subjective camera. ⊘ **p. 163** Science-fiction writer Arthur C. Clarke has claimed that "Virtual Reality won't merely replace TV. It will eat it alive" (cited by Rheingold, 1991, back cover). As a prediction of the success of this technology, Clarke is likely to be quite wrong, at least for the foreseeable future, but he is right in the sense that virtual reality remediates television (and film) by the strategy of incorporation. This strategy does not mean that virtual reality can obliterate the earlier visual point-of-view technologies; rather, it ensures that these technologies remain at least as reference points by which the immediacy of virtual reality is measured. Paradoxically, then, remediation is as important for the logic of transparency as it is for hypermediacy.

Another category of refashioning must be mentioned here: the refashioning that occurs within a single medium—for example, when a film borrows from an earlier film, as *Strange Days* borrows from *Vertigo* or when a painting incorporates another painting, as in Courbet's *Interior of My Studio*. This kind of borrowing is perhaps the most common, because artists both know and depend most immediately on predecessors in their own medium. This borrowing is fundamental not only to film and painting, but also to literature, where the play within a play (from *Hamlet* to *Rosencrantz and Guildenstern Are Dead*) or the poem within a poem or novel (from the *Odyssey* to *Portrait of the Artist*) is a very familiar strategy. In fact, this is the one kind of refashioning that literary critics, film critics, and art historians have acknowledged and studied with enthuasiasm, for it does not violate the presumed sanctity of the medium, a sanctity that was important to critics earlier in this century, although it is less so now. Refashioning within the medium is a special case of remediation, and it proceeds from the same ambiguous motives of homage and rivalry—what Harold Bloom has called the "anxiety of influence"—as do other remediations. Much of what critics have learned about this special kind of refashioning can also help us explore remediation in general. At the very least, their work reminds us that refashioning one's predecessors is key to understanding representation in earlier media. It becomes less surprising that remediation should also be the key to digital media.

Media theorist Steven Holtzman (1997) argues that repurposing has played a role in the early development of new media but will be left behind when new media find their authentic aesthetic:

In the end, no matter how interesting, enjoyable, comfortable, or well accepted they are, these approaches [repurposing] borrow from existing paradigms. They weren't conceived with digital media in mind, and as a result they don't exploit the special qualities that are unique to digital worlds. Yet it's those unique qualities that will ultimately define entirely new languages of expression. And it's those languages that will tap the potential of digital media as new *[original italics] vehicles of expression. Repurposing is a transitional step that allows us to get a secure footing on unfamiliar terrain. But it isn't where we'll find the entirely new dimensions of digital worlds. We need to transcend the old to discover completely new worlds of expression. Like a road sign, repurposing is a marker indicating that profound change is around the bend.* (15)

From the perspective of remediation, Holtzman misses the point. He himself appeals to a comfortable, modernist rhetoric, in

Mediation and Remediation

2

It is easy to see that hypermedia applications are always explicit acts of remediation: they import earlier media into a digital space in order to critique and refashion them. However, digital media that strive for transparency and immediacy (such as immersive virtual reality and virtual games) also remediate. Hypermedia and transparent media are opposite manifestations of the same desire: the desire to get past the limits of representation and to achieve the real. They are not striving for the real in any metaphysical sense. Instead, the real is defined in terms of the viewer's experience; it is that which would evoke an immediate (and therefore authentic) emotional response. Transparent digital applications seek to get to the real by bravely denying the fact of mediation; digital hypermedia seek the real by multiplying mediation so as to create a feeling of fullness, a satiety of experience, which can be taken as reality. Both of these moves are strategies of remediation.[1]

There are two paradoxes at work here. One is that hypermedia could ever be thought of as achieving the unmediated. Consider again the music spectacle CD-ROMs like the *Emergency Broadcast Network* with its surfeit of images and sounds that bombard the viewer. The idea of excess has been part of the popular music culture for decades. At first the excess was achieved simply by turning up the volume, until the sound could be felt as well as heard. More recently, the stage productions of popular musicians have emphasized visual spectacle and the acknowledgment of multiple media. The excessive, highly self-conscious video style of MTV is one result, and the music spectacle CD-ROMs obviously remediate MTV. The excess of media becomes an authentic experience, not in the sense that it corresponds to an external reality, but rather precisely because it is does not feel compelled to refer

1. The logic of remediation we describe here is similar to Derrida's (1981) account of mimesis, where mimesis is defined not ontologically or objectively in terms of the resemblance of a representation to its object but rather intersubjectively in terms of the reproduction of the feeling of imitation or resemblance in the perceiving subject. "Mimesis here is not the representation of one thing by another, the relation of resemblance or identification between two beings, the reproduction of a product of nature by a product of art. It is not the relation of two products but of two productions. And of two freedoms. . . . 'True' *mimesis* is between two producing subjects and not between two produced things" (9).

2. Greenberg's account of modernism has been challenged by many critics, among them T. J. Clark (1983), who criticizes Greenberg for not recognizing what Clark sees as modernism's essential qualities of negation and ideological critique. Clark's argument is refuted by Michael Fried (1983), who sees Clark as subscribing to a kind of essentialism that Greenberg too endorses. For Fried, modernism is not about "the irreducible essence of *all* painting," but rather "those conventions which, at a given moment, alone are capable of establishing [a] work's identity as painting" (227). In arguing that all mediation is remediation, we do not mean that remediation is the irreducible essence of either digital media or mediation generally, but rather that at our historical moment, remediation is the predominant convention at work in establishing the identity of new digital media.

to anything beyond itself. As with MTV, the viewer experiences such hypermedia not through an extended and unified gaze, but through directing her attention here and there in brief moments. The experience is one of the glance rather than the gaze, a distinction that Bryson (1983) has drawn in order to understand the semiotics of Western painting (cf. Bryson 1981). The aesthetic of the glance also makes the viewer aware of the process rather than just the product—both the process of creation and the process of viewing. For example, the Emergency Broadcast Network's CD-ROM conveys the feeling that we are witnessing, and in a way participating in, the process of its own construction. By emphasizing process, digital hypermedia become self-justifying. With their constant references to other media and their contents, hypermedia ultimately claim our attention as pure experience. In this claim, and perhaps only in this claim, hypermedia remind us of high modern art.

High modern visual art was also self-justifying, as it offered the viewer an experience that he was not expected to validate by referring to the external world. Modern art also promised authenticity of experience, and it emphasized the process of putting paint on canvas. As Greenberg (1986) described it, "[modern] painting and sculpture can become more completely nothing but what they do; like functional architecture and the machine, they *look* what they *do*" (34).[2] Digital hypermedia also look what they do. On the other hand, modern art often worked by reduction and simplification rather than excess. In that sense, digital hypermedia (and MTV) are closer in spirit to the excessive rhetoric of early modernism than to the visual practice of high modernism. The rhetoric of cyberspace is reminiscent of the manifestos of Filippo Tommaso Marinetti and the futurists. Moreover, the cyberspace enthusiasts have a similar relationship to technologies of representation that Marinetti and the futurists had to technologies of motive power (race cars, airplanes, etc.).

The second paradox is that just as hypermedia strive for immediacy, transparent digital technologies always end up being remediations, even as, indeed precisely because, they appear to deny mediation. Although transparent technologies try to improve on media by erasing them, they are still compelled to define themselves by the standards of the media they are trying to erase. The wire, Lenny claims, "is not like TV only better"; in saying this, of course, he affirms the comparison that he denies. The wire does improve on television, because it delivers "lived" experience, as television promises and yet fails to do. Similarly, interactive computer games such as *Myst* (and its sequel *Riven*) and *Doom* define their reality through the traditions of photography and film. *Doom* is regarded as authentic because it places the user in an action-adventure movie, *Myst* and *Riven* because of the near photorealism of their graphics and their cinematic use of sound and background music. In general, digital photorealism defines reality as perfected photography, and virtual reality defines it as first-person point-of-view cinema.

It would seem, then, that *all* mediation is remediation. We are not claiming this as an a priori truth, but rather arguing that at this extended historical moment, all current media function as remediators and that remediation offers us a means of interpreting the work of earlier media as well. Our culture conceives of each medium or constellation of media as it responds to, redeploys, competes with, and reforms other media. In the first instance, we may think of something like a historical progression, of newer media remediating older ones and in particular of digital media remediating their predecessors. But ours is a genealogy of affiliations, not a linear history, and in this genealogy, older media can also remediate newer ones.[3] Television can and does refashion itself to resemble the World Wide Web ⊘ **p. 189**, and film can and does incorporate and attempt to contain computer graphics within its own linear form. ⊘ **p. 153** No medium, it seems, can now function independently and establish its own separate and purified space of cultural meaning.

To suggest that at our present moment all mediation is remediation is not, however, to suggest that all of our culture's claims of remediation are equally compelling or that we could necessarily identify all of the strategies through which digital media remediate and are remediated by their predecessors. The double logic of remediation can function explicitly or implicitly, and it can be restated in different ways:

• *Remediation as the mediation of mediation.* Each act of mediation depends on other acts of mediation. Media are continually commenting on, reproducing, and replacing each other, and this process is integral to media. Media need each other in order to function as media at all.

• *Remediation as the inseparability of mediation and reality.* Although Baudrillard's notion of simulation and simulacra might suggest otherwise, all mediations are themselves real. They are real as artifacts (but not as autonomous agents) in our mediated culture. Despite the fact that all media depend on other media in cycles of remediation, our culture still

3. It is in this sense of older media remediating newer ones that our notion of remediation can be distinguished from the Hegelian concept of sublation (*Aufhebung*), in which prior historical formations (like pagan religions) are sublated or incorporated by newer formations (like Christianity). But as Slavoj Žižek (1993) points out, the interesting move in thinking about Hegelian sublation is to look at those moments when the newer formation is still "in its becoming," when it is perceived as something of a scandal. It is in part the attempt to understand remediation at such a historical moment that we are endeavoring in this book (284–285, n. 34.)

needs to acknowledge that all media remediate the real. Just as there is no getting rid of mediation, there is no getting rid of the real.

• *Remediation as reform.* The goal of remediation is to refashion or reha- bilitate other media. Furthermore, because all mediations are both real and mediations of the real, remediation can also be understood as a pro- cess of reforming reality as well.

REMEDIATION AS THE MEDIATION OF MEDIATION

Readers may already see an analogy between our analysis of media and poststructuralist literary theory of the past four decades, for Derrida and other poststructuralists have argued that all interpretation is rein- terpretation. Just as for them there is nothing prior to writing, so for our visual culture there is nothing prior to mediation. Any act of medi- ation is dependent on another, indeed many other, acts of mediation and is therefore remediation. In his work on postmodernism, Fredric Jameson (1991) has traced out the connection between the "linguistic turn" and what he calls "mediatization." Jameson describes the spatiali- zation of postmodern culture as "the process whereby the traditional fine arts are *mediatized:* that is, they now come to consciousness of them- selves as various media within a mediatic system in which their own internal production also constitutes a symbolic message and the taking of a position on the status of the medium in question" (162). Jameson's mediatization of the traditional fine arts is a process of remediation, in which media (especially new media) become systematically dependent on each other and on prior media for their cultural significance. What Jameson describes as mediatization may be true not only of postmodern new media but also of prior visual media as well. What he identifies as new and truly postmodern in fact reflects an attitude toward mediation that, while dominant today, has expressed itself repeatedly in the gene- alogy of Western representation.

Jameson himself seems to recognize this genealogy.

It is because we have had to learn that culture today is a matter of media that we have finally begun to get it through our heads that culture was always that, and that the older forms or genres, or indeed the older spiritual exercises and medita- tions, thoughts and expressions, were also in their very different ways media products. The intervention of the machine, the mechanization of culture, and the mediation of culture by the Consciousness Industry are now everywhere the case, and perhaps it might be interesting to explore the possibility that they were al-

ways the case throughout human history, and within even the radical difference of older, precapitalist modes of production. (68)

Jameson still insists that there is something special about the mediatization of our current culture: visual media are challenging the dominance of older linguistic media. The most powerful form of this "critical and disruptive challenge" is video, whose "total flow" threatens the physical and temporal differences that constitute linguistic meaning— even as the "available conceptualities for analyzing" media like video "have become almost exclusively linguistic in orientation."[4] Proclaimed by Jameson the dominant medium of our postmodern age, video simultaneously depends on and disrupts literary and linguistic theory. For Jameson, literary theory, and by extension the traditional humanist enterprise, is redefined by popular visual culture. In fact, television, film, and now computer graphics threaten to remediate verbal text both in print and on the computer screen—indeed, to remediate text so aggressively that it may lose much of its historical significance.[5]

In *We Have Never Been Modern* (1993), Bruno Latour takes us further in understanding the role of postmodern theory in our media-saturated, technological culture. For Latour, as for Jameson, contemporary theory gives a special status to language and interpretation: "Whether they are called 'semiotics,' 'semiology' or 'linguistic turns,' the object of all these philosophies is to make discourse not a transparent intermediary that would put the human subject in contact with the natural world, but a mediator independent of nature and society alike" (62). Contemporary theory thus makes it difficult to believe in language as a neutral, invisible conveyor of fully present meaning either between speaker/writer and listener/reader or between subjects and objects, people and the world. Instead, language is regarded as an active and visible mediator that fills up the space between signifying subjects and nature. But language is not the only mediator; it operates just as visual media operate in their tasks of remediation. Postmodern theory errs in trying to isolate language as a cultural force, for it fails to appreciate how language interacts with other media, other technologies, and other cultural artifacts. For Latour, the phenomena of contemporary technoscience consist of intersections or "hybrids" of the human subject, language, and the external world of things, and these hybrids are as real as their constituents—in fact, in some sense they are more real because no constituent (subject, language, object) ever appears in its

4. Jameson's (1991) concept of "total flow" relates to the concept of the "televisual," which Tony Fry (1993) describes as "an ontological domain" of which "almost everyone, everywhere," lives within its reach. For Fry, and for the other authors collected in *RUA/TV,* the "televisual" signals "the end of the medium, in a context, and the arrival of television as the context" (11–13). Where Jameson still sees video as a medium, Fry aims to offer new "conceptualities" for analyzing the ontology of the televisual. (For a critique of this ontological argument, see Auslander, 1997a.)

5. In *Teletheory,* published in 1989 and therefore before the advent of the World Wide Web, Gregory Ulmer made an influential attempt to refashion academic discourse for what he characterized as the "age of video." In this new, highly mediated environment, he argued, academic discourse must abandon its claim to critical distance and become more like television (10–11). He has subsequently revised his argument to take in new media as well.

6. Prior to *We Have Never Been Modern* (1993), Latour's fullest account of the heterogeneous network that links together humans, language, and the external world is in *Science in Action* (1987).

7. In *The Media Equation* (1996), Byron Reeves and Clifford Nass argue not only that media are real objects in the world, but that "media equal real life" (6). Drawing on their own extensive empirical research, the authors have conclusively demonstrated that people relate to media in the same way in which they relate to other people or places. For Reeves and Nass, the media equation has five variables: manners, personality, emotion, social roles, and form. Each of these variables, they argue, affects the way in which people relate to media and should inform the design choices made by media technologists and developers. This important book supports and complements our contention that media and reality are inseparable. Where Reeves and Nass focus largely on the psychological and sociological implications of how people relate to media, our concern is primarily with the cultural, historical, and formal relationships between people and media, and, more important, among media themselves.

8. For Cavell on modernist painting and acknowledgment, see *The World Viewed* (1979, 108–118). The relations among Cavell, Fried, and Greenberg are complex. See note 2 for Fried's Cavell-inspired criticism of Greenberg and T. J. Clark.

pure form, segregated from the other constituents.[6] The events of our mediated culture are constituted by combinations of subject, media, and objects, which do not exist in their segregated forms. Thus, there is nothing prior to or outside the act of mediation.

REMEDIATION AS THE INSEPARABILITY OF REALITY AND MEDIATION

Media function as objects within the world—within systems of linguistic, cultural, social, and economic exchange.[7] Media are hybrids in Latour's sense and are therefore real for the cultures that create and use them. Photography is real—not just as pieces of paper that result from the photographic process, but as a network of artifacts, images, and cultural agreements about what these special images mean and do. Film is real; its reality is constituted by the combination of the celluloid, the social meaning of celebrity, the economics of the entertainment industry, as well as the techniques of editing and compositing. The reality of digital graphics and the World Wide Web is attested to by the web of economic and cultural relationships that have grown up in a few years around the products from Netscape and Microsoft.

Modern art played a key role in convincing our culture of the reality of mediation. In many cases, modern painting was no longer about the world but about itself. Paradoxically, by eliminating "the real" or "the world" as a referent, modernism emphasized the reality of both the act of painting and its product. Painters offered us their works as objects in the world, not as a representation of an external world. By diminishing or denying painting's representational function, they sought to achieve an immediacy of presentation not available to traditional painting, where immediacy had been achieved by concealing signs of mediation. Modern art was often regarded as real or authentic, precisely because it refused to be realistic, and the example of modern art reminds us of the need to distinguish mediation and remediation from representation. Although the real and the representational are separated in modern art, modern art is not therefore less immediate. Modern painting achieves immediacy not by denying its mediation but by acknowledging it. Indeed, as Cavell has noted, building on the work of Greenberg and Michael Fried, one of the defining characteristics of modernist painting is its insistence on acknowledging the conditions of its own mediation.[8]

The reality of modernist painting extends beyond the work itself to the physical space that surrounds it. As Philip Fisher (1991) has argued, "The colonizing of this space between the surface of the canvas and the viewer has been one of the most aggressive features of the 20th century" (37). As we can learn from a visit to any traditional museum, the space between viewer and canvas is controlled, institutionalized, and policed as a special, real kind of space, which people walk around or wait before entering. The colonization of museum space has extended to the space between a photographer or videographer and the object of her mediating technology. When a tourist is taking a photograph or making a video, for example, we treat the line of sight between the camera and the object as if it were a real obstruction; we walk around it, bend under it, or wait until it is gone. We make these gestures not only out of politeness, but also to acknowledge the reality of the act of mediation that we are witnessing. In this case, the act of mediation functions in a system of pedestrian traffic circulation like a tree, a wire, or a traffic light (which is also an act of mediation whose reality we acknowledge). Mediations are real not only because the objects produced (photos, videos, films, paintings, CD-ROMS, etc.) circulate in the real world, but also because the act of mediation itself functions as a hybrid and is treated much like a physical object.

Finally, just as there is nothing prior to the act of mediation, there is also a sense in which all mediation remediates the real. Mediation is the remediation of reality because media themselves are real and because the experience of media is the subject of remediation.

REMEDIATION AS REFORM

The word *remediation* is used by educators as a euphemism for the task of bringing lagging students up to an expected level of performance and by environmental engineers for "restoring" a damaged ecosystem. The word derives ultimately from the Latin *remederi*—"to heal, to restore to health." We have adopted the word to express the way in which one medium is seen by our culture as reforming or improving upon another. This belief in reform is particularly strong for those who are today repurposing earlier media into digital forms. They tell us, for example, that when broadcast television becomes interactive digital television, it will motivate and liberate viewers as never before; that electronic mail is more convenient and reliable than physical mail; that hypertext brings interactivity to the novel; and that virtual reality is a more "natural" environment for computing than a conventional video screen.[9] The assumption of reform is so strong that a new medium is now expected to justify itself by improving on a predecessor: hence the

9. In *The Soft Edge* (1997), Paul Levinson uses the term *remediation* to describe how one medium reforms another (104–114). Levinson's intriguing theory is teleological: media develop "anthropotropically"—that is, to resemble the human. For Levinson, remediation is an agent of this teleological evolution, as we invent media that improve on the limits of prior media. Thus, writing makes speech more permanent; the VCR makes TV more permanent; hypertext makes writing more interactive; and so on. The development Levinson describes, however, is always progressive. We are arguing that remediation can work in both directions: older media can also refashion newer ones. Newer media do not necessarily supersede older media because the process of reform and refashioning is mutual.

need for computer graphics to achieve full photorealism. The assumption of reform has not been limited to digital media. Photography was seen as the reform of illusionistic painting and the cinema as the reform of the theater (in the sense that early films were once called "photoplays").

It is possible to claim that a new medium makes a good thing even better, but this seldom seems to suit the rhetoric of remediation and is certainly not the case for digital media. Each new medium is justified because it fills a lack or repairs a fault in its predecessor, because it fulfills the unkept promise of an older medium. (Typically, of course, users did not realize that the older medium had failed in its promise until the new one appeared.) The supposed virtue of virtual reality, of videoconferencing and interactive television, and of the World Wide Web is that each of these technologies repairs the inadequacy of the medium or media that it now supersedes. In each case that inadequacy is represented as a lack of immediacy, and this seems to be generally true in the history of remediation. Photography was supposedly more immediate than painting, film than photography, television than film, and now virtual reality fulfills the promise of immediacy and supposedly ends the progression. The rhetoric of remediation favors immediacy and transparency, even though as the medium matures it offers new opportunities for hypermediacy.

Remediation can also imply reform in a social or political sense, and again this sense has emerged with particular clarity in the case of digital media. A number of American political figures have even suggested that the World Wide Web and the Internet can reform democracy by lending immediacy to the process of making decisions. When citizens are able to participate in the debate of issues and possibly even vote electronically, we may substitute direct, "digital" democracy for our representational system. Here too, digital media promise to overcome representation. Even beyond claims for overt political reform, many cyberenthusiasts assert that the web and computer applications are creating a digital culture that will revolutionize commerce, education, and social relationships. Thus, broadcast television is associated with the old order of hierarchical control, while interactive media move the locus of control to the individual. That digital media can reform and even save society reminds us of the promise that has been made for technologies throughout much of the twentieth century: it is a peculiarly, if not exclusively, American promise. American culture seems to believe in technology in a way that European culture, for example, may not. Throughout the twentieth century, or really since the French Revolution, salvation in Europe has been defined in political terms: finding the appropriate (radical left or radical right) political formula. Even traditional Marxists, who believed in technological progress, subordinated that progress to political change. In America, however, collective (and perhaps even personal) salvation has been thought to come through technology rather than through political or even religious action.

Contemporary American culture claims to have lost much of its naive confidence in technology. Certainly postmodern theory is ambivalent about, if not hostile to, technology, but postmodern theory is European, and largely French, in its origins and allegiances. On the other hand, the whole fringe of rhetorical hangers-on that has grown up around computer technology is defined by its commitment to technological salvation. What remains strong in our culture today is the conviction that technology itself progresses through reform: that technology reforms itself. In our terms, new technologies of representation proceed by reforming or remediating earlier ones, while earlier technologies are struggling to maintain their legitimacy by remediating newer ones. The cyberenthusiasts argue that in remediating older media the new media are accomplishing social change. The gesture of reform is ingrained in American culture, and this is perhaps why American culture takes so easily to strategies of remediation.

Finally, remediation is reform in the sense that media reform reality itself. It is not that media merely reform the appearance of reality. Media hybrids (the affiliations of technical artifacts, rhetorical justifications, and social relationships) are as real as the objects of science. Media make reality over in the same way that all Western technologies have sought to reform reality. Thus, virtual reality reforms reality by giving us an alternative visual world and insisting on that world as the locus of presence and meaning for us. Recent proposals for "ubiquitous" or "distributed" computing would do just the opposite, but in the service of the same desire for reform. ⊘ **p. 212** Instead of putting ourselves in the computer's graphic world, the strategy of ubiquitous computing is to scatter computers and computational devices throughout our world—to "augment reality" with digital artifacts and so create a "distributed cyberspace." Its advocates see such a strategy "as a way to improve on the 'flawed' design in ordinary reality," in which "objects are largely 'dead' to distinctions we care about. Television sets and stereo systems are socially insensitive; they do not turn themselves down when we talk on the phone" (Kellogg, Carroll, and Richards 1991, 418).

Latour has argued, however, that for hundreds of years we have been constructing our technologies precisely to take our cultural distinctions seriously. Although he would probably agree with the enthusiasts for distributed computing that "the 'distinctions' people care about can be viewed as virtual worlds, or . . . information webs," these enthusiasts miss the point when they want to make a categorical distinction between distributed cyberspace and other current and past technologies (Kellogg, Carroll, and Richards 1991, 418). For Latour (1992) the idea of technologies that embody our cultural values or distinctions has been a feature not only of modern but of "amodern" or "premodern" societies as well.

The advocates of ubiquitous computing express grandiloquently the implied goal of all advocates and practitioners of digital media: to reimagine and therefore to reform the world as a mediated (and remediated) space. Again this is not new. For hundreds of years, the remediation of reality has been built into our technologies of representation. Photography, film, and television have been constructed by our culture to embody our cultural distinctions and make those distinctions part of our reality; digital media follow in this tradition. Nor will ubiquitous computing be the last expression of remediation as reform—as the burgeoning promises made on behalf of "push media" already remind us.

Networks of Remediation

3

Television, film, computer graphics, digital photography, and virtual reality: our culture recognizes and uses all of these technologies as media. This cultural recognition comes not only from the way in which each of the technologies functions in itself, but also from the way in which each relates to other media. Each participates in a network of technical, social, and economic contexts; this network constitutes the medium as a technology.

What Is a Medium?

We offer this simple definition: a medium is that which remediates. It is that which appropriates the techniques, forms, and social significance of other media and attempts to rival or refashion them in the name of the real. A medium in our culture can never operate in isolation, because it must enter into relationships of respect and rivalry with other media. There may be or may have been cultures in which a single form of representation (perhaps painting or song) exists with little or no reference to other media. Such isolation does not seem possible for us today, when we cannot even recognize the representational power of a medium except with reference to other media. If someone were to invent a new device for visual representation, its inventors, users, and economic backers would inevitably try to position this device over against film, television, and the various forms of digital graphics. They would inevitably claim that it was better in some way at achieving the real or the authentic, and their claim would involve a redefinition of the real or authentic that favors the new device. Until they had done this, it would not be apparent that the device was a medium at all.

In the past fifty years, we have seen the digital computer undergo this process of "mediatization." The programmable digital computer was invented in the 1940s as a calculating engine (ENIAC, EDSAC, and so on); by the 1950s, the machine was also being used for billing and accounting in large corporations and bureaucracies. At that time, proponents began to understand the computer as a new writing technology; that was in fact the message of the artificial intelligence movement, which began as early as 1950 with A. M. Turing's famous essay, "Computing Machinery and Intelligence." The important cultural contribution of artificial intelligence was not that the computer could be a new kind of mind, but rather that it could be a symbol manipulator and could therefore remediate earlier technologies of arbitrary symbol manipulation, such as handwriting and printing.

As long as computers remained expensive and rare, available only to a limited group of experts in large institutions, their remediating functions were limited. In the 1970s, the first word processors appeared, and in the 1980s the desktop computer. The computer could then become a medium because it could enter into the social and economic fabric of business culture and remediate the typewriter almost out of existence.

Although the computational device itself, even the "user-friendly" word processor, was not a medium, that device, together with its social and cultural functions, did constitute a new medium. (Furthermore, in the 1980s and 1990s the digital computer has taken on new technical and social functions and is being constituted as a second medium, or series of media, for visual or sensory representation.)

The cultural work of defining a new medium may go on during and in a sense even before the invention of the device itself. The technologists working on the device may have some sense of where it might fit in the economy of media, what it might remediate, as fifteenth- and sixteenth-century printers did in their project to remediate the manuscript and as the inventors of photography did in the nineteenth century. Or they might be working on a device for a different purpose altogether, and they or someone else might realize its potential for constituting a new medium. In some cases the potential might emerge only slowly as the device evolved and changed (as with radio and the telephone). All sorts of cultural relationships with existing media are possible. The only thing that seems impossible is to have no relationship at all.

The cultural studies of popular media (for example, *Media Culture* by Douglas Kellner) have been right to insist on close ties between the formal and material characteristics of media, their "content," and their economic and social functions. Indeed, the various elements are so tightly bound that they can never be entirely separated; a medium is a hybrid in Latour's sense. To say, for example, that the commercial funding of American television is the cause of its insipid content (or induces individuals to identify with dominant ideologies, or whatever) is already to separate the technical form of television (as the creation and distribution of programs on television sets) from its economic expression. In fact, commercial financing is an inseparable aspect of the medium of American television, as are its many social uses (TV dinners, occupying the children, defining shopping habits). We do not mean that one could not design a different system, say public financing, but rather that, in the unlikely event that it were ever established, public financing would redefine American television as a technology or medium. This does not mean that the mode of financing *causes* American television to be what it is, but rather that the character of a technology such as television is articulated through a network of formal, material, and social practices.

Whenever we focus on one aspect of a medium (and its relationships of remediation with other media), we must remember to include its other aspects in our discourse. In the case of film, for example, when we look at what happens on the screen (in a darkened theater), we can see how film refashions the definitions of immediacy that were offered by stage drama, photography, and painting. However, when the film ends, the lights come on, and we stroll back into the lobby of, say, a suburban mall theater, we recognize that the process of remediation is not over. We are confronted with all sorts of images (posters, computer games, and videoscreens), as well as social and economic artifacts (the choice of films offered and the pricing strategy for tickets and refreshments). ◈ **p. 173** These do not simply provide context for the film itself; they take part in the constitution of the medium of film as we understand it in the United States today. We must be able to recognize the hybrid character of film without claiming that any one aspect is more important than the others. This is the claim implicit in most cultural studies analyses of popular media: that film and television embody or carry economic and cultural ideologies and that we should study media principally in order to uncover and learn to resist their ideologies

(Kellner, 1995). Although it is true that the formal qualities of the medium reflect their social and economic significance, it is equally true that the social and economic aspects reflect the formal or technical qualities.

THE MATERIAL AND ECONOMIC DIMENSIONS OF REMEDIATION

The economic aspects of remediation have already been acknowledged and explored by cultural theorists. Each new medium has to find its economic place by replacing or supplementing what is already available, and popular acceptance, and therefore economic success, can come only by convincing consumers that the new medium improves on the experience of older ones. At the same time, the economic success of workers depends on the new medium's acquired status. Thus, web designers currently command higher salaries than technical writers and graphic designers for print; it is in their interest to promote the belief that digital media can not only replace printed documents, but vastly improve on them.

Similarly, the whole entertainment industry's understanding of remediation as repurposing reveals the inseparability of the economic from the social and material. The entertainment industry defines repurposing as pouring a familiar content into another media form; a comic book series is repurposed as a live-action movie, a televised cartoon, a video game, and a set of action toys. The goal is not to replace the earlier forms, to which the company may own the rights, but rather to spread the content over as many markets as possible. Each of those forms takes part of its meaning from the other products in a process of honorific remediation and at the same time makes a tacit claim to offer an experience that the other forms cannot. Together these products constitute a hypermediated environment in which the repurposed content is available to all the senses at once, a kind of mock *Gesamtkunstwerk*. For the repurposing of blockbuster movies such as the Batman series, the goal is to have the child watching a Batman video while wearing a Batman cape, eating a fast-food meal with a Batman promotional wrapper, and playing with a Batman toy. The goal is literally to engage all of the child's senses.

We can also consider repurposing in microeconomic terms as the refashioning of materials and practices. When artists or technicians create the apparatus for a new medium, they do so with reference to previous media, borrowing and adapting materials and techniques whenever possible. Thus, Gutenberg and the first generation of printers borrowed the letterforms and layout from the manuscript and constructed the printed book as the "manuscript only better." They borrowed the materials too. Paper had long been used for manuscripts, and techniques of binding remained the same (Steinberg, 1959). After winning their rather easy battle of remediation, printers in the late fifteenth and early sixteenth centuries moved away from the manuscript model by simplifying letterforms and regularizing the layout. A manuscript page was dark with the ink of letters formed by hand; these printers learned to use ink sparingly to achieve a highly legible page. In the case of photography, Talbot, one of the pioneers, justified his invention because of his dissatisfaction with a contemporary device for making accurate perspective drawings by hand, and the name "camera" was his remediation of the *camera lucida* (Trachtenberg 1980, 27; Kemp 1990, 200). Film technicians and producers remediated both photography and the practices of stage plays. We have noted that early films were once called photoplays, which expresses this combined remediation; the term *mise-en-scène* was also borrowed from stage production to refer to the film director's control of the visual appearance. In computer graphics, paint programs borrowed techniques and names from manual painting or graphic design practices: paintbrush, airbrush, color palette, filters, and so on. World Wide Web designers have remediated graphic design as it was practiced for printed newspapers and magazines, which themselves in some cases have reappropriated the graphic design of the World Wide Web.

The Social Dimension

The remediation of material practice is inseparable from the remediation of social arrangements, in the first instance because practitioners in the new medium may want to claim the status of those who worked in an earlier medium. Film stars hope to be seen as artists, as skilled as stage actors, and, at least from the 1950s on, many film directors want to be regarded as "authors" of their films. In turn, actors and directors of television dramas want their work to be accorded the status of dramatic film. On stage, in film, or on television, the mark of being a true author or actor is "moving" the audience: offering an experience that the audience finds authentic. Film and television actors and directors could also lay claim to improving on stage drama, in the sense that their newer media handle popular subjects in accessible ways and appeal to a public that twentieth-century stage drama could no longer attract. Meanwhile, computer game makers hope that their interactive products will someday achieve the status of first-run films, and there is even an attempt to lure film stars to play in these narrative computer productions. Game makers can cite the wide appeal of their games as evidence of the success of their remediations.

The status of the photographer in the nineteenth and twentieth centuries presents a more complicated case. In their rivalry with painting, some photographers (such as Henry Peach Robinson) sought to be regarded as artists, while others (such as Lewis Hine, Edward Weston, and August Sander) promoted themselves instead as social historians or even natural scientists. Their internal disagreements were over both the material and formal basis of their medium and the social nature of the remediation that photography undertook. Meanwhile, the viewer was being refashioned into the role of photographer. Daguerre himself suggested that "everyone, with the aid of the daguerreotype, will make a view of his castle or country-house; people will form collections of all kinds, which will be the more precious because art cannot imitate their accuracy and perfection of detail. . . . The leisured class will find it a most attractive occupation, and although the result is obtained by chemical means, the little work it entails will greatly please ladies" (Trachtenberg 1980, 12–13). Daguerre had from the outset a sense of the social aspects of remediation that his invention would entail, although his "everyone" seemed to include only men and women of the leisured class. The formal remediation—that the daguerreotype captures more detail than a painting—meant that the technology would better serve the needs of the wealthy collector, an emerging, nineteenth-century type. Daguerre may not have been precisely right with his prediction. With Eastman, photography later became a pastime for a larger and less wealthy middle class.[1] The important point is that even one of its inventors realized very early that photography was about social practices as well as technical details.

The two logics of remediation have a social dimension for the viewers as well as the practitioners. We have so far used the term *immediacy* in two senses: one epistemological, the other psychological. In the epistemological sense, immediacy is transparency: the absence of mediation or representation. It is the notion that a medium could erase itself and leave the viewer in the presence of the objects represented, so that he could know the objects directly. In its psychological sense, immediacy names the viewer's feeling that the medium has disappeared and the objects are present to him, a feeling that his experience is therefore authentic. Hypermediacy also has two corresponding senses. In its epistemological sense, hypermediacy is opacity—the fact that knowl-

1. Eastman had figured out how to automate or "blackbox" not only the mechanical but also the commercial aspects of his photographic system (Latour 1987, 115, 122, 124, 131).

edge of the world comes to us through media. The viewer acknowledges that she is in the presence of a medium and learns through acts of mediation or indeed learns about mediation itself. The psychological sense of hypermediacy is the experience that she has in and of the presence of media; it is the insistence that the experience of the medium is itself an experience of the real. The appeal to authenticity of experience is what brings the logics of immediacy and hypermediacy together.

This appeal is socially constructed, for it is clear that not only individuals, but also various social groups can vary in their definitions of the authentic. What seems immediate to one group is highly mediated to another. In our culture, children may interpret cartoons and picture books under the logic of transparent immediacy, while adults will not. Even among adults, more sophisticated groups may experience a media event as hypermediated, while a less sophisticated group still opts for immediacy. In the mid-1990s a film became widely available (even in video stores) that purported to show the autopsy by American doctors of an alien creature. When both sides in the UFO debate pored over the film, their argument really concerned the logic by which the film should be read. Critics were looking for signs of mediation or staging—for example, that the telephone on the wall was of the wrong kind for the supposed date of the autopsy. Believers, on the other hand, were trying to establish that the film was a transparent recording of a "real" event. All debates about UFO films and photographs turn on the question of transparency.

The experience of hypermediacy also depends on the social construction of the media used. Staged rock productions are hypermediated events, which no one interprets as transparent in the sense that the media are to be forgotten or erased. But by entering into an immediate relationship with the media themselves—the sound, the lights, the televised images—rock fans achieve an experience they regard as authentic. Others remain distanced from that experience, either repelled or simply unmoved. This distancing depends at least in part on social grouping. For example, those on the American religious right are compelled by their construction of rock music to remain distanced. They may claim that the sinfulness of rock music lies primarily in its lyrics, but it is the nature of hypermediated experience that really troubles them. Rock music expects, if it does not require, that the viewer/listener be intimately involved in the hypermediacy—that she "abandon herself" to the music. This abandonment is all the more threatening because there is nothing offered beyond the medium—no world into which the user can enter—as there is in conventional representational media, such as linear-perspective painting. What rock music seems to offer (and indeed what Wagnerian opera offered to the nineteenth-century German audiences, or flute music in the Lydian mode to Plato's Greeks) is pure experience, pure authenticity, real in a sense that the listener's perception cannot itself be deceived.

Photography provides an important example of the social debate that can surround the logics of immediacy and hypermediacy. When Niepce, Daguerre, Talbot, and others claimed immediacy for their new medium, they were seeking to control its social construction. A long and complicated debate followed, with important figures such as Baudelaire arguing in opposition, but in general the case for immediacy succeeded, and Western societies accepted the idea that a photograph truly captures the world. Digital photography is now challenging that claim to immediacy ⊘ **p. 104**, so that a new kind of hybrid is emerging whose social and practical meanings have to be reworked. Even prior to the advent of digital photography, there has been an argument for decades about whether the Western technologies of drawing and photography are governed by convention or by the intrinsic principles of human vision and Euclidean space: whether these techniques capture the world scientifically, as it appears "in the light." Although strict social constructionists and many other postmodern writers take it as dogma that linear-perspective representations are as artificial and arbitrary as any others, some psychologists and art historians still believe otherwise. An empirical test of the question has been to show perspective drawings, photographs, or films to subjects from cultures (often in Africa) that had never seen them. The results of the relatively few experiments have been mixed. When shown a photograph or perspective drawing for the first time, subjects sometimes had trouble interpreting the images, although after a few minutes or a few tries they could handle the images more easily. In other experiments subjects have had little trouble understanding films that employ editing conventions (Hagen 1980, vol. 1; Messaris 1994).

Such experiments suggest to us that neither the social nor the technical aspect of mediation should be reduced to the other. Both Western and African subjects clearly use their innate visual systems to process the information in the image, but it is also clear that the images are socially constructed. For the Westerners, photography and linear-perspective drawing are media that are constructed as transparent. The images are transparent, however, only because Westerners have already learned to overlook, or "look through," the conventions that they appear on paper and offer a static, monocular view. When the same images were handed to the African subjects, they were at first experienced as hypermediated. Some of the subjects had never seen paper before, so that the very idea of paper carrying an image was foreign to them (Messaris 1994). After that initial phase, when the subjects had adjusted and could read the images "properly," the media would still not necessarily be transparent in our sense, because the African subjects would not have had the opportunity to build the collective response that Western culture now has to perspective painting, photography, and realistic film. However, the fact that the subjects could learn so quickly to interpret the images in the Western fashion indicates that the images do take advantage of properties of the propagation of light that are the same in the developing countries as in the West. What counts as transparent or as hypermediated depends on social construction, but the social construction of immediacy is not arbitrary or oblivious to technical details. It has been relatively easy to construct linear perspective as transparent and natural, precisely because the construction can mobilize the (Western) physics of light and vision.

The social dimension of immediacy and hypermediacy is as important as their formal and technical dimensions. However, there is no need to deny the importance of the latter in order to appreciate the former, no need to reduce the technical and psychological dimensions to the social. It is not helpful to seek to reduce any aspect of media to any other. This applies equally to the economics of media, to which traditional Marxists (and capitalists) seek to reduce all other aspects. Furthermore, by seeking to recognize all aspects of media and mediation, we can best respond to, although we cannot conclusively settle, the vexing question of technological determinism.

The Work of Art in the Age of Remediation

Before taking up the question of technological determinism, we need to say more about remediation's political dimension. Remediation is not replication or mechanical reproduction; however, we cannot discuss its social and political dimensions without pausing to reflect on Walter Benjamin's influential essay "The Work of Art in the Age of Mechanical Reproduction" (1969). Benjamin's argument is that mechanical reproduction produces a fundamental change in the nature of art, a change that destroys the artwork's "aura" by removing it from the context of ritual and tradition in which art had been historically embedded.

Citing photography and especially cinema, Benjamin posits that technology creates a new kind of political or revolutionary potential for mass art, a potential that can also be dangerous, as his concluding discussion of Marinetti and the futurists warns us.

Benjamin's argument that technologies of mechanical reproduction are politically enabling has its counterpart today in the claim by some enthusiasts that new media, particularly the Internet, will bring about a new kind of democracy. For example, according to Howard Rheingold (1994), "The political significance of [computer-mediated communication] lies in its capacity to challenge the existing political hierarchy's monopoly on powerful communications media, and perhaps thus revitalize citizen-based democracy" (14). In the most extreme version of this argument, we find John Perry Barlow proclaiming in his "Declaration of Independence" (http://www.eff.org/pub/Publications/John.Perry.Barlow/barlow_0296.declaration   April 17, 1998) that cyberspace is a new political territory in which the laws of industrial capitalism no longer apply and that a new political order lies on (or perhaps just beyond) our monitors. These Internet and new media enthusiasts are more naive, or at least less subtle, than Benjamin, for they are arguing that digital technology offers us a transparent democracy, in which the medium of political representation disappears and citizens can communicate their political will directly with each other or with their government. Benjamin believed that film educates its mass audience through a more complex dynamic.

Benjamin begins with the assertion that film technology, or mechanical reproduction in general, breaks down the aura of the work of art by eliding or erasing the distance between the work and its viewer. Removed from the cathedral or museum, the work of art is now closer to the viewer. At first glance, Benjamin seems to be suggesting that mechanical reproduction is responding to and even satisfying a desire for transparent immediacy—that removing the aura makes the work of art formally less mediated and psychologically more immediate. On the other hand, Benjamin's mechanical reproduction also seems to evoke a fascination with media. In the case of film, he describes the viewer as distracted by the rapid succession of scenes, as simultaneously entranced and aroused by the mediation of film. For just this reason, Benjamin contrasts seeing a film with viewing a painting. Unlike a filmgoer, the viewer of a painting is absorbed into the work, as if the medium had disappeared. Perhaps for Benjamin, the immediacy offered by film is the immediacy that we have identified as growing out of the fascination with media: the acknowledged experience of mediation.

Furthermore, film for Benjamin is a medium that demonstrates the inseparability of technology and reality. He emphasizes the complicated apparatus surrounding the production of film, as a result of which there is no unity or wholeness in the surrounding scene. It requires elaborate camera work, editing, and other forms of reproduction to make film appear seamless, to make its mediation disappear. Ironically, although filmmakers work hard to conceal the signs of material and technological mediation, their final product calls attention (through the rapid succession of images) to its aesthetic, temporal, and formal mediation in a way that traditional painting does not. For Benjamin, the painter and the cameraman practice very different crafts:

The painter maintains in his work a natural distance from reality, the cameraman penetrates deeply into its web. There is a tremendous difference between the pictures they obtain. That of the painter is a total one, that of the cameraman consists of multiple fragments which are assembled under a new law. Thus, for contemporary man the representation of reality by the film is incomparably more significant than that of the painter, since it offers, precisely because of the thoroughgoing permeation of reality with mechanical equipment, an aspect of reality which is free of all equipment. And that is what one is entitled to ask from a work of art. (233–234)

Benjamin encourages us to reformulate his question: What are we entitled to ask from a work of art in an "age of remediation"? Benjamin still seems to believe both that it is possible to get past mediation to "an aspect of reality which is free of all equipment" and that political revolution may come about through such an achievement. In a period such as ours today, in which media and the process of mediation are more frankly acknowledged and appreciated, the aesthetic goal and its political consequences seem to be different. The work of art today seems to offer "an aspect of reality which cannot be freed from mediation or remediation," at the same time that new media seek to present us precisely with "an aspect of reality which is free from all mediation." Thus remediation does not destroy the aura of a work of art; instead it always refashions that aura in another media form.

TECHNOLOGICAL DETERMINISM
If Benjamin's essay has often been read as an expression of the technological determinism implicit in classical Marxist thought, more recent scholars have been concerned to avoid the charge of determinism. Even two decades ago, British Marxist Raymond Williams (1975) made an

influential argument against the notion that new technologies "are discovered, by an essentially internal process of research and development, which then sets the conditions for social change and progress" (13). He was protesting against a view that was popular in the 1960s and 1970s and remains so today. Whether they are blaming or praising technology, politicians, futurologists, and the print and electronic media fall easily into the rhetoric of technological determinism. Enthusiasts for cyberspace such as John Perry Barlow credit the Internet with creating a new culture, while conservative politicians speak as if the Internet itself had called forth a new form of pornography. Meanwhile, Williams and others have convinced almost all historians, social scientists, and humanists, with the result that technological determinism has been one feature of traditional Marxism rejected by postmodern theory and cultural studies. Whenever it is made, the charge is now considered fatal: nothing good can come of technological determinism, because the claim that technology causes social change is regarded as a justification for the excesses of technologically driven capitalism in the late twentieth century.

Williams was reacting above all to McLuhan's (1964) then influential theory of media as "extensions of man." For Williams, McLuhan had isolated and abstracted media from their social contexts, as if media could work directly on some abstract definition of human nature. Williams (1975) objected that in McLuhan's work, "as in the whole formalist tradition, the media were never really seen as practices. All specific practice was subsumed by an arbitrarily assigned psychic function, and this had the effect of dissolving not only specific but general intentions. . . . All media operations are in effect dissocialised; they are simply physical events in an abstracted sensorium, and are distinguishable only by their variable sense-ratios" (127). In *Understanding Media* (1964) McLuhan did often claim that media change us, and he continues to influence popular versions of technological determinism today. Although he was regarded as a radical in the 1960s, McLuhan has now been adopted as a patron saint of the information industry. In the 1960s, his phrase "global village" sounded like a justification of social protest and "flower power." Today, communications giants happily borrow the phrase in their advertising. The idea that new electronic technologies of communication will determine our social organization is clearly not threatening to corporations that produce and market those technologies.

In *Understanding Media,* on the other hand, McLuhan often notices intricate correspondences involving media and cultural artifacts.

Although Williams is right that McLuhan returns repeatedly to the claim that media bring about cultural change, the chapters of *Understanding Media* are filled with contemporary as well as historical examples, from popular and literary culture. Some of McLuhan's correspondences are still worth considering, for they point to the ways in which one medium remediates others (especially print, radio, film, and television). Often the remediations involve the social practices that accompany media—for example, how a contemporary American family views television or film. We can let go of the premise of cause and effect and still examine the interrelationships among media for which McLuhan argues. We need not be afraid of McLuhan's "formalism," as long as we remember that technical forms are only one aspect of technologies that are simultaneously social and economic. McLuhan's notion that media are extensions of the human sensorium can even be regarded as an anticipation of Donna Haraway's cyborg. McLuhan did bring to our attention the fact that media take their meaning through interactions with the senses and the body, although feminist writers since the 1970s have elaborated this idea in ways that McLuhan did not envision. In short, we can reject McLuhan's determinism and still appreciate his analysis of the remediating power of various media.

We need to keep in mind, however, the other half of Williams's critique. Williams (1975) also warned against the notion of "determined technology [which] has a similar one-sided, one-way version of human process. Determination is a real social process but never . . . [functions] as a wholly controlling, wholly predicting set of causes" (130). He argued that social forces "set limits and exert pressures, but neither wholly control nor wholly predict the outcome" (130).

In an effort to avoid both technological determinism and determined technology, we propose to treat social forces and technical forms as two aspects of the same phenomenon: to explore digital technologies themselves as hybrids of technical, material, social, and economic facets. Thus, virtual reality is not only a head-mounted display and computer hardware and software; it is also the sum of the entertainment and training uses to which this hardware and software is put, and it is the institutional and entrepreneurial capital devoted to these uses. Finally, virtual reality enacts a subjective, point-of-view aesthetic that our culture has come to associate with new media in general. These facets of the cultural meaning of virtual reality are so closely associated that it is unproductive to try to tease them apart. Like a quark, no one facet can exist in isolation; any argument forceful enough to detach one facet from its network of affiliations would necessarily bind that facet into some other cultural network. Because our digital technologies of representation are simultaneously material artifacts and social constructions, there is no need to insist on any aspect as cause or effect.

It is difficult, however, to hold in relief all the aspects of a technology at any one rhetorical moment. Readers of this book will find sentences in which a technology is used as the subject of an action verb. We have tried to avoid the most egregious generalizations of the kind that make McLuhan so appalling to Raymond Williams and his followers. When we do write something like "digital media are challenging the status of television and film," we are asking readers to treat this as shorthand. A longer, and less felicitous, version would be that "the individuals, groups, and institutions that create and use digital media treat these media as improved forms of television and film." Media *do* have agency, but that agency is constrained and hybrid. To say that digital media "challenge" earlier media is the rhetoric of technological determinism only if technology is considered in isolation. In all cases we mean to say that the agency for cultural change is located in the interaction of formal, material, and economic logics that slip into and out of the grasp of individuals and social groups.

Nevertheless, our rhetoric and our strategy foreground new media in a way that may prove unacceptable to many postmodern theorists, because of their suspicion, inherited in large part perhaps from the influential Frankfurt School, that high technology has become a principal obstacle to social progress and economic justice. We cannot hope to allay this suspicion; in fact, if our argument is successful, we will exacerbate it. We believe that the cultural significance of the new digital media cannot be condemned or praised in isolation, precisely because these media are hybrids that draw on so many aspects of our culture. To condemn new media is to condemn contemporary culture itself—in a kind of jeremiad that has made a few humanists wealthy but has not helped to explain our current cultural moment. We are attempting to explore, not to pass judgment on, the twin logics of remediation at work on the eve of the twenty-first century.

The Remediation of the Gendered Gaze

One more key theoretical issue remains to be touched on: the implications of gender for our understanding of remediation. Among the best-known illustrations of the Renaissance theory of linear perspective is the Dürer woodcut in which the male draftsman objectifies and mathematically dissects his female model (cf. Alpers 1982, 184–185, 187;

Figure 3.1 A draftsman drawing a nude from Albrecht Dürer, *Unterweysung der Messung,* Nuremberg, 1538.

Haraway 1997, 182–183). (See fig. 3.1.) In this image, the artist's desire for immediacy is evident in his clinical gaze, which seems to want to analyze and control, if not possess, its female object. The woodcut suggests the possibility that technologies of transparent immediacy based on linear perspective, such as perspective painting, photography, and film, or computer graphics and virtual reality, may all be enacting the so-called male gaze, excluding women from full participation as subjects and maintaining them as objects.

Beginning with Alberti's window, transparent immediacy itself may be a gendered notion. Martin Jay (1988) has suggested that Albertian technical perspective joined with Descartes's philosophical dualism to constitute "Cartesian perspectivalism"—a way of seeing that characterized Western culture at least until the coming of modernism in the twentieth century ⊗ **p. 21**. Evelyn Fox Keller and Christine Grontkowski (1996) have associated Descartes's dualism with the privileging of the visual and also with Western, masculinist science (187–202). They also point out that "there is a movement among a number of feminists to sharpen what, until now, had only been a vague sentiment . . . : that the logic of the visual is a male logic. According to one critic [Luce Irigaray], what is absent from the logic . . . is women's desire" (187). For these feminists, then, the desire for visual immediacy is a male desire that takes on an overt sexual meaning when the object of representation, and therefore desire, is a woman, as in the Dürer woodcut.

Film is the medium for which feminist theorists have delivered perhaps the most powerful and sustained critique of the male gaze. In the 1970s, in a now-classic essay, Laura Mulvey argued that Hollywood film almost inevitably enacts that way of looking, because both the camera work and the narrative structure cause the viewers to identify with the usually male main character and to join him in his visual examination of women:

The actual image of woman as (passive) raw material for the (active) gaze of man takes the argument a step further into the content and structure of representation, adding a further layer of ideological significance demanded by the patriarchal order in its favorite cinematic form—illusionistic narrative film. . . . Although none of these interacting layers is intrinsic to film, it is only in the film form that they can reach a perfect and beautiful contradiction, thanks to the possibility in the cinema of shifting the emphasis of the look. The place of the look defines cinema, the possibility of varying it and exposing it. This is what makes cinema quite different in its voyeuristic potential from, say, striptease, theatre, shows, and so on. Going far beyond highlighting a woman's to-be-looked-at-ness, cinema builds the way she is to be looked at into the spectacle itself . . . . Cinematic codes create a gaze, a world and an object, thereby producing an illusion cut to the measure of desire. (1989, 25)

The desire of which Mulvey speaks certainly seems to be what we call the desire for immediacy, which then becomes a male desire to possess, or perhaps to destroy, the female. The case is clearest in detective films, such as Hitchcock's *Vertigo* (1958), in which the detective follows, observes, and not coincidentally falls in love with the women he is asked to investigate. Through Hitchcock's transparent style, we share the detective's gaze and perhaps his desire for both cognitive and sexual immediacy, which is the real subject of the film. ▷ **p. 150** Mulvey suggests that film is the definitive medium for representing this desire, because only film can offer a mobile and shifting point of view. She exaggerates somewhat. Striptease (and perhaps the theater in general) would also seem to build the way woman is to be looked at into the spectacle itself. What else is striptease, in fact, but a highly stylized structure for gazing at women? Nevertheless, film's claim to immediacy is that it defines and controls the structure of the gaze with greater precision. Mulvey is in fact arguing that film remediates striptease and the theater (we would add photography and painting) through its ability to change point of view, and, because of this remediation, it offers a new path to satisfying a familiar desire.

It may well be that film and other technologies of transparent immediacy enact a gendered form of looking. On the other hand, visual media can pursue other routes to immediacy than perfect transparency. Television's claim to immediacy depends not only on its transparency (conventional television is not as visually precise as film), but also on its ability to present events "live." ◁ **p. 187**. The immediacy of such new media as computer games and the World Wide Web is supposed to come through interactivity—the fact that these media can change their point of view in response to the viewer or user. Indeed, interactivity even forms part of virtual reality's claim to immediacy. Finally, there is the immediacy that comes through hypermediacy—an immediacy that grows out of the frank acknowledgment of the medium and is not based on the perfect visual re-creation of the world. In such cases, we do not look *through* the medium in linear perspective; rather, we look *at* the medium or at a multiplicity of media that may appear in windows on a computer screen or in the fragmented elements of a collage or a photomontage. We do not gaze; rather, we glance here and there at the various manifestations of the media. This immediacy is not based on a desire to control and appropriate the female form, or any form, and may not be univocally gendered.[2]

Even within the cinema, there can be a hypermediacy of which Mulvey does not take adequate account. Recent film theorists such as Linda Williams (1995, 1–22) have criticized Mulvey's influential view for not attending to the multiplicity of possible viewers and viewing positions. Early film defined an alternative viewing position, which Tom Gunning (1995) has called the "cinema of attractions," and to which recent Hollywood film is returning with the help of computer graphics. ◁ **p. 155** Other theorists argue that we need to understand the filmic gaze in the context of other media or mediated experiences— for example, in the early days of film, the pleasures of strolling along boulevards and through arcades, of looking into shops, and of visiting museums and other exhibits (Friedberg 1995, 59–83; Schwartz 1995, 87–113). Vanessa Schwartz goes on to compare our contemporary cinema to the mediated spaces of shopping malls. ◁ **p. 174** Paul Young (1998) has argued that some early films were concerned with the potential rivalry of the telegraph, wireless, and radio. In other words, from its beginnings the cinema has entered into remediating relationships with a variety of other forms, and these relationships may encourage ways of looking other than the appropriating male gaze.

Networks of Remediation

2. For psychoanalysis, immediacy may not be gendered in any univocal way. In Freudian terms, the desire for immediacy may well be a kind of prephallic desire to unite with the mother or return to the womb. This desire can be shared by women. Even in Lacanian terms, the desire for wholeness—the desire to get back behind the psychic split defined by the mirror stage—is something that both men and women can feel, although in different ways.

The model offered by Christian Metz and Laura Mulvey treats the cinema as a medium in isolation. In fact, they understand the viewer's experience of film as one of enforced isolation: he sits in a darkened theater and falls under the imaginary spell of the cinematic apparatus. However, in our media-saturated culture, we see film through other media and other media through film in a play of mutual remediations. The experience of transparent immediacy remains important in contemporary Hollywood film, but it is not the sole experience that even Hollywood film offers. Even for a male viewer, a recurring fascination with the medium distances and frames the viewing experience; the viewer oscillates between a desire for immediacy and a fascination with the medium. This distancing and framing occur not only for the spectator in the darkened theater, but also during all the other manifestations that precede and follow that supposedly isolated experience: the previews playing on monitors in the lobby of the theater; the home viewing of whole films on videocassette; the appearance of trailers, film stills, and information on the World Wide Web; and so on. These agents of remediation are at work for older films as well as contemporary ones. Perhaps it was still possible in 1958 to view *Vertigo* in relative isolation from other media. (In its early days, television remediated vaudeville and live theater more often than it remediated film. ◈ **p. 185**) But now even old films are caught in the logic of hypermediacy. In the mid-1990s a remastered version of *Vertigo* was released for the theater, and part of the remastering process included digital enhancing. The movie is available on videocasette and on laser disk, and a search of of the Web reveals well over two-thousand web documents that mention Hitchcock's *Vertigo,* some of which include film stills.

As a result of such remediations, we may all experience film and other visual media with something of that multiple consciousness or "double desire" that Teresa de Lauretis (1984, 155) ascribes to the female spectator, who is necessarily shut out from any simple participation in the transparent male gaze (cf. Doane 1991, 17–32). The remediation of the male gaze is apparent in *Strange Days,* when Lenny experiences a wire recording of a brutal rape and murder simultaneously from the points of view of the male assailant and his female victim. ◈ **p. 163**. The violent potential of the male gaze is not denied, but it is certainly complicated by the remediating power of the wire. The male gaze can be distanced and framed by new media as well—for example, in the Amsterdam webcam, which purports to monitor the windows of rooms occupied by prostitutes (fig. 12.12). Although such a webcam seems perfectly to enact the male gaze, no one could find this site even mildly erotic. The viewer may certainly be curious about what is going on behind the shades, but his desire for immediacy must pass quickly into a fascination with the medium. ⊘ **p. 208**

Furthermore, it is not clear whether the desire for immediacy must necessarily be expressed in the scopophilia of the male gaze. For if the male gaze takes as its sole purpose to control and possess the female, then the desire for immediacy implies another kind of looking as well. In formal terms, the desire for immediacy is the desire to get beyond the medium to the objects of representation themselves. Different media may enact this desire in different ways. Although linear-perspective painting and film may keep the viewer distant from what he views, in virtual reality the viewer steps through Alberti's window and is placed among the objects of representation. Similarly, the desire for sexual immediacy could aim for a voyeuristic examination of the objects of representation or a union with them. If the aim is voyeuristic, then the spectator is practicing the traditional male gaze. However, if the aim is union, then the desire for immediacy could be interpreted in Lacanian terms as the longing gaze of the mirror stage—a desire to return to an original state of union (with the mother) prior to the split that defined the subject and simultaneously privileged the male realm of the Symbolic over the realm of the Imaginary. The desire for immediacy then becomes the desire to return to the realm of the Imaginary and could well be shared by female spectators.

Finally, if the male gaze is exclusively an exercise in control and possession, the question remains whether such a gaze can be sustained in contemporary visual media, which are constantly remediating one another and therefore reminding us of the futility of believing that any technology of representation can fully erase itself. We may wonder whether the male gaze was ever represented unproblematicaly even in apparently transparent media. If we look back at the Dürer woodcut, we see that it too is hypermediated, at least to the extent that it does not simply enact the male gaze but represents it. After all, we do not look through the draftsman's eyes in a first-person, point-of-view shot; instead, we see the draftsman in the act of gazing. Since this image is not a motion picture, we cannot have the establishing-shot, point-of-view-shot, reaction-shot sequence that would enact the male gaze more straightforwardly. Instead, we are made conscious of our position as spectators, for our perspective enables us to appreciate the dissecting character of the draftsman's gaze. The subject of this woodcut is the technique of linear perspective itself, which is what makes the image so amenable to a feminist critique. Once again, the desire for immediacy passes into a fascination with media. In this case, the conventional, heterosexual male gaze leaves itself open to another, hypermediated kind of looking.

All this suggests a psychosexual interpretation of the dichotomy between transparent immediacy and hypermediacy. Transparent immediacy attempts to achieve through linear perspective a single, "right" representation of things. Linear perspective becomes the normal and normative way of looking at the world, while hypermediacy becomes the sum of all the unconventional, unusual, and in some sense deviant ways of looking. Hypermediacy is multiple and deviant in its suggestion of multiplicity—a muliplicity of viewing positions and a multiplicity of relationships to the object in view, including sexual objects. Lorraine Gamman (1989, 12) has suggested that the female gaze can be distinguished from the male gaze by its multiplicity—so much so that it may be not be appropriate to speak of the female gaze at all, but rather of a series of looks from various perspectives.

At the same time, Judith Butler (1990) has argued that heterosexuality itself depends on homosexuality for its cultural meaning. While the socially accepted practice of heterosexuality seeks to exclude other sexual practices as deviant, it is precisely this exclusion that enables heterosexuality to define itself as normal and normative: "For heterosexuality to remain intact as a distinct social form, it *requires* an intelligible conception of homosexuality and also requires the prohibition of that conception in rendering it culturally unintelligible. Within [Butler's revised notion of] psychoanalysis, bisexuality and homosexuality are taken to be primary libidinal dispositions, and heterosexuality is the laborious construction based upon their gradual repression" (77). In the same way, we might argue that linear perspective, which enacts the heterosexual male gaze, depends on hypermediacy, which is defined as an "unnatural" way of looking at the world. As the sum of all unnatural modes of representation, hypermediacy can then be used to justify the immediacy of linear perspective. It would be for this reason that hypermediacy always reemerges in every era, no matter how rigorously technologies of transparency may try to exclude it. Transparency needs hypermediacy.

The chapters in part II are not in any sense meant to be comprehensive studies; instead, they illustrate the process of remediation in about a dozen contemporary media. We will observe how digital media, such as computer games, the World Wide Web, and virtual reality, refashion their predecessors and each other in their efforts to convince us of their transparency or to confront us with a striking variety of media and mediations. We will see how established media, such as film and television, respond by trying to incorporate digital media within their traditional formal and social structures. There is, by the way, nothing wrong or even unusual in an older medium's attempt to refashion a younger one. The relative age of a technology is certainly a factor in its cultural meaning. For example, supporters of the printed book use its venerable age to claim a special status. And the fact that the classical cinema predates computer games by a hundred years gives it a repertoire of visual techniques that computer games in fact want to appropriate. The longevity of film also gives it a tradition as a collective social experience, to which supporters of film can appeal. For our traits of immediacy, hypermediacy, and remediation, historical affiliations among media do indeed matter; however, there are other formal and social affiliations for which the chronology is not important. All currently active media (old and new, analog and digital) honor, acknowledge, appropriate, and implicitly or explicitly attack one another. Various media adopt various strategies, which are tried out by designers and creators in each medium (and sometimes in each genre within a medium) and then sanctioned or discouraged by larger economic and cultural forces.

We have not tried to organize the following chapters in any strict chronological or thematic order. In some cases, chapters are juxtaposed to highlight certain affiliations, but readers are invited to sample the chapters in any order that suits their own interests in or sense of the comparisons and the contrasts among media.

The term *computer game* covers a range of forms, including violent action games, strategy games, role-playing and narrative games, erotic and frankly pornographic applications, card games, puzzles and skill-testing exercises, and educational software. Some of these forms are clear repurposings of early games. Some computer games restage famous board games, from Monopoly to Trivial Pursuit; others enact war games (including reenactments of World War II, the Civil War, and so on), which were first introduced and are still played as intricate board games. There are digital versions of every popular American sport from golf to football, which remediate on at least two levels. Because sports themselves are staged events and at the same time televised performances, the computerized versions can refashion our experience of both.

Computer games are delivered on a variety of platforms, which are themselves multiply remediating artifacts: arcade machines, video units that connect to a television set, CD-ROM (or DVD) applications for desktop computers, games sites and servers on the Internet to be received by desktop computers or televisions with set-top boxes, and portable games units. In all their forms and with all their modes of delivery, digital games illustrate the commodification of the computer.

ARCADE AND VIDEO GAMES

Games were introduced first in arcades and then as home video units in the early 1970s (Herz 1997, 14), a time when only organizations and businesses could afford fully programmable mainframes and minicomputers. (The first do-it-yourself computer kits, such as the Altair 8800, also date from this time, but they were of interest only to skilled hobbyists.) The ongoing development of arcade and home games paralleled or anticipated the development of the desktop computer and its interface. These games in fact repurposed the mainframe and the mini as well as the desktop computer, with an implicit suggestion that gaming, or at least an immediately responsive, graphical interface, is what computing should really be about.

As games became more graphically sophisticated, the desktop computer did too, so that the remediations were at times mutual. Sometimes the desktop computer would run ahead of the games (the Macintosh interface in 1984 was more graphically sophisticated than many contemporary games); sometimes the visual presence and interactive strategies of the games would suggest new paths for the desktop interface. Finally, the portable units, such as the Nintendo Game Boy introduced in 1989 (Herz 1997, 21), repurposed the pocket calculator and the portable computer, with a claim to immediacy of experience through the intense, almost hypnotic involvement of the user.

The earliest games in arcades were not at all photorealistic; indeed, they just managed to break out of one dimension into the second. Although the famous game Pong consisted of nothing more than lines and circles on an empty field, it nevertheless liberated the user from the conventions of contemporary computers, which were still programmed with punched cards or at best through a dumb terminal with a command-line interface. In Pong, it was as if the circles and lines had flown off the command line and could ricochet around the screen (fig. 4.1). Although the graphics were primitive, Pong and other first-generation games were hypermediated in that they called attention to an interface that seemed at the time to be moving at a frenetic pace. No one confused Pong with a game of tennis or Ping-Pong in the physical world. Nevertheless, it was a genuine surprise to watch a dot on the screen behave like a ball, bouncing off each striking paddle or ricocheting off the side of the screen and returning on an appropriate trajectory. There was a vast difference between this graphic behavior and the operations of a traditional computer, which manipulated symbols and presented its results only in rows of alphanumeric characters on the screen or on perforated printer paper. The game suggested new formal and cultural purposes for digital technology.

Soon the arcade games became fully two-dimensional, with figures cruising, running, or hopping around as inhabitants of an electronic Flatland, thus anticipating and then later refashioning the desktop interface as it evolved in the 1980s. In the popular PACMAN, for example, the amoeba-like figures can be seen as weird desktop icons, repurposed from the sedate task of representing data files and directo-

Figure 4.1 Pong, an early video game. © 1998, Sherri Locker/FOX News. Used by permission.

ries and set in motion to gobble up or be gobbled (fig. 4.2). Like all the other action games from this era, PACMAN is completely opaque; there is nothing behind or beyond the interface, as there appears to be with a perspective painting or photograph. The game is an interface, and so for the player the immediacy of the experience can come only through acknowledging the medium. ◈ **p. 31**

Action games in arcades, on video units, and on computers have continued to require the user's intimate involvement with the interface. Some developers have created more visually complicated games without showing any particular concern to pursue transparency. Others have worked toward a three-dimensional transparency, toward producing in the user a feeling of immersion through linear perspective and a first-person point of view. In addition to remediating the computer itself, these games also remediate television and film. In fact, the distinction between the more hypermediated and the more transparent games often turns on whether the primary remediation is television or film.

Video games are played on a repurposed television set, one in which an attached control unit transforms the screen into a different medium. Such video game systems constitute a commodity different from broadcast television shows—one intended for a particular group (boys in their pre- and early teens) and packaged and paid for in a differ-

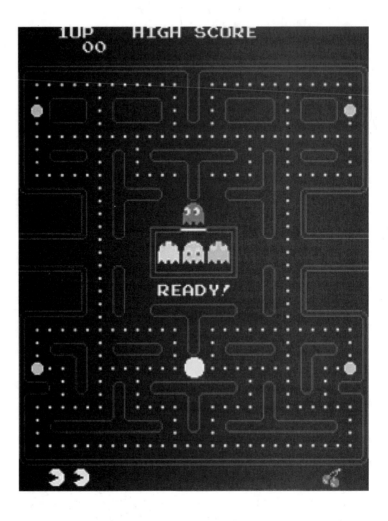

Figure 4.2 PACMAN, an early video game.

ent way. The game units co-opt broadcast television to offer a kind of entertainment whose characteristics include simple but violent narratives and tightly coupled interaction between the player and the screen. At least for its audience of young users, the interactivity is an improvement over conventional television. Although the remote control for a conventional set allows the viewer only to change channels, reduce the sound, and make other relatively minor alterations in the video stream, the joysticks, keyboards, and trackballs of the games refashion and magnify the player's sense of control. Video games, as well as the action-style arcade and computer games, nevertheless continue to show the influence of conventional television.

Television operates more often under the logic of hypermediacy than does film. For a variety of reasons, television readily acknowledges itself as a medium, and action-style games are like television in this willingness to acknowledge their own mediation. Like television, these games function in real time: either the player tries explicitly to "beat the clock" or faces some other limitation, such as the amount of ammunition, which defines the rushed pace of the game. Finally, like television, these games are about monitoring the world. Television and video cameras monitor continuously the visual scene at which they are pointed. ▷ **p. 187** In the same way, players of action-style games are called on to conduct an ongoing surveillance. They are assigned explicitly or implicitly the role of security guards, whose simple task is to shoot anything that appears threatening. Because the ultimate threat is that the enemy will destroy the equilibrium of the system and eventually halt the game by destroying the player himself, the player must constantly scan the visual field and direct his fire appropriately. Ideologically, the player is asked to defend or reestablish the status quo, so that even though the violence of the games appears to be antisocial, the ultimate message is not. It is a message that has prevailed from the early games such as *Space Invaders* in the 1970s to such games as *Doom* and *Quake* in the 1990s (fig. 4.3). For decades, action games have played out the most aggressive form of televisual monitoring.

In the 1980s, first arcade games and then video and computer games began to exploit three-dimensional graphics and so to define a space that could be continuous with the user. Designers could then make the games remediate not only the monitoring function of all video, but also the narrative functions of television and film. An early example was *Dragon's Lair,* which contained short segments of linear video (Herz 1997, 147). Arcade games and video games have not exploited the possibilities of interactive narrative as have computer games, however, probably because the arcade and the living room are too public and noisy. Interactive narrative games favor a single user with the time and the solitude to solve puzzles and make choices. These more thoughtful games remediate film rather than video.

INTERACTIVE FILM

Graphic, role-playing computer games derive their narrative structure from earlier textual games (*Zork* and similar adventure games), which themselves come from fantasy literature, such as Tolkien's *The Lord of the Rings.* Their visual tradition is that of three-dimensional graphics and ultimately, therefore, the tradition of realistic, perspective painting. Such games seek the real, sometimes through transparency and sometimes through hypermediacy—sometimes by encouraging the player to look through the surface of the screen and sometimes by dwelling on the surface with its multiplicity of mediated objects. This combination is what makes Tolkien's trilogy such an attractive model for game designers and players. Although the books describe a world of fantastic events and characters with a photorealistic attention to detail, the text calls attention to itself with its antiquated prose and poetry. The elements of immediacy and hypermediacy combine to create an effect that many computer game designers have consciously or unconsciously imitated. This is the case with the extraordinarily popular and influential *Myst,* which is compelling because it simultaneously remediates several media on several levels (cf. Smith forthcoming). *Myst* combines three-dimensional, static graphics with text, digital video, and sound to refashion illusionistic painting, film, and, somewhat surprisingly, the book as well. Almost certainly without the conscious intent of its authors, *Myst* turns out to be an allegory about the remediation of the book in an age of digital graphics.

The logic of immediacy requires that the acts of mediation be concealed, and *Myst* is about concealment, about hidden puzzles whose solutions open up new graphic worlds and bring the player closer to

Figure 4.4 Myst island contained within the Myst book. © 1993 Cyan Inc. Myst ® Cyan Inc. Reprinted with permission.

solving the mystery of the father and his two sons. "Myst" is not only the name of the game, but also the name of the book that tumbles into a crevice during the game's cinematic opening credits. The book then opens to reveal the island, as books in movies in the 1930s often opened to reveal a picture that then became the first scene of the film (fig. 4.4). There is a whole library on Myst island, some of whose books describe worlds that the father has created. Two strange volumes actually contain his evil sons—we can see them as noisy video images inside the pages of the books—while the father, named Atrus, is trapped elsewhere (fig. 4.5). The concealment in *Myst* comes through containment, replication, and changes of scale. Like a series of nested Russian dolls, the Myst book contains the island, which in turn contains the library, which contains the books, which contain the sons. At the same time, the game makes unwitting allusions to the literature of generational conflict from the *Oresteia* to *Finnegans Wake*. The game and the allusions begin with the literal fall of Atrus into the crevice, where the falling father morphs into the falling book. The father thus becomes the book that becomes the game. Eventually the player discovers that the two volumes that contain the brothers are incomplete: their videos are faulty because their pages have been scattered. So the player must hunt for these pages throughout the *Myst* worlds. If the player retrieves a

Figure 4.5 One of the sons of Atrus in *Myst.* © 1993 Cyan Inc. Myst ® Cyan Inc. Reprinted with permission.

certain page from another world, she can gain access to a chamber where the father has been imprisoned by his sons. The father then goes back to the library and apparently destroys the two books that hold his sons. If the player makes the mistake of trusting either son and places all of the blue or red pages in one son's book, then that son escapes and the player must take his place, trapped in the book.

The allegory is obvious: the book as a text should be replaced by the book as a window onto a visually realized world. Books operate best (or as best they can) under the logic of immediacy, but computer graphics are more immediate and therefore better. If the player wins by helping the father destroy the brothers' books, she transcends the book as a texture of symbols and is allowed to remain in the world of computer graphics. If she fails, she is trapped forever in the book itself—the worst possible fate in the age of graphics. In the course of playing, what the Myst player is actually discovering are the moments and strategies by which the computer game remediates the printed book.

In denying the book, *Myst* is also affirming the book's great rival in the twentieth century: film. *Myst*'s refashioning of film is subtle. The game offers very little digitized video (although the video it offers is strategically important) and instead presents the player with a series of tableaux that change only when she clicks. Still, there is no question that the game draws heavily on such detective films as *Vertigo* and *Chinatown,* which present the detective as voyeur. *Myst* is an interactive detective film in which the player is cast in the role of detective. It is also a film "shot" entirely in the first person, in itself a remediation of the Hollywood style, where first-person point of view is used only sparingly—except in special cases, such as *Strange Days* recently and some film noir in the 1940s. (See Telotte, 1989.) Like many of the other role-playing games, *Myst* is in effect claiming that it can succeed where film noir failed: that it can constitute the player as an active participant in the visual scene. As Lenny in *Strange Days* might put it, *Myst* is trying to be "like film only better."

Myst tries to improve on film by redefining the standard by which we judge film. In many instances of remediation, the new medium must try to convince the viewer to accept a new standard, for the older medium is inevitably superior when judged by its own traditions. In *Myst,* for example, the mystery is singularly lacking in the rhythmic variations we find in the traditional film. If anything, the game's narrative stillness is like the arrested time in such unusual (and by Hollywood standards unsuccessful) films as Antonioni's *L'Avventura, Blow-up,* and *The Passenger. Myst* sustains almost to the end the single moment in which the detective is on the verge of making a discovery, although our viewing habits from film tell us that that moment cannot last indefinitely. We expect some revelation and probably some violence, and our expectation is the source of the game's quiet suspense. When we enter a dark passage on Myst island, we expect a creature to come out of the darkness at us—but nothing ever comes.

Unlike in Antonioni's films, however, resolution *is* possible in *Myst,* through the solution of a series of puzzles. These puzzles constitute the player as a detective only in the shallow sense, for they do not move the player deeper into the mystery, into a mystery of self. When the player does find and free the father, she does not learn anything about herself. And unlike in *Blow-up,* the player of *Myst* ultimately rejects the logic of mediation in favor of the logic of the transparent, which the father Atrus affirms by destroying the books.

The purpose of *Myst*'s remediation of film is not principally to comment on film; the creators of *Myst* may not even be aware of specific affiliations of their game to films made a generation ago. However, the game is undeniably an exercise in cinematic point of view, and even the vaguest acquaintance with the Hollywood style is enough for a player to appreciate *Myst*'s appropriation and remediation of it. The feeling of immediacy in *Myst,* as in other games of this genre, is generated in large part by the player's expectations derived from the medium of film. It is not really as if the player were on Myst island, which after all looks like no island on earth; it is as if the player were in a film about Myst island. The game can only attempt to satisfy the viewer's desire for immediacy by seeming to put her in a film. Her sense of immediacy comes only through an awareness of mediation.

Myst is by no means the only example of a computer game that remediates film, although it is unusually resonant with the history of film. Myst's sequel, *Riven,* appears to reiterate the strategy of the first game, employing the same interface of pointing and clicking through static images (and in some cases video). But the images are more photo-realistic and the game in general is even more calculated in its pursuit of immediacy.

We might also have examined *The Last Express,* which is more overtly filmic than *Myst* or *Riven.* Although the characters and backgrounds are graphic stills and animations (in some cases generated from filmed figures by motion capture), the mise-en-scène and the "camera shots" are entirely consistent with the Hollywood style (fig. 4.6). The player clearly feels herself to be in a film—as usual, a film of mystery or detection. The plot recalls Hitchcock or Graham Greene: the player is given the role of an American expatriate who must assume the identity of his friend aboard the Orient Express on the eve of World War I. At the beginning, the American character knows nothing about the plot in which he is implicated with the discovery of his friend's murder. In typical Hitchcock fashion, he must learn more while avoiding arrest by the police and whatever danger killed his friend. He must learn in real time as the train moves across Europe—by walking up and down the corridors, meeting people who seem to know him, and eaves-dropping on conversations that may provide useful information. One of the most compelling features of *The Last Express* is the way in which a filmic sense of plot is integrated with the monitoring function that computer games have in common with television.

In addition to such resonant examples as *Myst* and *The Last Express,* there are now hundreds of less innovative games, many based explicitly on Hollywood originals. Some of these, such as *Blade Runner,* use three-dimensional graphics to recreate the atmosphere and cinematic style of the original film. Others string together segments of live-action film, as does *Star Trek Borg: The Interactive Movie,* which is shot entirely from the first-person point of view of the player as a character.

Figure 4.6 Cinematic sequence in *The Last Express.* Graphics/images courtesy of The Last Express ®, a game by Jordan Mechner. © 1997 Broderbund Software, Inc. All rights reserved. Used by permission.

Just as photorealism has defined reality as being in a photograph, interactive films define it as being in a movie. In games such as *Borg,* the player as character is addressed by fellow characters in the scenes, and her choices change the course of events. Typically, conventional filmed scenes establish the narrative line, while the player's action at various decision points will determine which filmed scenes will be presented next. Although the interaction between the player and the filmed scene is clumsy, the goal of this genre is to close such gaps and give the player the sense that she has "fallen into a movie." Role-playing computer games are attempting to move from hypermediacy to immediacy by concealing the signs of their mediation.

SEX, VIOLENCE, AND COMPUTER GAMES

Computer games have become popular visual media, and so erotic and violent computer games are open to the same pressure for public censorship that affects film and television. The charge that the games promote violence in society has been repeated since the early 1980s, even by a surgeon general of the United States (Herz 1997, 184), when action games became graphically sophisticated. In addition, religious conservatives and some feminists are critical of erotic games. Computer games come under attack precisely because they remediate the two genres (film and television) that American society has come to regard as immediate and therefore potentially threatening. Books are not censored as strictly as film and television because for our visual culture the written word does not have the immediacy that a moving picture has.

In fact, mainstream American culture seems to have established a hierarchy of media according to their assumed immediacy, a hierarchy revealed in particular by erotic representation. Written or printed pornography without illustrations is regarded as the least immediate. Graphic pornography, such as comic books and illustrated sex manuals, comes next. The major cultural line is clearly crossed with photography. Erotic photographs are subject to censorship or possible criminal charges in ways that graphic art and books no longer are. This cultural reaction stems from a belief in the immediacy of photography. The assumption is that the human models must have actually performed the act revealed in the photograph and that the image is caused by the reflected light that traveled from their bodies to the film. It is as if the erotic impulse could pass through the photograph to touch the viewer. Film and video are even more threatening because they are regarded as photographs in motion.

The place of digital technology in this hierarchy has been shifting over the past two decades. When the technology was used primarily to store and retrieve alphanumeric information, the closest analogy was the book. When digital technology became graphic, it could take on the cultural status of erotic picture books or photographs. Now, computer applications are setting these erotic graphics and digitized images in motion, with, as always, the promise of an interactivity not possible with linear video. As the computer offers greater visual immediacy, it becomes a greater threat to those in our culture who fear erotic immediacy.

Pornography has been among the first expressions of two recent media, the VCR and the graphical World Wide Web, as well as the stereoscope in the nineteenth century. It is true that in the last two centuries practitioners of each new visual medium have sought out content that will demonstrate its powers of immediacy, so that pornography has been one (tempting) test of immediacy. Today, enthusiasts for computer graphics and virtual reality hold out eroticism as an indication of progress, when they speak of cybersex or "teledildonics" (Rheingold 1991, 345–353). Depictions of violence offer another test of immediacy, one that for our culture is somehow felt to be less threatening than sex. Hence, scenes of violence permit popular film, television, and now computer games to demonstrate their powers of immediacy before a wider audience.

Designers in digital media can choose to represent sex through either the logic of transparency or the logic of hypermediacy. The obvious impulse is to seek immediacy through transparency, to try to erase the interface from the user's consciousness so that the experience seems as authentic as possible. In fact, in choosing to remediate film, the computer game designer is also choosing to reenact the sexually aggressive male gaze that has been associated with traditional film. ◇ **p. 78** Erasure of the medium is difficult for computer games, as it is for film, because in both the experience must be represented visually without the crucial sense of touch. Feminist critics have argued that film and computer environments are disembodied visual experiences. ◇ **p. 236** In the case of film, the camera work—point-of-view shots, unusual camera angles, and so on—is used to attempt to make up for the lack of the body. These shots are set up in the name of transparency but often create a hypermediated effect. There is, for example, an erotic cliché in Hollywood cinema, in which the camera moves with such intimacy over entangled bodies that it is difficult to determine exactly what part of whose body is being viewed. The bodies become abstract forms, making the viewer aware of the medium of film. It is perhaps not surprising that film would use detailed editing to strive for the immediacy of sex. Computer games, which still cannot match professional film in camera work and editing, rely instead on their special claim to immediacy through interactivity. They allow the player to intervene in the action and so to define a role unlike the one offered by film, video, or photography.

One of the early erotic programs, *Virtual Valerie,* offers a simple branching structure and graphics primitive by today's standards. It remains interesting, however, for the way in which it oscillates between transparency and hypermediacy. Terry Harpold (1998) has called *Valerie* an example of "programmed failure," because the first release was programmed to reboot the computer if the player failed to satisfy Valerie. This failure abruptly denies the player any illusion of immediacy and reminds him that he is merely interacting with a computer program.

Erotic computer games, such as *Valerie,* promise immediacy through transparency, but this promise is always compromised by the failure of the interface to remain transparent, just as film or video sex is compromised by its failure. The result is often, perhaps always, that the program reverts to its other strategy of hypermediacy—poking fun at its own failure or using multimedia or self-conscious camera work to call attention to itself as a medium. Representations of violence also revert to hypermediacy, in computer games as in film. The violence is stylized, performed by cartoon-like characters and controlled by elaborate, "unrealistic" rules of interaction (with joystick, keyboard, or mouse). Games that depict flight simulation in jet fighters (such as *A-10 Attack!*) revel in the hypermediacy of violence, as the players must destroy their targets by engaging the complicated cockpit controls of the jet.

THE SOCIAL SPACES OF COMPUTER GAMES

Arcade games, home video games, and desktop computer games each operate within their own social space. Arcade games are usually grouped in a commercial space, such as a shopping mall or an airport. ⊚ **p. 166** An arcade hall is a collection of mechanical, mechanical-electronic, and fully electronic games, in which the electronic versions remediate the earlier mechanical forms such as pinball. All the games together create a frenzied atmosphere of light and sound, the young adolescent equivalent of nightclubs, which the players are too young to visit. Nightclubs, of course, with their rock music and elaborate lighting effects, are also experiments in hypermediacy. Home video games must be played where the television is located, which is often a relatively large and public room. Although only one or two people can actively participate, everyone who sits in or walks through the room shares the experience of the game. In an action game, everyone in the room gets caught up in the act of monitoring the environment. As with conventional television, the home video game becomes the focus of the room's attention and redefines the social space. Desktop computer games, played where the computer is located in an office or perhaps a bedroom, are comparatively antisocial, for they are often designed for a single player.

On the other hand, desktop games may use networking to expand their social space beyond the confines of the office or bedroom (Foster 1997). *Myst*, with no network connection and providing only for a solitary player occupying a single (though mobile) point of view, cannot begin to address the social dimension of film, the collective experience of an audience. Ironically, the violent and tremendously popular *Doom* (and its successor, *Quake*) is in this sense more socially conscious than *Myst*. With *Doom* you can play with one or more networked partners, with whom you share the work of eliminating monsters, and, if you get in the way of the other players' weapons, you too can be eliminated. *Doom* defines community as a community of killers, the high-tech version of a tribe of paleolithic hunters. Like MUDs and MOOs, *Doom* is socially shared in another sense. It allows experienced users to build new architectural "levels," in which the game of destruction can continue. There is an entire community of such users on the Internet who construct and share the vast environment that *Doom* has become. The game's capacity to absorb authors and forge them into a community is in fact an implied improvement over traditional cinema, in which the viewers cannot reshape or add to the narrative structure. Networked games make a claim to improve on the social practice not only of other computer games, but of television and film as well.

The Internet promises to assimilate the social space of gaming to the space of MUDs and MOOs, as computer games connected to the network can serve as sites for "virtual communities." According to its promotional web site, the role-playing game *Ultima Online*

allows literally thousands of people to exist simultaneously in the same fantasy game world over the Internet.

Players can enjoy true social interaction with other participants in real time—form adventuring parties, engage in battles with other players, take on perilous quests, or chat in a tavern over a goblet of virtual wine.

Other elements of the game constantly evolve—a functioning virtual ecology drives monsters to roam in search of food if it's scarce, and world events are inter-related through a closed economic system and limited resources.

Ultima Online *allows players to indulge in a continuous, ever-changing game world, complete with day and night, light and shadow effects, 3-D terrain and 16-bit color SVGA graphics. (http://www.owo.com/info/index.html January 11, 1998)*

Like MUDs and MOOs, *Ultima Online* and other such game worlds promise transparent immediacy through real-time interactive graphics or text. (Yet promises of transparency and hypermediacy are surprisingly juxtaposed. *Ultima*'s virtual kingdom comes complete with "day and night" as well as sixteen-bit color graphics.) Like other manifestations of cyberspace, a networked role-playing game such as *Ultima Online* offers its players a world parallel to, yet distinct from, their contemporary social and physical space, a world with its own ecology, economics, and perhaps even physics. The rhetoric of escape is common among enthusiasts for many forms of cyberspace: virtual reality, MUDs and MOOs, role-playing games, and even newsgroups and email. All of these manifestations are supposed to provide a new and authentic experience while at the same time they divorce us from the physical world.

Digital Photography

If computer graphics is sometimes called on to refashion the photo-graph ⊘ **p. 119**, photography is also used to refashion computer graph-ics. Many remediations are reciprocal in the sense that they invite us to imagine each medium as trying to remediate the other. In such cases, deciding which medium is remediating and which is remediated is a matter of interpretation, for it comes down to which medium is re-garded as more important for a certain purpose.

If an image is captured with a digital camera, there is no chemi-cal process as with analog photography. Instead, the image is recorded by photosensitive cells and never exists except as bits. Is such an image a photograph or a computer graphic? If the image began as a conven-tional photograph and was scanned into the computer and digitally re-touched, is it then a photograph or a computer graphic? In what is called digital photography, the result is an image that is advertised as a photograph and meant to be read as such by the viewer. The digital photographer, who captures images digitally, adds computer graphic elements to conventional photographic images, or combines two or more photographs digitally, still wants us to regard the result as part of the tradition of photography. For the photographers and their audi-ences, digital photography (like digital compositing and animation in traditional film) ⊘ **p. 146** is an attempt to prevent computer graphic technology from overwhelming the older medium.

Computer photorealism is trying to achieve precisely what dig-ital photography is trying to prevent: the overcoming and replacement of the earlier technology of photography. And yet success in overcoming photography would have consequences that the computer graphics spe-cialists do not necessarily foresee, given that most graphics specialists remain realists as well as photorealists. If they could achieve perfect photorealism, then they could create "photographs" without natural light. An image could be synthesized to meet the viewer's desire for immediacy without the need for the objects in the image to have existed or to have been together at any time, which was exactly the condition that Roland Barthes considered the definition of photography in *Camera Lucida*. Complete success in computer photorealism would make nonsense of the term *photorealism*, because no one could any longer believe in a causal connection between the image and the world. Such success would remediate the term *photorealism* out of existence, which is the most radical form of remediation possible.

PHOTOGRAPHIC TRUTH

Digital photography poses a similar threat for those who believe that the traditional photograph has a special relationship to reality. William J. Mitchell (1994) acknowledges the power of digitally manipulated photographs and yet finds that power troubling: "For a century and a half photographic evidence seemed unassailably probative. . . . An interlude of false innocence has passed. Today, as we enter the postphotographic era, we must face once again the ineradicable fragility of our ontological distinctions between the imaginary and the real, the tragic elusiveness of the Cartesian dream" (225).

What Mitchell calls the postphotographic era, we characterize as an era in which photography and digital technologies are remediating each other. But in any case photographic "truth" was not unassailable even in the nineteenth and early twentieth centuries. Impressionists claimed that their paintings captured the truth of light better than photographs could. ⊚ **p. 125** Furthermore, as Mitchell himself documents, in the nineteenth and early twentieth centuries, so-called combination printing could make photographs deceptive. For example, during World War I, two young girls took pictures with cardboard cutouts and managed to convince much of the English public that fairies existed (fig 5.1).

It is remarkably appropriate that these photographs have themselves become the subject of further remediation in the film *Fairy Tale: A True Story* (1997). The film uses computer graphics to let us see the fairies flying around the garden and the girls' room and then presents the girls' photographs as reproductions of what we have already seen to be "real" in the film itself. The original photographs and the 1917 incident were themselves the occasion for the film, but now the film seems

Figure 5.1 Cottingly fairy photograph, 1917. Brotherton Collection, Leeds University Library.

to reverse the relationship. The film and its computer graphics seem to validate the photographs and in the process the characters' and our desire for immediacy.

The truthfulness of the photograph is the issue addressed in the CD-ROM *Truths and Fictions* by the Mexican photographer Pedro Meyer (1995). He offers a collection of forty photographs together with audio and textual commentaries and supporting materials, some of which have been part of a conventional gallery exhibit. The CD-ROM in fact remediates an art gallery in which Meyer's photographs might hang. There is implied rivalry in this remediation—the suggestion that the CD-ROM can present this work more effectively to viewers. As their labels indicate, most of the photographs have been "digitally altered," and the result is a variety of different styles. Some of the photographs are explicit digital collage. Others are realistic except for the appearance of a fantastic, presumably digital, element, such as an angel. In this respect, they are almost visual equivalents of the magic realism of Latin American authors like Gabriel Garcia Marquez. Looking at some of the photographs, we cannot be sure what the computer has changed, for nothing in the picture is unambiguously impossible in the world of light. Meyer's alterations often involve subtly combining two or more photographs, as is the case with *Emotional Crisis* (fig. 5.2). In this case, it is the digitally created wiggle in the striping that attracts our attention; we cannot know that the billboard that gives the photograph its title has been digitally cut from another photograph and

Figure 5.2 Pedro Meyer, *Emotional Crisis (Texas Highway, 1990/1993), altered black and white image.* © Pedro Meyer. All rights reserved. Used by permission.

pasted here. Finally, Meyer labels some of the photographs "unaltered black and white image[s]."

The fact that we know that some of Meyer's photographs have been digitally altered calls the status of all the photographs into question. The images labeled "unaltered" seem as artificial as the others. In fact, because these unaltered images are presented next to the altered ones, it is they (the unaltered) that do some of the most interesting work of remediation. One (*Cardboard People*) shows a man posing before a photographer with cardboard figures of Ronald Reagan and a beautiful woman. Another (*Mona Lisa in the Wax Museum*) shows a woman painting a copy of the *Mona Lisa* from another copy that is before her (fig. 5.3). With their multiple planes and replications of images, *Mona Lisa* and *Cardboard People* are explicitly hypermediated. They represent the desire for immediacy by multiplying media (photographs or paintings) in the image itself, although, if we can believe Meyer, they do so within the single medium of a conventional photograph.

In *Truths and Fictions* Meyer is making Mitchell's point that with the advent of digital technology the photograph has lost the simple relationship to the real that it previously enjoyed. Because the truthfulness of any photograph is now in question, Meyer's composite photographs are supposed to reveal truths (for example, about the banality of American culture) that are more compelling than the factual record to which photography used to lay claim. In an audio track on the CD-ROM, Meyer tells us how to read some of the images and makes

clear his political agenda. The computer allows him to put images together to sharpen his critique of American culture or, in the Mexican photographs, to challenge by subtle disruptions in the surface of the image assumptions about third-world poverty. We can appreciate here the political dimension of remediation. With his digital reworkings, Meyer remediates the traditional photograph into an image that is supposed to be more authentic because of its clarified or intensified ideological message. The CD-ROM is at the same time a political remediation of the museum exhibit, because Meyer can offer aural hyperlinks on the CD that explain the political meaning of the images.

With the creation of digital images like those in *Truths and Fictions,* the status of photography itself has so changed that we are now troubled by Meyer's claim that *any* of his images are "unaltered." How could exposing photographic film to light, developing the negative in a chemical bath, and transferring the result to paper ever constitute an unaltered image? Because of our heightened awareness, for which Meyer and other digital photographers are responsible, we can hardly look on any photograph without taking note of our desire for immediacy. Every photograph becomes not only a failed attempt to satisfy that desire, but also to some extent a representation of that failure. Meyer is trying to exploit our desire for an authentic and immediate political response to the complex images that his camera captures. Here too, Meyer is trying to improve on traditional photography, which he and many others (for example, John Tagg in the *Burden of Representation*) would also regard as an art with a political or ideological dimension. His digital reworkings offer to clarify the political meaning of these images, and in this sense the digital result can be simpler than the analog original.

PHOTOGRAPHING THE DESIRE FOR IMMEDIACY

It is not any one digital photograph that is disturbing. We are disturbed because we must now acknowledge that *any* photograph might be digitally altered. Digital technology may succeed—where combination printing and other analog techniques have not succeeded in the past—in shaking our culture's faith in the transparency of the photograph. However, altered images become a problem only for those who regard photography as operating under the logic of transparency. If the viewer believes that a photograph offers immediate contact with reality, he can be disappointed by a digitally altered photograph. The reason is that the logic of transparency does not accord the status of reality to the medium itself, but instead treats the medium as a mere channel for placing the viewer in contact with the objects represented. Yet a digital photograph can be as transparent as an analog one. The process of digitizing the light that comes through the lens is no more or less artificial than the chemical process of traditional photography. It is a purely cultural decision to claim that darkening the color values of a digitized image by algorithm is an alteration of the truth of the image, whereas keeping an analog negative longer in the developing bath is not.

With this in mind, we can see how digital techniques suggest a new way of understanding all photography. Instead of dividing the world of photography into true and deceptive images, or even into "untouched" and altered images, we can distinguish photographs on the basis of their claims to immediacy. A photograph may be either an expression of the desire for immediacy or a representation of that desire. The photograph that presents itself to be viewed without irony expresses the desire for immediacy, while a photograph that calls attention to itself as a photograph becomes a representation of that desire.

No one has explored the notion of photography as a desire for immediacy more eloquently than Roland Barthes in *Camera Lucida* (1981). For Barthes, photography is special. "More than other arts, Photography offers an immediate presence to the world" (84). Barthes denies the traditional interpretation that photography grows out of perspective painting, precisely because he wants to insist on the immediacy of photography:

It is often said that it was the painters who invented Photography (by bequeath-ing it their framing, the Albertian perspective, and the optic of the camera ob-scura). I say: no, it was the chemists. For the noeme "That-has-been" was possible only on the day when a scientific circumstance (the discovery that silver halogens were sensitive to light) made it possible to recover and print directly the luminous rays emitted by a variously lighted object. The photograph is literally an emanation of the referent. From a real body, which was there, proceed radia-tions which ultimately touch me, who am here. (80)

So photography is not "like painting only better," but is truly transparent:

The realists, of whom I am one and of whom I was already one when I asserted that the Photograph was an image without a code—even if, obviously, certain codes do infect our reading of it—the realists do not take the photograph for a "copy" of reality, but for an emanation of past reality: a magic, not an art. (88)

What makes Barthes's qualified and complicated realism so in-teresting is the way he uses it to articulate the theme of desire. The most moving picture in *Camera Lucida* is the one that Barthes describes in words but does not show us: a picture of his mother as a child, which becomes for him the expression of his own desire to be reunited with a mother who has just died. For Barthes, a photograph is always an ex-pression (not a representation) of loss, of death in fact, because it is an emanation of a past that cannot be retrieved: "All those young photog-raphers who are at work in the world, determined upon the capture of actuality, do not know that they are agents of Death" (92). Although Barthes does not discuss digital photography, clearly any reworked pho-tograph can no longer enjoy this simple and powerful relationship to the past. It becomes instead an image of a second order, a comment on a photograph or on photography itself, and therefore a representation of the desire for immediacy.

At first, then, there seems to be a simple dichotomy: digital photography is hypermediated, while analog photography is transpar-ent. Digital photography appears to complicate and even to mock the desire for immediacy that traditional photography promises to satisfy. On the other hand, because a digital photograph can sometimes be re-garded as transparent, it too can express our desire for immediacy. And because an analog photograph can be reworked and combined with other photographs, it can become a second-order expression, a conscious representation, of that desire. Each technology can perform the cultural function apparently belonging to the other, because transparency always implies hypermediacy, and vice versa.

Digital photography alters our understanding of the prior history of photography. This is the most radical achievement of experimenters like Meyer, far more radical than their overt political message: that they can help to redefine the cultural significance of a past technological moment. We now find ourselves looking at traditional photographs with a nostalgia for the time when digital technology did not exist and could not therefore intervene between the viewer and his desire. At the same time we become conscious of the interventions and choices required even in the analog photography of the nineteenth and early twentieth centuries. It is no accident that the voices (of theorists like Nelson Goodman in *Languages of Art*) against the immediacy of photography grew strong in the 1960s and became increasingly insistent in the following decades, for this was exactly the period in which the mechanical and digital manipulation of photographs became increasingly sophisticated. It is no accident that the French original of Barthes's nostalgic and pessimistic *Camera Lucida* appeared in 1980 (as the first desktop computers were being developed and marketed), at almost the last moment when any sophisticated writer could still claim that an analog photograph was not a representation but an emanation of its subject.

Photorealistic Graphics

6

Photorealistic computer graphics seeks to create a space that is purified of all references to itself as a medium and to other media, and yet it never seems to be able to maintain that purity. Instead, it must appeal to us through the traditions of linear-perspective painting and photography. ▷ **p. 21:** We cannot look at a digital image with eyes innocent of these traditions. Computer graphics specialists acknowledge their dependence on these traditions when they take as their model a painting or photograph rather than "real life." Realistic painters, such as Jan Vermeer, invite such remediation, precisely because their paintings seem to have solved the problem of immediacy that computer graphics also wants to solve. As soon as graphics specialists begin to make this comparison and become concerned with the relative powers of representation of the computer and its predecessors, the logic of hypermediacy has begun to operate. ▷ **p. 31**.

REMEDIATING VERMEER

We can see how easily immediacy passes into hypermediacy by comparing three images. The first (fig. 6.1) is Vermeer's *The Music Lesson,* and the other two (figs. 6.2 and 6.3) are remediations of the Vermeer painting.

The second image (fig. 6.2), a doll's house–sized scale model of the Vermeer painting, is almost a *tableau vivant,* or "living picture." Built by an art critic and scholar, Philip Steadman, to demonstrate the naturalness of Vermeer's handling of linear perspective, the model is real in the sense that it exists as materials in physical space. Vermeer is thought to have used a camera obscura and perhaps even a real room to create his painting (Kemp 1990, 194–196). Steadman reproduces

Figure 6.1 Jan Vermeer, *A Lady at the Virginals with a Gentleman* [*The Music Lesson*]. The Royal Collection. © Her Majesty Queen Elizabeth II. Used by permission.

Vermeer's picture in wood in order to show that a three-dimensional reality could or did lie behind Vermeer's painting. His model makes the world into a medium for representing the painting rather than the reverse.

The third image (fig. 6.3) is a computer graphic generated by creating a mathematical rather than a physical model—one consisting of polygons, textures, and algorithms for linear perspective, illumination, and shading. Steadman presumably wanted to "vindicate" Vermeer by showing his fidelity to reality. The computer graphic image chooses to imitate the Vermeer painting because the painting is itself regarded as a fine imitation of the real. However, there is an identifiable motive of rivalry as well. The creators of this graphic want to measure their model (in particular, its ability to produce lighting and shading effects) against a master painter—to demonstrate that the computer

Figure 6.2 Model of Vermeer's *The Music Lesson.* © Philip Steadman. All rights reserved. Used by permission.

can approach painting and to suggest that it might one day surpass it. Their desire to compete with the Vermeer is the opposite of Steadman's scholarly remediation.

Nevertheless, the doll's house and the computer graphic have much in common as representations. Both begin to operate under the logic of transparent immediacy, and yet both end up being hypermediated and so draw our attention to the medium that they sought to cancel. The doll's house makes no representational sense at all, until we place it beside the Vermeer work and understand that its maker is trying to arrange a small part of the physical world in agreement with the painting. The computer graphic too invites a comparison with the picture. Both of these remediations therefore recognize the reality of media. ▷ **p. 58** They acknowledge the Vermeer painting as a real object in the world to be reproduced, and such acknowledgment is the key

Figure 6.3 Computer graphic modeled on Vermeer's *The Music Lesson.* © 1987 John Wallace (Cornell University, Program of Computer Graphics).

to the logic of hypermediacy. Finally, in trying to demonstrate their transparency by assimilating themselves to the painting, the two remediations add two more almost, but not quite, perfect reproductions to the world. They confirm the reality of media by adding to the fund of media. The fact again is that in this book, all three of these figures are photographic reproductions, illustrating how visual media proliferate as they seek to reproduce other media. The multiplication seems to go on indefinitely. Multiplication and replacement are characteristics of hypermediacy, but even transparent forms of photorealism cannot avoid multiplying themselves and attempting to replace other media.

Immediacy implies hypermediacy in photorealistic graphics, as in photography and perspective painting. The viewer needs the context provided by other media in order to appreciate the immediacy that is being offered. These technologies of visual illusion require the viewer's conscious or unconscious collusion in order to work their magic (cf. Kubovy 1986, 55ff.; Hagen 1980, vol. 1).

VARIETIES OF PHOTOREALISM

Computer graphic photorealism needs at all costs to avoid inconsistencies or breaks in the illusion. It constructs the real as a plenitude, which is one reason that the photograph is used as a model. Consider the fullness of the digital image (fig. 6.4) of Mahogany Hall, the celebrated brothel in the Storyville district of New Orleans in the 1910s (Rose 1974, 80). The furnishings and textures that fill the space are not quite indistinguishable from a photograph, but they give us the impression that the way to the photoreal is simply to add more detail. Digital photorealists want to move more and more pixels or polygons on to the screen in order to bring the image up to the limit of resolution of the human eye. One computer graphics expert, Alvy Ray Smith, has defined reality as 80 million polygons (Rheingold 1991, 168). (In fact, Smith defined reality as 80 million polygons *per second:* this is virtual reality or "filmic" realism rather than static photorealism.) However, if digital photorealists want to paint reality as simple and unitary, our

Figure 6.4 Mahogany Hall computer graphic. http://www.animalu. com/images.htm January 28, 1998. © Jeff Alu, AnimAlu Productions. Used by permission.

culture always seems to complicate the relationship of its media to the real, and this is especially true for digital media. Behind each apparently unified photorealistic image lies another image—a photograph or painting that serves as a model or an analogy, and behind digital photorealism there lies another form of visual representation, manual photorealism.

The photorealist movement in art grows out of the pop art of the 1960s; its practitioners, such as Ralph Goings, Richard Estes, and Charles Bell, create minutely accurate paintings based on photographs. It is possible that neither group of photorealists—the computer graphics experts or the painters—has heard of the other, although they share the same enterprise, the remediation of photography. Both groups rely on the cultural assumption that the photograph has a special relationship to reality. This special relationship has been justified by appealing to the automaticity of the photographic process, which draws its images with Talbot's "pencil of nature." ⊗ **p. 25** Although no viewer could believe that the photograph is the same thing as the world it depicts, he can be encouraged to look through the medium, on the grounds that the medium holds a record of the light rays that would have reached his eye had he been placed where the camera was. Neither painting nor computer graphics can appeal to the "natural" agency of light itself. In fact, in the very attempt to duplicate photography in oil or in pixels, photorealism renders photography no longer special. The act of remediation depends in this way on a foundation of transparency that it itself denies.

The manual photorealists (or at least their interpreters) are explicit about their goal of remediating photography, as we learn from Linda Chase's essay (1988) on Goings: "Since the invention of photography, artists have used photographs as both a tool and an inspiration in their work, but the Photo Realists were the first to unapologetically translate the information from one medium to another, to make paintings that were not simply based on photographs, but were paintings of photographs" (8).

In the case of Goings and other photorealists, to make paintings of photographs is a process of self-remediation, because the painters themselves take the photographs that they then remediate on canvas or paper. Furthermore, just as they are remediating photography, the manual photorealists are redefining painting. They are borrowing from and reforming earlier American realist painting and at the same time reacting against the abstract expressionism that is regarded as the ultimate achievement of high modernism. Chase (1988) points out that

for most of the Photo Realists in the early years, a major issue was the use of the photograph as a method of bypassing or obviating those choices that traditional realists made in translating the three-dimensional object to the two-dimensional plane of the canvas. The desire to bypass these choices was tied up with the desire to present the image as factually and objectively as possible, but it was also tied up with the desire to be free of the exigencies of self-expression with a capital "S" that had become a cliché and also a trap. (20)

Although the photorealists invoke the medium of photography against expressionist painting, they do not abandon painting in favor of photography, as others have done. Instead, they use photography to reform modernist painting, while implicitly reforming photography itself in their own paintings. They also enact yet another version of the definition of self through mediation. Stanley Cavell (1979) noted that with both romanticism and modernism, the artist's goal was to achieve presentness or immediacy by insisting on the presence of his own self in his art. ◐ **p. 234** Goings rejects this route to immediacy, when he says that "in the twentieth century, tremendous emphasis has been piled on imagination and originality, and self-expression—the triumvirate of Modernist art. When . . . I realised that this grand style of painting I had been teaching and trying to do was a dead end for me, I began to question these things. If everything is self-expression, then self-expression is no big deal" (in Chase 1988, 20).

Goings and other photorealists seem to be returning to the strategy of transparency in order to achieve immediacy—except that in vigorously reforming earlier painting and photography, these artists make us intensely aware of the medium and ultimately of themselves as mediators. We look not only through the canvas, but very much *at* the canvas in order to discover how the careful effacing is achieved and whether we can see "flaws," places where the paint reveals itself.

Photorealistic paintings are not immediate perceptual experiences; rather they are paintings about immediacy, about photography as immediacy, as Chase (1988) acknowledges: "Photo Realism is an art of many ironies—not the least of which is that the artist seeks a directness in relation to the visually experienced world through the use of secondary source material, and that he achieves a heightened sense of reality by reproducing an illusion of an illusion. With his use of the photograph, the artist actually gains a double immediacy" (8).

What Chase calls "double immediacy" we could call hypermediacy. The photorealist asks us to define the photograph as the real and then attempts to see how close he can bring us to that predefined reality. He is not willing to take us all the way, however, for he exhibits his paintings, not the photographs on which they are based. He must retain us in the realm of painting in order to represent the desire for immediacy. Here as elsewhere, the logic of hypermediacy is to represent the desire for transparent immediacy by sublimating it, by turning it into a fascination with the medium. So again in this case, hypermediacy becomes the representation of the desire for immediacy and unavoidably of the artist as the seeker after immediacy.

Photorealists seem to understand their paintings' role as hypermedia as well as the irony that their paintings appear to be unmediated. On the other hand, computer graphics experts generally do not. Because digital photorealists are computer specialists, trained as scientific engineers and not generally as humanists or artists, they do not worry about the tradition of the modern or the question of self-expression. Their remediations of photography are simpler expressions of homage and rivalry. Computer graphic images rely on our culture's belief in the immediacy of photography in order to make their own unself-conscious claim to immediacy. Photography is appealed to in order to bring computer graphics up to a higher standard of visual fidelity. Although manual and digital photorealisms confront some of the same technical problems, their different understanding of the task of remediation suggests that we must interpret these two practices differently. Photorealist paintings read as statements of contemporary American realist art—intensely detailed, denying (and yet affirming through the act of denial) the modernist motive of self expression. Computer graphic images, on the other hand, often seem to achieve that absence of self-expression that Goings claims to be after in his paintings. This great difference and the many lesser similarities become apparent when we compare examples.

Ralph Goings's painting *Still Life with Creamer* (fig. 6.5, plate 4) can be viewed, like many realistic computer graphics, as a study in illumination, specular reflection, and refraction. At first glance we might well mistake this ironic still life for a photograph. As we look closer, we can detect a surreal shine in the ketchup bottle and the salt and pepper shakers on the left. Although they are glass, they look plas-

tic, and they seem to flatten out and detach themselves from the picture plane as we gaze at them. It turns out that the painter, like the computer graphics specialist, cannot always duplicate the shading and texturing effects that a straight photograph teaches us to regard as realistic.

In manual photorealism, as in computer graphics, the clever choice of objects of representation can help the illusion tremendously, as it does in Charles Bell's *Marbles IX* (fig. 6.6, plate 5). This painting is also a study in illumination, reflection, and refraction, but it is more abstract than Goings's and looks much more like a ray-traced computer graphic. Chrome and glass spheres floating over specularly reflective surfaces have been common motifs in computer graphics, because these shapes and textures lend themselves to techniques of ray tracing. Compare Bell's marbles to the ray-traced computer graphic spheres in fig. 6.7 (plate 6). Bell's work imitates a photographic style (the extreme close-up) that does not correspond to what we see with the unaided eye. It would be hard to hold one's focused eye close enough to such marbles to obtain precisely this view, and in fact, without a tradition of photographic close-ups, we might have some difficulty understanding this image. For that very reason, the image is all the more successful as photorealism: it looks so much like a photograph, because it does not look like anything else.

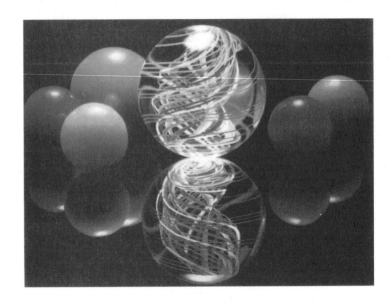

Figure 6.6 Charles Bell, *Marbles IX, 1982.* © Louis K. Meisel. Used by permission.

Figure 6.7 A ray-traced computer graphic image. Created by Sherry G. Strickland.

Plate 1 A computer graphic rendering of the nave of Chartres cathedral. Created by John Wallace and John Lin, using Hewlett Packard's Starbase Radiosity and Ray Tracing software. Copyright 1989 Hewlett Packard Co.

Plate 2 A page from a Book of Hours, circa 1450.© Robert W. Woodruff Library, Emory University. Used by permission.

Plate 3 Arkansas: the splash (opening) screen for a multimedia celebration of the state. A digital parody of medieval illumination (Plate 2).

Plate 4 Ralph Goings, *Still Life with Creamer.* Photorealist paintings like this one explicitly remediate photography. © Louis K. Meisel. Used by permission.

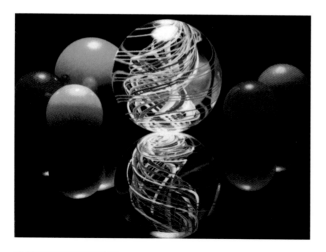

Plate 5 Charles Bell, *Marbles IX, 1982.* This photorealistic painting not only remediates photography, but it also closely resembles computer-graphic photorealism (plate 6). © Louis K. Meisel. Used by permission.

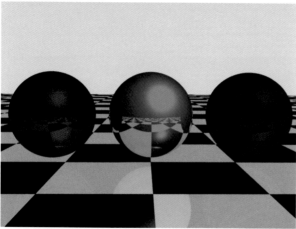

Plate 6 A ray-traced computer-graphic image. An exercise in computer-graphic photorealism: the spherical shapes facilitate the technique known as "ray tracing." Created by Sherry G. Strickland.

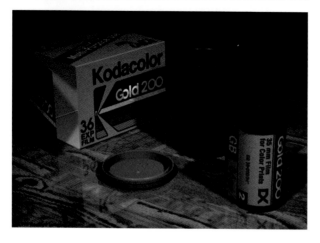

Plate 7 *Kodak Film.* A computer graphic that frankly acknowledges its remediation of photography. © Todd Siechen, RealEyz Imaging. Used with permission.

Plate 8 Robert Lowell, *Vanishing Point*. A work of digital art that vacillates between transparent immediacy and hypermediacy. ©Robert Lowell. Used by permission.

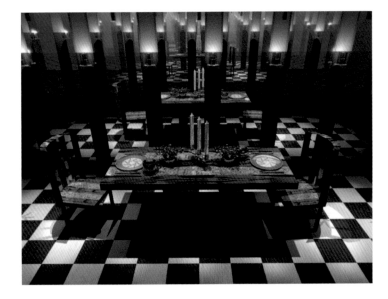

Plate 9 Uri Dotan, *Hummingbird*. Digital art that recalls the European modernist tradition. http://www.wmgallery.com/dt1095. html January 28, 1998. © 1993, Uri Dotan, represented by The Williams Gallery, Princeton, New Jersey. Used by permission.

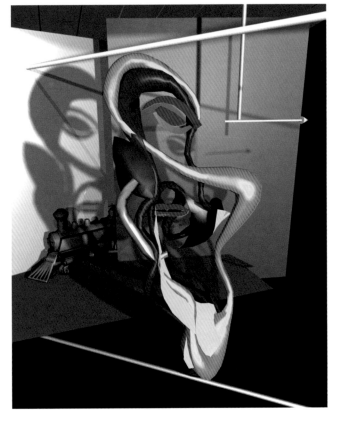

Plate 10 Lisa Johnston, *Sattelight*. A digital remediation of photo-montage. ©Lisa Johnston. Used by permission.

Plate 11 Chris Nordling, *Netwash 6.9*. A hypermediated collage of images and texts taken from the Internet. © Chris Nordling. Used by permission.

Plate 12 Tobias Richter, *Atlantis, My Love.* A science fiction/fantasy graphic that pays homage to the genre of fantasy illustration in print. © Tobias Richter. Used by permission.

Plate 13 Chris Thomas, *The Many Brains of Media.* An allegory of the remediation of film, video, and audio by new digital media. © 1993 Inverse Media, LLC. Used by permission.

Plate 14 (a) A still life photograph. (b) The "fresco" filter. (c) The "cutout" filter. (d) The "graphic pen" filter.
Digital algorithmic filters can refashion this photograph to imitate various painting or graphic styles. © 1998 Lori Levy and Jay David Bolter.

a.

b.

c.

d.

Plate 15 The balcony from the virtual acrophobia experiment. The goal of this virtual reality system was to induce in its subjects a clinical fear of heights. Courtesy of Professor Larry Hodges, GVU Center, Georgia Institute of Technology.

Plate 16 *The Creating Killer Web Sites* splash (opening) screen. This page and the whole web site refashion traditional, printed graphic design for the World Wide Web. http://www.killersites.com January 28, 1998. © 1998 David Siegel. Used by permission.

Plate 17 A telepresence application: A micro-surgical robot. *Presence,* Cover 2, 4 (Fall, 1993): MIT Press. Image by Tilemachos D. Doukoglou and Serge R. Lafontaine. Used by permission.

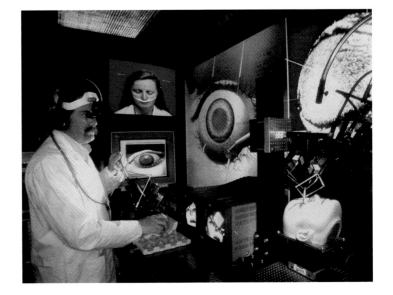

REALISTIC FAILURES

In many cases the same elements appear imperfect (not convincingly photographic) in both the computer graphics and the paintings. Often the colors are too bright, the illumination too crisp, and any sense of atmosphere absent. The computer photorealists would say that their models of shading and illumination are still not adequate. Although the painters can do somewhat better, their shadings too are sometimes unconvincing. The frequent result is textures that seem fabricated, such as the plastic-looking ketchup bottle and shakers in the Goings picture, or the false texture of the skin in almost every case where human beings appear. In computer graphics, too, shiny, artificial surfaces dominate. The plastic and chrome are often flawless, whereas skin, cloth, and un-polished wood are not, as if to confirm the traditionalist's bias that the computer cannot render any human or natural textures. The digital ani-mators of the film *Toy Story* were wise to make toys the main characters, for these were mostly plastic and appeared to be almost photorealistic, while the few human characters in the film would have looked like toys in any case. ▷ **p. 147**

Successful algorithms for shading and illumination (using tech-niques of ray tracing and radiosity) are more difficult than the algo-rithms for perspective projection. The problem of perspective has effectively been solved for computer graphics. The debate among art historians and psychologists (Kubovy 1986, Elkins 1994, Hagen 1996) about the validity of various kinds of perspective has relatively little influence on the graphics community. The problem of perspective is also solved for the manual photorealists, because they can rely on the perspective lines generated by the photographs from which they are working. We might even argue for a parallel between the computer graphics community today and the earlier artistic community of im-pressionists and postimpressionists. The nineteenth-century artists had conceded linear perspective to photography and were rather concerned about color and light, which the cameras of their day could not capture convincingly. As the received history of impressionism would have it, "photography could produce black and white prints, but artists could do better and seize the immediacy and actuality of life and vision through the use of brilliant and varied colours and shimmering light effect" (Sérullaz 1978, 12). Although computer graphics artists have not conceded perspective, they too must now deal with light and the visual textures it produces.

Figure 6.8 Mahogany Hall, circa
1916. Photograph by Ernest
Bellocq.

On the other hand, the failure to achieve photorealistic light
and color can itself become part of the meaning of the image, which
then passes from immediacy to hypermediacy. If we look again at the
Mahogany Hall graphic (fig. 6.4), we can see that it is the shading and
textures, not the perspective, that fail. The failure is the beginning of a
fascinating chain of remediations, for we have photographs with which
to compare the graphic, including the historical parlor of Mahogany
Hall itself (fig. 6.8). The Mahogany Hall graphic bears only a generic
resemblance to this photograph. The graphic seems to incorporate a
waiting room from another New Orleans brothel (fig. 6.9). The graphic
is therefore a conscious refashioning of these early documentary photographs. At one level, the computer graphic promises greater access to
the real, because it can present the room in full color instead of the
high-contrast black and white of the photographs. However, precisely
because of our cultural faith in photography—we still believe that photographs taken "in the light" have somehow been touched by the objects depicted ⊳ **p. 106**—this colored image does not seem as real to
us as a grainy photograph.

The computer graphic then comes to look more like a painting
than like a photograph, and we are led to read it in the tradition of

Figure 6.9a Detail of Mahogany Hall computer graphic (figure 6.4).

Figure 6.9b Photographic detail from the Arlington, a brothel in the Storyville district of New Orleans.

realistic Western painting. We begin to notice, for example, the reme-diation of Dutch art in the mirror-like shield in the waiting room (fig. 6.4) and in the pictures texture-mapped on the wall above the piano. Such a remediation could not have been accomplished if the image had succeeded in becoming for us a conventional photograph. Precisely be-cause it fails, the image heightens our desire for immediacy rather than satisfying it, and the fact that it is a picture of a whorehouse encourages us to regard it as an allegory of desire. What is conspicuously lacking are people (notoriously hard for both manual and digital photoreal-ists)—the prostitutes and their patrons. The occupants of the room have gone (up the stairs to the left?), and only the furniture and decora-tions remain, particularly the shining shield and the pictures, which establish this hypermediated image as a representation in structure as in content of the desire for immediacy.

It turns out, however, that the prostitutes have not been erased from the image's genealogy. The photograph of Mahogany Hall (fig. 6.8) was taken by Ernest Bellocq, who also photographed the prosti-tutes (Rose 1974, 59–60). Bellocq's intimate photoportraits of the prostitutes of the Storyville district of New Orleans perfectly captured the desire for immediacy. And these photographs were remediated in the 1970s in Louis Malle's film *Pretty Baby,* in which the immediacy of Bellocq's art—we see the prostitutes sitting for him—becomes the film's central metaphor. *Pretty Baby* therefore stands in relation to Bel-locq's portraits as the recent film *Fairy Tale* stands in relation to the Cottingly photographs. ◈ **p. 106** The photographs begin as apparently simple expressions of the desire for immediacy, but as they are taken up in a chain of remediations, they become examples of our fascination with media. Thus, on the one hand, the original Bellocq photographs would seem to enact the male gaze and its desire for immediacy ◈ **p. 78;** on the other hand, the chain of remediations complicates our response to both Bellocq and his photographs. We are inclined to look not only through the photographs, but also at them and at the formal and cul-tural circumstances of their creation. The hypermediacy of the film and computer graphics has its effect on the immediacy of the Bellocq originals.

The movement from immediacy to hypermediacy is a charac-teristic of both manual and digital photorealism (and of digital photog-raphy as well). The photorealistic painters would not deny the heightened awareness of two media (painting and photography) that pervades their paintings, while computer graphics researchers and art-

Figure 6.10 *Kodak Film* © Todd
Siechen, RealEyz Imaging. Used
with permission.

ists are less articulate about, or perhaps not even conscious of, the double logic of remediation. We need to distinguish, however, between computer graphics researchers and computer graphics artists. The researchers create new techniques, which eventually become embodied in commercial software, while the artists or illustrators are skilled users of that software. The artists, whose work is everywhere now in films, on CD-ROMs, and on the Web, may have a variety of goals, but some at least seem to be more concerned with carrying through the project of photorealism than are the researchers. The researchers want to create "models" that can be viewed from any perspective; the artists want to create single images. Computer artists can sometimes work in a similar spirit to the manual photorealists, although as long as they lack a knowledge of the modernist tradition, they cannot remediate twentieth-century painting in the same way.

Meanwhile, popular computer graphics is full of unintended ironies in its remediation of photography. A computer graphic of a Kodak film box and canister (fig. 6.10, plate 7) is almost perfectly photorealistic. It is successful because it recalls a special genre of photography, common in advertising, in which the surreal colors and textures and the absence of extraneous detail serve to focus our attention on a featured commodity. This genre of photography does not correspond to anything we see in daily life (except on billboards and in magazines), and precisely for that reason the computer image seems so

Digital Art

7

Chapter 6 took up the work of computer graphic photorealists, who think of themselves not as artists but as engineers or scientists creating a new technology. That is precisely the distinction between the manual photorealists and the computer photorealists: the manual photorealists offer their work as art, not engineering. ▷ **p. 119** In this chapter, we examine the digital products—by computer graphics designers, professional artists, and amateurs—that do present themselves as art. By digital art we mean static graphic images made with pixels rather than oils or watercolors. Such images are created with the aid of two- and three-dimensional graphics programs, and they may remediate all sorts of traditional visual art, from oil-based painting to pen-and-ink illustrations, photographs, and collage and photomontage. The result may be destined for print or for display in a multimedia application or on a web site. Digital art is eclectic, as the figures in this chapter indicate. It may be highly realistic or hypermediated: it may be an image that was generated entirely in the digital domain, or it may contain elements from other media that have been scanned in and modified.

Vanishing Point presents a realistic, although not quite photorealistic, table and chairs in perspective and with the sculpted look and shiny plastic textures we associate with three-dimensional graphics programs (fig. 7.1, plate 8). Furthermore, the table and chairs are copied repeatedly and fade into a surreal background, so that the whole image seems to be an exercise in computer graphic shading and illumination. It is as if the artist tried to achieve transparency in the foreground of the picture and then abandoned the attempt in a flourish of hypermediacy in the background. Indeed, we can almost read this

image as an allegory of the way in which the desire for immediacy passes into the fascination with media.

The next three images are all modernist in their remediating influences, for the modernist tradition is still what our culture most easily identifies as high visual art. *Hummingbird* does not remediate any specific painting, but it does recall various European modernist painters and techniques (fig. 7.2. plate 9). The clean, mechanical form of the hummingbird reminds us of Marcel Duchamp's *The Bride* and other highly mediated cubist or futurist painting from the early part of this century. *Sattelight* seems to be a digital photomontage, in which a photograph of a satellite has been scanned in, altered, and assembled with other purely digital elements (fig. 7.3, plate 10). Digital art can thus be openly hypermediated, as it also is in *Netwash6.9,* which its composer characterizes as "a collage of images and text grabbed from the Infobahn during the week ending June 9th [1996]" (fig. 7.4, plate 11). *Netwash6.9* is self-referential: it takes as its content the medium (the Internet) on which the image itself appears.

There are affiliations of technique among all these images. They are, of course, composed of discrete pixels, and most of them were created using standard three-dimensional modeling and rendering programs. Each image is doing its own work of remediation, and it is above all the practice of remediation that unites the diverse forms that go under the name of digital art.

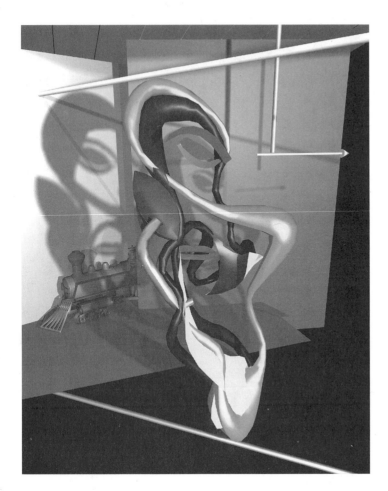

Figure 7.2 Uri Dotan, *Humming-bird.* http://www.wmgallery.com/dt1095.html January 28, 1998. © 1993, Uri Dotan. Represented by The Williams Gallery, Princeton, New Jersey. Used by permission.

FANTASY AND ALLEGORY

Digital art often refashions popular illustration—above all, science fiction and fantasy illustration from comic books and pulp-fiction book covers. These digital images are often photorealistic in the sense that they make use of rendering programs to obey the principles of perspective and shading. But the content is fantastic: desolate moons with strangely colored skies through which planets rise and set or giant (plastic) insects that cruise the weird canyons. We see an example in fig. 7.5 (plate 12). Although the scene is in perspective, we could not mistake this picture for a photograph, nor is that the goal. Such impossible scenes are both an homage and a challenge to the tradition of fantasy illustration in print. In computer graphics as in print, fantasy illustra-

Figure 7.3 Lisa Johnston, *Sattelight.* © Lisa Johnston. Used by permission.

tion expresses a strong desire for immediacy, the desire that one's waking or dreaming imagination should come true. In this case, it is the dream of space enthusiasts to visit other worlds containing futuristic cultures.

There is nothing in this fantastic image to suggest that it is meant to be read ironically. Popular digital art is often serious and sometimes carries an obvious message. Naive allegory is common, as we see, for example, in the computer game *Myst* with its allegory of the end of the book. ◉ **p. 94** The image in fig. 7.6 (plate 13), found on the Internet, could almost serve as a frontispiece for this book. This image is an allegory of remediation, in which the three jars represent the media of film, video, and audio, now united by the remediating spark of computer digitization. There is a further remediating element, the allusions to the filmed version of *Frankenstein:* the brains in jars, lightning spark, and the castle-like wall behind. The new Prometheus that comes forth here is realistic digital visual technology. The whole picture is in

Figure 7.6 Chris Thomas, *The Many Brains of Media.* © 1993 Inverse Media, LLC. Used by permission.

linear perspective and displays its photorealism in the refracted light of the jars.

Perhaps the reason popular digital art favors such blatant allegory is that allegory permits digital designers to pursue visual immediacy (through three-dimensional effects) and to deliver a message at the same time. If digital art is about repetition, cutting and pasting, and establishing visual analogies among objects, allegory establishes lines of analogy between the visual objects and the elements of a verbal message. This technique means that the image, as in the Frankenstein example, does not have to abandon the logic of immediacy in order to tell its highly mediated story. Furthermore, the allegory itself guarantees the viewer a clear and seemingly authentic message and validates the viewing experience.

DIGITAL ART AND THE AUTOMATIC

Once it has been digitized, any image can undergo a whole repertoire of transformations, which for our culture are regarded as distortions: rotation, shearing, morphing, and filtering. These operations, which make the viewer aware of the computer as a medium, will turn transparent images into hypermediated ones. Such algorithmic transformations raise the question of agency in digital art: whether the digital artist is to be regarded as the agent of the image in the same way as a traditional painter or whether her role is more like that of a photographer. The question of photographic agency has always been complex, because light or nature seems to be responsible for imprinting the image on the film. The work of Pedro Meyer and other digital photographers calls into question the status of the photograph, but they could not raise the question if our culture did not continue to assume that the analog photograph had a special capacity for the immediate reproduction of reality. ⓓ **p. 106** Once the photographer presses the button, the camera seems to work automatically. It is this automaticity that produces the contingent or accidental element in the photograph, which is then taken as its trademark of the real. Like traditional painting, however, digital art does not seem to generate the contingent in the same way.

On the other hand, more like the digital photographer and less like the painter, the digital artist works at several technological removes from the image. The digital artist draws or paints with a set of programmed tools: the application itself, the various toolboxes from which the application is composed, and the computer's operating system. All of these layers of programming operate more or less automatically under the digital artist's control. The analogy for painting would be the chemistry of the paints themselves and the making of the canvas or other surface; however, our culture does not usually consider the way in which paint sets up on canvas to be automatic. In some ways, however, the programmed character of digital media is different from the automatic character of photography. Digital automaticity offers the artist more opportunity and more time to intervene as the image is being created. The analog photographer establishes all the conditions, and then the mechanism takes over for the short but crucial moment of exposure. The digital artist intervenes again and again, defining digital objects in the image, mixing and adding colors in layers, subjecting parts of the image to a dozen different algorithmic filters, and so on. Although some of these actions may require nothing more than choosing a menu item, others need considerable manual dexterity. All of them at some point will release the computer to perform a programmed action. In terms of the relationship of the creator to the image, digital art seems to be painting placed on top of photography. In its attempt to achieve immediacy, digital art therefore shares something with both photography and painting.

ART: HIGH AND LOW, OLD AND NEW

Digital art repositions the artist with respect to her materials and at the same time provides her with an opportunity to redefine her cultural status. In the case of fantasy illustrations and computer games, it sometimes seems odd even to call her an artist. The question of her name and cultural position is part of the remediation that digital media are working in the visual arts. The artist Richard Wright (1995) notes that

> it is now possible to buy a modest software package that applies filters to digital images to give them the appearance of having been created by an artist's hand. One called Gallery Effects by Aldus includes sixteen "master effects" to turn scanned photographs into "Charcoal, Watercolor, Fresco, Film Grain," and many others. The software is advertised as "Everything you need to transform images into art." High art has been brought into the domain of computer media, but now it is merely a style. (92–93)

The digital techniques that Wright is describing can (literally) illustrate a larger cultural development: that we are coming to regard what was once high art as a series of stylistic choices.

There is no longer a rigid cultural hierarchy by which, say, a portrait in oils is always superior to an ink-drawn illustration for a comic book (or "graphic novel," as comic books are now sometimes called). Digital graphic artists may choose to adopt and refashion styles that in the past were characterized as high art, but they would have difficulty claiming that this choice necessarily raises their work above popular illustration. Instead of elevating her, the decision to work in the tradition of high art simply puts the artist into a relatively small "special interest group." As Wright suggests, it is technically easy for a digital artist to mix styles or move from one stylistic register to another.

a.

b.

c.

d.

Figure 7.7 (*a*) A still life photograph. (*b*) The "fresco" filter. (*c*) The "cutout" filter. (*d*) The "graphic pen" filter. © 1998 Lori Levy and Jay David Bolter.

At one level, the medium is uniform: the only thing the artist can do is to specify color values at the various pixels of the bitmap. (In comparison, paint on canvas is far more complex, for paints can differ in texture as well as color and can be applied with a variety of techniques.) Beyond the great limiting necessity that a digital image must be composed of discrete color values, the blank bitmap can accommodate many styles equally well. The ease with which the bits can be manipulated by two- and three-dimensional graphics programs reinforces the notion that styles are individual choices and not cultural or aesthetic imperatives. Popular styles coming from fantasy or science fiction illustration are then as legitimate as a classical perspective style or as modernist collage. As we see in fig. 7.7 (plate 14), filters encourage users to adopt a strategy of remediation through parody, where parody becomes as easy as a couple of menu commands. It becomes equally legitimate to attempt to purify the graphic space by pursuing one style exclusively or to combine various styles that were previously quite separate. In digital art, the logics of transparency and hypermediacy are often placed side by side.

Furthermore, whether transparent or hypermediated, digital styles are no longer regarded as "inner necessities," as they were regarded by nineteenth- and even twentieth-century art critics. However, to say that all styles and all combinations are now equally valid is not to say that they are all popular and successful. Obviously styles derived from fantasy illustration, naive realism, pop art, and art deco are going to be far more popular than those that come from modernist collage or abstract expressionism. On the other hand, it is not quite true to say that our culture has abandoned the distinction between high and low art. Popular culture often wants to deny traditional high art a claim to superior status, but still to appropriate its cachet and vocabulary, as it does, for example, with the terms *digital art* or *computer art*. The web sites that characterize themselves as art are often in a popular vein or are simply sites for graphic design. By calling themselves "art" and their creators "artists," these sites are asserting that their styles are legitimate. They are doing what remediators always do: borrowing names and forms from earlier media while claiming to be as good as or better than the media from which they are borrowing.

At the same time, a struggle is going on over the social status and appropriate background for the makers of the new digital art. Traditional artists trained in classical, manual techniques have to establish their credentials in the new medium. Wright (1995) notes that

> *once technological culture had become unavoidable through its prevalence in popular forms like videographics, computer games, and music, it was as though the time had come for digital media to now be saved from its vulgar origins and a process of aesthetic upliftment to begin. . . . By the beginning of the nineties there were numerous calls for artists to become more and more involved in new media, computer technology, and electronic imaging, to use their "unique powers of creativity and imagination" to show what computers could do when put to "nondestructive ends." (94–95)*

Yet Wright is talking about calls from within the artistic community itself, specifically by that group of artists and critics who are trying to find their way into the new medium. A search of the web site Yahoo!

shows how many "naive" graphic designers are portraying themselves as digital artists. The challenge to traditional visual artists does not come only from these new media designers. Wright goes on to complain that

in 1992 [Ars Electronica, the major European festival for digital art] deliberately set out to restrict prizewinners to those working in computer-specific artistic genres (effectively defining computer art as algorithmic art), with the result that nearly all that year's prizewinners were people who wrote their own software. A peculiar result of this policy was that most winners were from computer science and engineering backgrounds, since they were the main group possessing the right technical abilities. . . . The likely prospect is that future "computer artists" will exclude not only those from marginal social groups, but also most artists as well. (96)

As the field of digital art is busy remediating a variety of modern forms, the struggle is ultimately over who should have the right to do this work of remediation.

ELECTRONIC ART

If we define digital art as the use of computer graphics to create static images, we need a broader term for the work shown at festivals such as Ars Electronica. Electronic art can employ traditional video and audio, as well as the computer, to create artistic installations and exhibits. If digital art is practiced by graphic artists whose work is often commercial or popular, electronic art is practiced by the heirs of traditional high art. The Ars Electronica festival has been held since 1979, before artists had easy access to sophisticated computer graphics, indeed before personal computers were readily available at all. In those early days, electronic art meant video installations and performances of electronic music, which belong to the late modernist tradition. Electronic artists today produce pieces that viewers may walk through, wear, or activate with their bodies. They combine digital graphics and virtual reality with avant-garde (rock) music and video. In these respects, electronic art is a fairly obvious extension, or perhaps in some cases a respectful remediation, of nonelectronic performance and installation art dating from the 1960s (or indeed of dada from early in the century). Nor are electronic artists at all worried about maintaining the purity of the digital medium, as they combine digital and analog forms and media, conceptual and physical spaces for the viewer to explore.

The Ars Electronica exhibits are presented in conjunction with a symposium, with its own futuristic modernist or postmodernist theme. In 1996, for example, the symposium celebrated Richard Dawkins and his concept of memes (http://web.aec.at/fest/fest96/fest96.html September 5, 1997). The exhibits included *Telegarden* by Ken Goldberg, in which users can tend a physical garden remotely through a web site robot; *Brain Opera* by Ted Machover, in which the audience participates in the final composition of the music; and Michael Redolfi's *Liquid Cities,* in which users actually swim in a pool and their movements affect the sound installations that they hear under the water. All such pieces are hypermediated and depend ultimately on a modernist aesthetic, in the sense that they offer the viewer/user a self-authenticating, interactive experience. Electronic installation art thus has a very different agenda from the digital art of popular illustration. The pieces in Ars Electronica, although not high brow in the traditional sense, are certainly esoteric and appeal mainly to other artists and critics. The pieces have affinities to web sites, computer games, and virtual and augmented reality systems built by computer scientists. For example, in Jeffrey Shaw's *The Legible City,* which appeared at the festival in 1989,

> the visitor can make use of a bicycle, to travel interactively in three-dimensional space consisting of videoprojections. [The space is a city whose outline corresponds to New York, Paris, Amsterdam, and others.] These cities are visualized as words and phrases with the help of a real-time three-dimensional computer graphics system. . . . The architecture of the city consists not of buildings, but of sequences of letters, words and sentences. . . . In this way the city of words becomes . . . a sort of three-dimensional book, which can be read in any direction and in which each visitor can put together his own stories, as he cycles along paths of his own choosing. . . . The face of the city is produced through a real-time 3D computer graphic simulation, whose images are projected on a three-by-four meter screen in front of the rider. The bicycle is anchored, but the rider determines the direction and speed of his journey by pedalling more quickly or slowly and by controlling the handlebars. (http://web.aec.at/fest/fest89/shaw.html September 5, 1997)

Shaw's piece obviously remediates television as well as the book: it makes television interactive, while making reading into a three-dimensional experience. Like the computer game *Myst* ⊗ **p. 96**, *The Legible City* is also an allegory of the book. In *The Legible City,* as in

Myst, the user begins by entering into a book, but Shaw's piece does not conceal the writing, as *Myst* does. Instead, it turns the city into a text to be read. *The Legible City* is therefore optimistic about the future of reading, while *Myst* is pessimistic. The more popular digital art, however, tends to agree with *Myst* that images should replace words, rather than the reverse.

Shaw's *The Legible City* exemplifies current trends in electronic art. It suggests that virtual reality technology and its first-person perspective can constitute an aesthetic experience: that electronic art is art, in what remains of the elite sense. Like the work of Stelarc and other installation and performance artists, *The Legible City* seeks to redefine the relationship between the body and the space of high technology. ◐ **p. 236** Shaw's work also refashions installation art itself through the medium of interactive computer graphics. And, like all other electronic art, and for that matter digital graphic art as well, it insists that a highly technical and technological piece can fulfill our desire for immediacy.

Arguably the most important popular artform of the twentieth century, film is especially challenged by new media. It is responding as has photography ⊳ **p. 104**: by trying to absorb computer graphics into its traditional structure. Furthermore, just as computer games seek to borrow the cachet of cinema by styling themselves as interactive film ⊳ **p. 94**, so Hollywood cinema is trying to co-opt our culture's fascination with new media by using digital graphics to refashion traditional, linear films.

ANIMATION

Animated films remediate computer graphics by suggesting that the traditional film can survive and prosper through the incorporation of digital visual technology. Full-length animated films, especially the Disney films of the past decade, are perfect examples of "retrograde" remediation, in which a newer medium is imitated and even absorbed by an older one. In addition to visual media, of course, animated films refashion stories, myths, and legends—from Greek mythology, to the story of Pocahontas, to Anastasia, to literary "classics"—often with great violence to the printed or oral versions. In fact, animated film cannibalizes and refashions everything it touches with a ferocity that is itself mediated and excused precisely because the genre is not "serious" and is supposed to speak to children.

For decades, animated films have been refashioning live-action Hollywood film, and they have continued to do so in the more recent Disney films. In *Beauty and the Beast* (1991), for example, computer graphics imitate tracking shots or other film conventions that were difficult or impossible to animate with purely manual techniques. The cartoon characters could still not be mistaken for live actors, and yet there are scenes in which the mise-en-scène and camera work have very much the look of live-action film. *Beauty and the Beast* is eclectic: it remediates not only live film, but also the Broadway musical of the 1950s and 1960s. Musically, stylistically, and even thematically, *Beauty and the Beast* is most closely modeled on the 1960 musical *Camelot.* The film resurrects the musical and at the same time through computer graphics works to redefine the relationship between live-action film and computer animation. The point is to make *Beauty and the Beast* immediate and authentic by appealing to familiar and established genres that we experience as immediate.

In comparison with the transparency of *Beauty and the Beast, Aladdin* (1992) is hyperkinetic and hypermediated. This animated film also refers to the same genres and media; however, *Aladdin* makes no attempt to blend all these media seamlessly and instead offers abrupt shifts that throw the various media into relief. Actor Robin Williams's Genie is the formal cause of these shifts, as he changes himself repeatedly and pulls the whole movie both visually and stylistically with him. *Aladdin* is fascinated with media, and in the character of the Genie, it is fascinated with its own ability to jump from genre to genre. There is an element of narcissism about the Genie, and therefore the movie—a fascination with its own changing reflection. (Perhaps narcissism is a general feature of works of blatant hypermediacy; the awareness of the various media leads to self-awareness and to a sense of satisfaction in the power of mediation.) The work as a whole is self-absorbed, concerned with displaying and exploring its own possibilities. On the other hand, transparent works do not dwell on the possibilities or the limits of their own powers of representation.

In one sense *Toy Story* (1995) returns to the strategy of *Beauty and the Beast* with its seamless presentation. There are no abrupt shifts in graphic style here; the whole piece has the smoothness of a properly functioning computer algorithm. Again the principal target of remediation is the live-action film and the traditional animated film. *Toy Story* is also, famously, the first full-length animation generated totally by computer graphic animation. Here the claim of remediation works in both directions. Computer graphics can now not only supplement manual methods—that claim was already made with the repeated improvements in *Beauty and the Beast* and *Aladdin*—but eliminate the traditional human technique entirely.

Toy Story also suggests a second, retrograde remediation, for if computer graphics can remediate conventional film, then film can remediate computer graphics by incorporation. (The film mischievously alludes to virtual reality with a sign in the front lawn of one of the houses indicating that it is for sale through "Virtual Realty.") *Toy Story* is, after all, a linear film intended to be viewed in the traditional way. It borrows the graphic power of digital media but removes the promise (or threat) of interactivity. *Toy Story* shows that the "new" digital film can maintain a conventional relationship with its audience—that linear media such as film and television can exploit the computer's power to create visually convincing worlds without the troubling notion that the user must be in control of these new worlds. This remediation of computer graphics by film has its economic and practical dimensions, since Disney and other major studios want to maintain the structure of their industry and retain their paying customers. Furthermore, although film animators will have to learn new skills, they, the script writers, directors, and actors (voices) can continue in something like their traditional roles.

These three Disney films (and numerous others) show how computer graphics is both disrupting and extending the tradition of Hollywood animation. Prior to digital graphics, cartoon studios had developed successful and identifiable styles that referred to but did not challenge live-action film. These styles could not achieve transparency in the sense of the Albertian window, because there was no hope of drawing by hand in perfect perspective twenty-four frames for each second of an eighty- or ninety-minute film. However, Disney did often aim for immediacy by evoking what the culture regarded as authentic emotional responses to the narrative, in such early, "heartwarming" classics as *Pinocchio* (1940), *Dumbo* (1941), and *Bambi* (1942). Other films, and certainly most of the short cartoons by the various studios, frankly adopted the strategy of hypermediacy, of making the audience aware of the artificiality of cel animation. The contrast between the animated styles and the traditional live-action film becomes most obvious in hybrids, such as *Space Jam* (1996) and the more sophisticated *Who Framed Roger Rabbit* (1988), in which cartoon characters with their traditional abilities to violate the laws of physics and perspective occupy the frame with live actors. The immediacy of the traditional Hollywood style is then violently juxtaposed to the hypermediacy of the cartoon.

In these hybrid films, traditional live action and animation meet. In *Toy Story*, something more radical happens when photorealistic computer graphics challenges live action on its own ground. Computer graphics now makes it possible to introduce into animation a consistent Hollywood-style camera technique, a moveable and shifting perspective. The latest animated films have found new ways to pursue both the desire for transparent immediacy and the fascination with media. In being able finally to compete with the "realism" of the Hollywood style, the animated film has also become increasingly aware of and confident of its own status as mediation.

TRANSPARENCY AND THE HOLLYWOOD STYLE

The Hitchcock film *Vertigo* (1958) predates the computer revolution in film by two decades—if we take the beginning of the revolution to be *Star Wars* (1977)—and yet it offers a perfect example of the techniques of representation that computer graphics animators and designers are now both imitating and changing. Most of *Vertigo* is shot in the Hollywood style, in which the point of view moves back and forth according to the narrative rhythm of the scene. There are a number of subjective shots when the detective, Scottie, is trailing Madeleine, whose strange behavior he has been asked to investigate. Here the subjective camera represents the detective as voyeur: we see what Scottie sees as both he and we try to make sense of Madeleine's actions. Inevitably Scottie cannot remain a voyeur, an outside observer; he must be drawn into the action as he intervenes to save her from drowning. (There is a clear parallel to *Strange Days,* in which the subjective camera in *Strange Days* also draws the character and us into political and personal disaster.) Most of the film therefore operates under the transparent immediacy of the Hollywood style. Whether the style is somehow natural or whether we are culturally determined to read it as natural is not the question. In either case, the style is transparent for Western viewers. Furthermore, as Laura Mulvey (1989) has argued, the shifting point of view encourages us (or at least male spectators) to be drawn into the film and to identify with the main character, in this case the detective himself, in his scopophilic relationship to the woman (cf. Modleski 1998, 87–100). ◁ **p. 78**

There are a few scenes in the film that are not transparent, however. When at key moments Scottie has attacks of vertigo, Hitchcock uses a peculiar camera technique to represent the sensation. We see a subjective camera shot of Scottie looking down, and then the camera is quickly tracked out while the lens zooms in (fig. 8.1). Because this effect is dislocating and "unnatural," we may be drawn in, but we are distanced at the same time—which is the significance of this ambivalent track-out/zoom-in. We suddenly become aware of the film as medium in precisely the way that the Hollywood style tries to prevent. These are moments in which hypermediacy interrupts the aesthetic of

Figure 8.1 (*top*) Scottie looks down. (*bottom*) Scottie's attack of vertigo. © 1998 by Universal City Studios, Inc. Courtesy of Universal Studios Publishing Rights, a division of Universal Studios Licensing, Inc. All rights reserved.

transparency. Scottie's problem throughout the film is in fact a problem of vision, and at the end, when he simultaneously conquers his vertigo and unravels the plot against him, his insight is rewarded by the fact that he can now look down a stairwell in a subjective camera shot without this dislocating special effect. The Hollywood style has apparently triumphed. (Yet the triumph is only apparent, for Scottie's desire for immediacy with Madeleine must ultimately be thwarted, because Madeleine does not and never did exist.)

Even before its final triumph, the Hollywood style is rejected in an extended sequence in the middle of the film. Scottie has a troubled dream—so troubled that he will wake into a year-long nervous breakdown. In the dream he sees a bouquet of flowers, and live action passes into animation, as the flowers become cartoon flowers and their petals separate. Still in the dream, Scottie suddenly sees Carlotta, a figure from a painting in his waking life, standing next to him in live action. For Scottie and for us as viewers, levels of representation are merging. We, and the dreaming Scottie, are watching remediation in action, as the painted depiction of a woman becomes a woman in the "reality" of the film itself. What is terrifying here is that these levels of representation refuse to stay put. If painted figures can become real, perhaps real figures can become mere paint (or perhaps characters can become animations in Toon Town, as in *Roger Rabbit,* or be trapped in books, as in the computer game *Myst*). ⊘ **p. 95** We also see Scottie's head flying through a psychedelic space. (fig. 8.2). (This image—together with the graphics of the opening credits, in which we see animated spirals that represent, and perhaps are meant to induce, vertigo—looks somewhat elementary today, because we are used to sophisticated computer graphic images in contemporary films.)

In *Vertigo,* as in other Hollywood films such as *Spellbound* (1945), hypermediacy is equated with dreams, mental disorder, or insanity. When characters are in mental balance, the camera is a transparent lens on the world; when something is wrong (when they are drunk or physically or mentally ill), the subjective camera offers a distorted view that makes us aware of the film as medium and often incorporates or refers to other media. Even today we can find films that follow the same practice (in which transparency is mental balance, while hypermediacy is mental dysfunction), although with less assurance and consistency than was possible in the 1950s. If a viewer accustomed to the traditional Hollywood of the 1950s were suddenly transported to the 1990s and set down in front of an MTV broadcast or an equivalent

moment in contemporary film, he might very well think that he is watching a representation of insanity.

COMPUTER GRAPHICS IN LIVE-ACTION FILM

What passed for decades as normal vision in film—Hollywood's traditional representation of immediacy through transparency—has certainly not been abandoned. Most films still offer us the carefully controlled point of view that still constitutes the real for film audiences in North America and, with certain different emphases, in Europe and elsewhere. As we have seen, designers of animated films have learned how to recreate this style with computer graphics instead of a mechanical camera. Live-action film directors and editors are also appropriating computer graphics. Sometimes graphics are used to enhance the film without acknowledgment, and sometimes the presence of the graphics is made visibly prominent. In a film such as *Terminator 2* (1991), the viewer is meant to see and appreciate the computer graphics that permit the evil robot to change shape. The audience is invited to interpret the film as a celebration of graphic technology, and in this respect the film must walk an interesting line. The graphics must be simultaneously remarkable and credible. When the creature emerges from the tiled pattern of the floor and reassumes its human form, the audience cannot believe that this is other than a graphic tour de force; it cannot believe it was recorded naturally in the light. The audience is asked to believe something rather different: that if there were such a robot, its visual metamorphoses would be as the computer represents them. In *Jurassic Park* (1993) and *The Lost World* (1997), the computer graphic creatures are meant to be photorealistic. These films too celebrate computer graphics, but they do so in the name of a not entirely naive transparency. Because no one has ever seen a living dinosaur, the viewer is invited to measure the graphics by what she regards as plausible for such huge animals, although her sense of plausibility comes largely from other films and fiction.

Digital compositing in Hollywood film often has as its goal to smooth over the ruptures in the raw footage by removing stunt wires and other visible traces of special effects or unwanted artifacts. When compositing restores the unbroken surface so that the film can be transparent to the viewer, it is working in the service of immediacy. However, when all computer techniques are taken into account, popular film is becoming progressively more hypermediated. Experimental or avant-garde film has always been hypermediated, in the sense that it has always made the user conscious of itself as a medium. Popular film has employed a variety of special effects, which may or may not have seemed transparent to the viewer, but such techniques have never been as varied and as prominent as they are today. In addition to live action (with all the technical nuances of lenses and cameras), a film may employ a combination of cel animation, motion capture, and two- and three-dimensional computer graphics, and some of this multiplicity will inevitably bleed through to the film's visible surface.

If the preference in earlier popular film, as in photography, was for a single unified style, popular film now seems more willing to reveal its multiple styles. Hypermediacy is certainly no longer the stylistic equivalent of insanity. With the introduction of digital techniques, the Hollywood style has expanded its representational palette from old-fashioned and still popular transparency to at least a moderate degree of hypermediacy and self-acknowledgment. In fact, films about media and mediation have become almost, but not quite, mainstream. A good example is Oliver Stone's *Natural Born Killers* (1994), which was controversial not so much for its cartoonish violence, but for its violent juxtapositions and remediations of television along with Hollywood film styles. Peter Greenaway's films, *Prospero's Books* (1991) and *The Pillow Book* (1995), are more esoteric examples, partly because they remediate the printed or written word in such a self-conscious fashion.

THE CINEMA OF ATTRACTIONS

In 1895 the Lumière brothers showed as one of their films in the Grand Café, *The Arrival of a Train at the La Ciotat Station.* The story is that audience members were so taken with the reality of the moving image of the train that they panicked and ran from the room. This would seem to be a perfect example of film as a transparent medium, but it also helps us to understand the subtle ways in which the logic of transparency can sometimes operate. The film theorist Tom Gunning (1995) has questioned the story and has suggested that the audience may have been awestruck, but was not so naive as to think that a train was about to burst into a basement room of the Grand Café. What astonished the audience, he thinks, was precisely the gap between what they knew to be true and what their eyes told them. They admired the capacity of the film to create so authentic an illusion in the face of what they knew to be true. Gunning argues that very early film was a "cinema of attractions" that played exactly on this discontinuity. He claims that the cinema of attractions predated narrative cinema, which eventually developed in the United States into the Hollywood narrative style. From the quotidian (the Lumière train) to the grotesque (the electrocution of an elephant), these very early films did not present themselves as fictional narratives, but simply offered the audience the marvel of realistic moving images. This function of early cinema fit in with a late-nineteenth-century taste for magic theaters and forms of trompe l'oeil.

Gunning's cinema of attractions illustrates how the logic of hypermediacy can assert itself within the logic of immediacy. The film was clearly advertised to be immediate and transparent. But if, as Gunning argues, the turn-of-the-century audience became conscious of the gap between what it knew and what it saw, then we could also say that the audience became conscious of its desire for immediacy. For such viewers, the cinema of attractions was immediate and hypermediated at the same time. The members of the audience oscillated between a sense of immediacy and an awareness of that sense: in other words, they experienced the same duality of looking *at* and looking *through* that is a feature of collage, photomontage, and "elite" modern art in general. Finally, it seems likely that the various members of the audience would have varied in the degree to which they were conscious of and could articulate their awareness. Perhaps there were some whose panic was caused by a simple belief in the reality of the image.

In any case, when narrative film and ultimately the Hollywood style superseded the cinema of attractions, it changed the terms in which the logics of transparency and hypermediacy would operate. In one sense, narrative films were less immediate than the cinema of attractions, because their stories were acknowledged to be fictions. The cinema of attractions seemed to depend on showing something that really happened, and the marvel was that the camera could capture the event. In narrative film, what the camera captures are actors playing out the story, and the audience is not expected to attend to the reality of the acting (that it took place in the physical world on a particular day). Instead, the reality effect comes through the narrative itself. It is real in the same ways in which written stories are regarded by our culture as real: true to life, emotionally authentic, and so on. Hypermediacy in turn comes though the use of stylistic techniques that violate the Hollywood conventions (the 180-degree rule, three-point lighting, and so on) that are now regarded as "natural." However, even during the ascendancy of the classic Hollywood style, the cinema of attractions never entirely disappeared. There were, for example, newsreels that preceded the main feature and often appealed to the audience's sense of wonder that something (an exotic location or a war scene) could have been captured on film at all. Even the Hollywood narrative film itself contained vestiges of the cinema of attractions. Gunning compares the cinema of attractions to other "thrilling" popular entertainments at the beginning of the twentieth century, especially the roller coaster, whose effect is visceral, making the spectator physically dizzy. Early film sought to produce something like this dizziness: "This vertiginous experience of the frailty of our knowledge of the world before the power of visual illusion produced that mixture of pleasure and anxiety which the purveyors of popular art had labelled sensations and thrills and on which they founded a new aesthetic of attractions" (Gunning 1995, 122).

In its narrative years, the Hollywood film tied the vertiginous experience to the plot and offered it both to the characters and to the audience. In the silent period, films were full of leaps, falls, and trips in careening cars, airplanes, and trains. The cliff-hanger was not only a technique for maintaining suspense from episode to episode, but also a reminiscence of the vertigo of early film. In later decades of Hollywood cinema, the reminiscences were perhaps subtler, but the vertiginous experience is still alluded to. This is another sense in which the classic *Vertigo* exploits the tension between transparency and hypermediacy. The sensation of vertigo is Scottie's awareness of his presence in high places; it is an intense experience of hypermediacy. It is also a relic of the cinema of attractions. It is interesting to recall how many Hitchcock films from the 1950s have characters dangling from high places or actually falling: *Rear Window* (1954), *To Catch a Thief* (1955), *Vertigo* (1958), and *North-by-Northwest* (1959). In the 1950s, too, new projection technologies were being introduced as restagings of the cinema of attractions. Film theorist Erkki Huhtamo (1995) notes that "the first Cinerama feature, *This is Cinerama* (1952), opened with a panoramic sequence shot from a roller coaster car. Cinerama publicly emphasized the cinema/amusement park connection by showing the cinema audience as if collectively squeezed on the front seat of the roller coaster" (163). Huhtamo later remarks, "Cinerama in the 1950s and Imax and Omnimax since the early 1970s have actually been attempts to reestablish the 'cinema of attractions' as an alternative mode of cinematic experience" (169).

Today the "typical" 35-mm or 70-mm Hollywood film is closer in spirit to the cinema of attractions than it has been in decades. (See also Manovich 1997, 55–57.) In Hollywood blockbusters, the weak narrative line is often simply the thread that ties together a series of car chases, firefights, or encounters with monsters. The set-piece attacks of the dinosaurs in *Jurassic Park* and *The Lost World* seek to invoke a sense of wonder in the contemporary audience similar to what Gunning describes for the French audience in the Grand Café. The audience for Steven Spielberg's films knows that the dinosaurs are animatronic or wholly computer generated, and the wonder is that these devices look so lifelike and interact so realistically with the human figures. This wonder works against the transparency of the story itself. When we see a female character within feet of a tyrannosaurus's moist eyes and flaring nostrils, we find ourselves thinking of the physical presence of the actress and wondering how the filmed image can make it seem as if a living dinosaur is standing next to her. We go to such films in large part to experience the oscillations between immediacy and hypermediacy produced by the special effects. Unlike the early cinema of attractions, the effects in today's films are, as most of the audience understands, computer-controlled or computer-generated remediations of traditional film.

Virtual Reality

9

Just as the World Wide Web best exemplifies the logic of hypermediacy ⓓ **p. 196**, virtual reality is the clearest (most transparent!) example of the logic of transparent immediacy. ⓓ **p. 21** Virtual reality is also the medium that best expresses the contemporary definition of the self as a roving point of view. ⓓ **p. 243** Finally, virtual reality has become a cultural metaphor for the ideal of perfect mediation, and other media are now being held to the standard supposedly set by virtual reality. In the name of transparency and presence, virtual reality applications are refashioning point-of-view editing, as it has developed in the Hollywood film tradition. In the name of hypermediacy, virtual reality games are refashioning the experience of the arcade. The results can be literally frightening for one class of users, exhilarating for another.

The End of Mediation

As a label for the digital revolution, the initials "VR" (virtual reality) have replaced the older "AI" (artificial intelligence). Just as artificial intelligence has served as the paradigm of the computer as symbol manipulator, virtual reality is now the paradigm for the computer as a graphics engine—even though the number of practical applications for virtual reality remains relatively small. The millennial rhetoric of artificial intelligence began soon after the invention of the digital computer, when in 1950 Alan Turing predicted that the computer would achieve a fully human intelligence by the year 2000. There are now numerous applications for artificial intelligence software and hardware and some computer researchers still remain committed to the paradigm, but our culture at large has lost interest. It is intrigued instead by the equally far-fetched prediction that we will soon be performing our work and enjoying our recreation while wearing head-mounted displays. If artificial intelligence in the 1950s and 1960s refashioned the computer from a mere adding machine into a processor of symbols, virtual reality is now refashioning the computer into a processor of perceptions.

Virtual reality operates most often under the logic of transparency. For enthusiasts, the perfect interface is one in which the user, wearing a head-mounted display, feels as if she has fallen through Alberti's window and into a world of computer graphics. For them the immediacy of virtual reality comes from the illusion of three-dimensional immersion and from the capacity for interaction. In the case of a traditional painting, photograph, or film, the viewer is located beyond the frame, looking in. In the case of such nineteenth-century technologies as the panorama and the stereoscope, the viewer did get some sense of immersion. But none of the earlier mainstream or marginal media were interactive in the way that virtual reality is; none of them changed the perspective depiction as the viewer turned his head (except perhaps the diorama in a different sense). Virtual reality can thus be seen to remediate all previous point-of-view technologies. This is not to say that virtual reality renders obsolete these earlier ways of seeing, but rather that enthusiasts understand virtual reality as the next step in the quest for a transparent medium. Virtual reality remains dependent on earlier point-of-view technologies for its cultural significance.

The dependence of virtual reality (as cyberspace) on its predecessors is made quite clear by the computer graphics expert Randall Walser:

Whereas film is used to show a reality to an audience, cyberspace is used to give a virtual body, and a role, to everyone in the audience. Print and radio tell; stage and film show; cyberspace embodies. . . . A spacemaker sets up a world for an audience to act directly within, and not just so the audience can imagine they are experiencing an interesting reality, but so they can experience it directly. . . . The filmmaker says, "Look, I'll show you." The spacemaker says, "Here, I'll help you discover." (cited by Rheingold 1991, 286)

Walser explicitly characterizes virtual reality, figured here as "cyberspace," as a medium coming out of and surpassing print, radio, drama, and film. For him, virtual reality achieves what its predecessors only promised: it finally disappears and leaves the viewer with the reality that is supposed to lie behind and beyond representation. However, the attempt to distinguish virtual reality from all other media seems instead to anchor virtual reality more firmly in the history of representation—by involving other media explicitly in its definition. Walser defines virtual reality as "film only better." Virtual reality could not, however, do away with film, television, and other media precisely because there would then be no standards against which to judge its remediations.

VIRTUAL REALITY AND THE REMEDIATION OF FILM

It was an inevitable and nevertheless highly original idea to create a virtual reality that would induce panic in its users. The accomplishment belongs to Larry Hodges and his colleagues at the Georgia Institute of Technology, who made virtual models of three high places: a balcony looking on to a street below (fig. 9.1, plate 15), a rope bridge stretched precariously between two tall buildings (fig. 9.2), and an elevator located in the interior courtyard of a hotel (fig. 9.3). As with other virtual models, the images themselves are not particularly convincing. What gives this virtual reality its sense of presence is the responsive character of the environment. Subjects can look out or down from the balcony, they can attempt to cross the bridge, and they can ride up and down the elevator. When clinical acrophobics are tested in this environ-

Figure 9.1 The balcony from the experiment in virtual acrophobia. Courtesy of Professor Larry Hodges, GVU Center, Georgia Institute of Technology.

Figure 9.2 The "Indiana Jones" bridge from the virtual acrophobia experiment. Courtesy of Professor Larry Hodges, GVU Center, Georgia Institute of Technology.

Figure 9.3 The elevator from the virtual acrophobia experiment. Courtesy of Professor Larry Hodges, GVU Center, Georgia Institute of Technology.

ment, they exhibit their familiar symptoms: sweaty palms, weak knees, and free-floating anxiety. Virtual reality turns out to be real enough to frighten them. Furthermore, the experiment shows that subjects could use the models as therapy, because through graded exposure, they gradually became less anxious (Strickland, Hodges, North, and Weghorst 1997).

This reaction would seem to vindicate the hopes of the cyberenthusiasts: that virtual reality can disappear as an interface and give the viewer the same emotions that she would feel in the real world. If virtual reality can evoke emotions, how can our culture deny that the experience of virtual reality is authentic? However, what this experiment really shows is that like other media, virtual reality can provide its own, self-authenticating experience—in this case, by remediating other point-of-view technologies and especially film.

The experiment in virtual acrophobia constituted a minidrama for each subject. Each run for each subject was like a narrative film shot entirely in the first person: there was only one character and usually a happy ending, in which the main character overcame her fear by confronting it. This same narrative can be found in Hitchcock's *Vertigo*. ◈ **p. 150** When the main character, Scottie, experiences his fear of heights, we as viewers see what he sees in that compelling, if brief, subjective shot that recedes and zooms in at the same time (fig. 8.1). The whole film can be regarded as a process of self-investigation by which Scottie is eventually cured of his fear.

The acrophobia experiment is in this sense a remediation of *Vertigo*. In the experiment, unlike the movie, the experience is interactive; the subject gets to play Scottie and decide whether she can make the climb all the way to the top. *Vertigo* is also a model for *Strange Days*, which alludes to the Hitchcock film in its opening sequence. In that sequence, the thief who is wearing the wire tries to jump from one rooftop to another, falls short, and sees his own approaching death as he rushes toward the pavement. In the beginning of *Vertigo*, Scottie, dangling from a high roof, looks down in terror at the street below, and as he looks we are given the first example of the unsettling vertigo shot. But we (and Scottie) look down for only an instant; *Strange Days* carries the vertigo shot to its logical conclusion, as we follow the victim all the way down to his abrupt end. And unlike *Vertigo*, which was made forty years ago, *Strange Days* is also overtly about virtual reality.

One way to understand virtual reality, therefore, is as a remediation of the subjective style of film, an exercise in identification through occupying a visual point of view. In our media-saturated culture, we can hardly avoid regarding virtual reality in this way, and that is perhaps why Hollywood filmmakers have offered us so many films that incorporate or refer to virtual reality, including *Brainstorm* (1983), *Lawnmower Man, Johnny Mnemonic, Disclosure,* and *Strange Days.* In their treatments, Hollywood writers grasped instantly (as did William Gibson in his novel *Neuromancer*) that virtual reality is about the definition of the self and the relationship of the body to the world. In almost every one of these films, VR-like devices give characters the experience of other characters' bodies and in doing so confuse or confound their sense of self and of gender. The theme is nowhere more successfully pursued than in *Strange Days,* and especially in a disturbing scene in which a victim is made to wear a wire while she is raped and murdered by an assailant who is also wired. ▷ **p. 78** Because the victim's wire is plugged into the output coming from her assailant, she sees and feels exactly what her assailant sees and feels. It is a strange and awful moment of specular reflection, in which the victim sees herself as other than herself, as in a mirror. In an act of ultimate violation, she is forced to assume the point of view of her assailant and therefore to become complicit in her own rape. She perceives herself not only as being attacked *by* a male subject but also as the object of her own attack *as* a male subject. She confronts her own death both immediately and as mediated by the ultimate technology of the wire.

The acrophobia experiment is an optimistic telling of the myth of transparency, in which the medium disappears so that the subject can confront and overcome her fear. The rape scene in *Strange Days* is a pessimistic version of the same myth, in which the victim becomes transparent to herself and is obliterated in the process. Both versions understand virtual reality as a technology for putting on new selves as one takes on a new visual perspective.

NEW TIMES SQUARE

A more playful application of virtual reality technology can be found in the proliferation of virtual arcades in major international cities like London and New York. One of the most elaborate is Too Much Is Not Enough on Broadway and Forty-second Street in the "New Times Square." Like all other virtual reality applications, the goal of such virtual arcade games is to provide the user with an experience of immediacy in which the medium becomes transparent. And like all other such applications, the desire for immediacy manifests itself in a form that refashions earlier media—in this case, the traditional arcade. Like its predecessors, Too Much Is Not Enough is filled with brightly lit, often loud machines, both lined up around the walls and scattered throughout the space. And like a conventional arcade, the games are tailored to the interests of adolescent males, focusing on sports, shooting, and speed. ⊗ **p. 102** Despite these similarities, it is the differences that are most striking.

One difference is the multiplicity of attendants, whose presence makes the virtual arcade reminiscent of a carnival or an amusement park, as well as an old-fashioned arcade. ⊗ **p. 173** All of the newer, explicitly VR-type games have attendants: to explain the games to newcomers; to make sure that users are buckled in to the flight simulators or race car simulators; to adjust users' VR helmets on games that are so equipped; and indeed to assuage the sense of vulnerability users might feel while wearing a VR helmet. Perhaps the game in which the user feels most vulnerable is one without a helmet, the virtual hang glider, where he lies down on his stomach. Physically, he is in the midst of a crowded arcade in New Times Square, but virtually he is on a simulated glider and navigates himself through a virtual Grand Canyon-like landscape while looking at the virtual landscape below.

Another difference from traditional arcades is the embodied nature of many of the games. In addition to the flight, race car, and hang glider simulators, there are games that simulate skateboards or jet skis, as well as golf and baseball simulators. The games that are the most graphically sophisticated are also the more embodied—so that the user feels himself physically flying a glider or driving, skiing, skateboarding through a virtual environment that he experiences visually. These games strive for immediacy through hypermediacy—by coupling the physical sensation of movement with a sophisticated, stylized visual representation of a virtual environment. In their explicit hypermediacy, these hybrid games remind us again that all virtual reality applications are in fact hypermediated. Virtual reality depends on our ability to compare it to both earlier visual media, such as film, and to earlier experiences of mediated environments, such as game arcades.

For decades, we have filled our theme parks, malls, and city streets with complementary and competing media; these spaces have refashioned and been refashioned by newspapers and magazines, radio, television, and film. Now our public spaces are entering into a further set of remediating relationships with multimedia as well as the "cyberspace" of the World Wide Web and other Internet communication services. The supposedly immaterial world of cyberspace is itself both a reflection and an extension of these public media spaces.

DISNEY AND THE REMEDIATION OF THE AMUSEMENT PARK

In the highly mediated spaces of amusement parks and theme parks, the logic of hypermediacy predominates. The parks themselves are full of sights and sounds from various media, and the attractions recall and refashion the experience of vaudeville, live theater, film, television, and recorded music. Since the founding of Steeplechase Park and Luna Park on Coney Island, amusement parks have functioned as both extensions of and places of escape from urban life. They have emphasized the immediacy and the legitimacy of the experience they offered; the physical exhilaration of a roller coaster ride needs no justification beyond itself. (The hypermediacy of the parks is reflected even in the postcards used to advertise and celebrate them. See figs. 10.1 and 10.2, and fig. I.14). Immediacy at Steeplechase Park was provided by the titillation of rides and devices that put men and women into contact, which had (and for that matter still has) mild sexual overtones (Adams 1991, 162). The early parks were often visually splendid. Luna Park, for example, "created an electric Baghdad with an architecture of swirling crescents and blazing minarets that combined chaos with splendor and bizarre fan-

Figure 10.1 "Greetings from Coney Island." Postcard from the 1910s.

Figure 10.2 "Dreamland Circus, Coney Island." Postcard from the 1910s.

tasy. Their 'pyrotechnic insanitarium' was in startling contrast to the drab, dingy tenement dwellings and mechanized, regimented work of the generally poor, immigrant urban multitudes" (Adams 1991, 162; see also Kasson 1978, 63ff.).

The hypermediacy of amusement parks has also been true of the sophisticated theme parks like Disneyland and Disney World, which surround visitors not only with the pure hypermediacy of electric light and sound but with specific references and remediations of particular Disney films, songs, and animated characters. There are also attempts at transparency in the narrative elements of theme parks. By recalling

Disney films and their characters, the parks offer visitors the opportunity to enter into these films either by taking rides that reenact moments of a film (a notion elaborated into entire theme parks by MGM and Universal) or by meeting the incarnations of famous characters from the animated films. While meeting a larger-than-life costumed Mickey Mouse may not constitute transparency for the adults, it does for the children, who in turn provide their parents with a suitably "heartwarming" moment. Although the careful staging of every aspect of the park seems calculated to remind visitors of the media that surround and embrace them, there is an almost contractual promise that the visit will provide an authentic emotional experience. Walt Disney once gave Billy Graham a tour of his park. When Graham observed that Disneyland was a mere fantasy, Disney is supposed to have replied: "You know the fantasy isn't here. This is very real. . . . The park is reality. The people are natural here; they're having a good time; they're communicating. This is what people really are. The fantasy is—out there, outside the gates of Disneyland, where people have hatreds and people have prejudices. It's not really real" (cited by Bryman 1995, 169–170). Even if the remark is apocryphal, the mediated spaces of Disney's parks embody this combination of cynicism and naiveté.

Although Disney did not invent the notion of the amusement park as a narrative space, he certainly understood better than anyone else how to make the theme park remediate other media. Disney had already pioneered another form of remediation, when he refashioned live-action film in the animated cartoon. ⊘ **p. 147** *Snow White* (1937) was the first full-length cartoon with a sustained narrative and therefore constituted a significant remediation of the Hollywood film. It was wildly successful and prompted Disney to try a further and even more ambitious remediation, *Fantasia* (1940), in which he sought to create a multimedia form that would popularize classical music while it elevated animation. Although he continued to make animated and eventually live-action films, he came up with his most ingenious and elaborate scheme for remediation in the 1950s, when he conceived of a theme park that would simultaneously refashion and be refashioned by television as well as film.

Disney financed the building of Disneyland through a deal with the network ABC in which he agreed to produce a television series. In the first broadcast of that series, he told viewers that "'Disneyland the place and Disneyland the show are all the same'" (Anderson 1994, 74–75; cf. Sorkin 1992, 67). As a clear case of economic repurposing, the remediation of the park by the television series was always honorific. When it was not promoting the theme park, the Disneyland series could promote its animated and live-action movies—for example, by presenting a pseudo-documentary about the making of the film *20,000 Leagues Under the Sea*. Meanwhile, the park itself remediated film in general and Disney films in particular. Christopher Anderson (1994) points out that the four areas of the park are physical expressions of four movie genres: "Fantasyland (animated cartoons), Adventureland (exotic action adventures), Frontierland (Westerns), and Tomorrowland (science fiction)" (74–75). In the 1950s the remediations between television and film were often charged with rivalry, because of the concern that television might displace film altogether. Disney had found a way by which television and film projects could reinforce each other: Disneyland became the physical ground on which the two could meet. At the same time, television's function of monitoring the world could be directed toward the Disney films and the park and therefore enhance the authenticity of the experiences of both. The television show appeared weekly before an audience of millions, while a new Disney film was released once a year or less often. Each film was an event that the child viewer might experience only once. With the ready availability of videocassettes, it is easy to forget the special character of film viewing before the 1980s. However, Disney understood this very well and for decades scheduled his full-length animated cartoons for rerelease every seven years, believing that a new audience of young viewers would be eager to see what their older siblings or parents had seen in previous cycles. Finally, most people might visit Disneyland itself only once or twice in their childhood. By monitoring the production of the movies and the activities of the park, television could insist on the uniqueness of the films and the park, while turning the anticipation of these experiences into a regular and ongoing process. The Disneyland park became one of the early instances of a product that was validated by being "as shown on television."

Disney television, film, and theme parks each made their own promise of authenticity of experience even as they validated the promise of the other two. The parks could appeal to the immediacy of physical presence. The rides themselves offer sound, light, and tactile sensations, as amusement park rides have always done, and the themes or narratives associated with the rides, the animated characters that roam the park, and the themed architecture all give the young visitor the exhilaration of being physically surrounded by media. Meanwhile, both the animated and the live-action Disney films are in general fantastic and contrived. What they offer is not the transparency of a plausible story, but rather the transparency and authenticity of emotion. Animated films, such as *Pinocchio* (1940) and *Bambi* (1942), as well as the animal films, such as *Old Yeller* (1957), provide emotional catharses for young viewers and constitute the real, as Disney suggested to Graham, as authenticity of communication and shared emotions. The television series depended for its claim to authenticity on its own "heartwarming" stories and animations, as well as its "behind-the-scenes" look at the park and the films.

THE THEME PARK, THE CITY, AND THE MALL

To reach the places of fantasy and adventure in Disneyland and Disney World, the visitor first walks down Main Street, which represents an idealized midwestern town, supposedly the refashioned image of Marceline, Kansas, where Disney lived as a youth (Bryman 1995, 127ff.). The parks celebrate the town as a commercialized media space, but this does not make Disneyland or Disney World any less a reflection of American town or city life, as the New Times Square in New York reminds us. ⊗ **p. 166** Real cities and towns are themselves media spaces, which theme parks reproduce and refashion. With their libraries, theaters, museums, and galleries, cities have always been locations for our culture's prestigious media. (When tourists arrive in famous cities, their major task is to visit such media locations.) Since industrialization, cities have also been the principal sites for the "new" media of mechanical, electric, and now electronic technology, such as movies and television. (Computers and applications software may be created in the Silicon Valley, but the new media titles themselves are often produced in the "Silicon Alley" of New York or in Los Angeles.) When we fly over the North American or European continents at night, cities and major towns are still marked out from the countryside by the concentration of electric light. Theme parks remind us that the city is a space that is both highly mediated and itself a kind of grand narrative. The first American theme park is often taken to be the "White City," an ideal of urban architecture built for the Chicago Columbian Exposition of 1892 (Adams 1991, 19–40). Disneyland and Disney World change the object of remediation from the elite, European architecture of the White City to the clapboard structures of the American Midwest, but they retain the idea that the theme park can reflect and reform an urban space.

Here is one way in which to understand Baudrillard's (1983) well-known claim that "Disneyland is presented as imaginary in order to make us believe that the rest is real, when in fact all of Los Angeles and the America surrounding it are no longer real, but of the order of the hyperreal and simulation. It is no longer a question of a false representation of reality (ideology), but of concealing the fact that the real is no longer real" (25). Disneyland the theme park teaches us to understand Los Angeles as a mediated space and a space of stories, as indeed all cities are (cf. Mitchell 1995). Admittedly, because of the film industry, Los Angeles is more overtly mediated than most other cities. Still, Disneyland and Los Angeles validate each other as mediated spaces, demonstrating that the media of which both are constituted are real and present in our world. Disneyland does not conceal; rather it exposes, even celebrates, the fact that contemporary American spaces are media spaces.

Disneyland, similar theme parks, and earlier amusement parks also recall urban traditions that take us back to the capital European city of the nineteenth century, Paris. As they stroll along Main Street and through the various kingdoms, visitors to Disneyland retrace and refashion the tradition of the Parisian stroller, or *flâneur*. In addition to the department stores and parks, this figure sought out the curious and extravagant sites that the city had to offer, and eventually the city built new sites for him: wax museums, for example, and even the morgue, where cadavers were put on public display (Schwartz 1995, 87–113). The cinema itself began when the Lumière brothers exhibited their films in a Parisian café, and early film, which Gunning (1995) has called the "cinema of attractions," became one of the extravagant sights for the flâneur to take in (114–133). ⊳ **p. 155** Even then the medium of film functioned as a remediation of the city's attractions. American amusement parks took up this tradition in the twentieth century, exhibiting the bizarre and the pathetic to their strolling patrons. And film was in the park too. When in 1905 Topsy, an aged elephant, was electrocuted before the public at Luna Park, Edison made a film of the event, itself a perfect example of the early American cinema of attractions.

Although city centers in Europe are still great mediated spaces, in the United States shopping malls are taking over this cultural function. Indeed the suburban shopping mall may even invade the city itself, as is the case in the renewal of New York's Times Square. ⊳ **p. 166** Accordingly, American theme parks have become not only small-scale versions of the city but grand-scale imitations of the shopping mall.

(The enormous Mall of America in fact contains within it a theme park, Camp Snoopy: fig. 10.3.) Like theme parks, malls also refashion both film and television. Scott Bukatman (1991) agrees with William Kowinski that "strolling through a mall is analogous to walking around inside a giant TV. One chooses from among an abundance of selections (stores equal channels), solicited by an array of colorful enticements and standardized slickness, overwhelmed by the overall electronic *buzz*" (67). And for Michael Sorkin (1992) the "new American city" is becoming a giant, anonymous shopping mall, which is taking on the homogenized quality of (American broadcast) television: "The new city threatens an unimagined sameness even as it multiplies the illusory choices of the TV system" (xiii). Sorkin's remark reminds us of the opening sentence of William Gibson's *Neuromancer.* Describing a Japanese version of the new American city, Gibson writes that its "sky . . . was the color of television tuned to a dead channel" (1). Nevertheless, for the mall goers, as for the committed television viewers, it is the subtle variations within that sameness that matter, for those variations generate the feeling of hypermediacy. The mall patron is surrounded by media as well as merchandise. In addition to the ubiquitous mall music, there are media for sale (televisions, VCRs, computers, radios, amplifiers, and computer game consoles) as well as media (television monitors and occasionally computers in kiosks) promoting the sale of everything else. (Around the corner from the mall, many bars and even some restaurants have also become hypermediated spaces with television monitors hanging from the ceiling—often several monitors tuned to different channels, all of whose audio is turned down so that music from a radio or a sound system can occupy the background.) Finally, most new film theaters are now located in malls, so that a trip through the mall becomes part of the experience of the movies (Friedberg 1995, 69ff.). As much as it celebrates other aspects of capitalism, the mall celebrates the hypermediacy of our culture and calls forth a postmodern version of the flâneur, whose gaze, as she walks amid all these competing media, is a series of fragmented, sidelong, and hypermediated glances.

THE HYPERMEDIACY OF NONPLACES

The shopping mall as a mediated space is simultaneously particularized and anonymous. Each mall is particular in the sense that it is filled with brand-name commercial products and media in the stores, films on view in the cineplex, and video games in the arcade. Yet despite efforts

Figure 10.3 Two rides at the Camp Snoopy amusement park inside the Mall of America. (*top*) The Screaming Yellow Eagle. (*bottom*) The Bloomington Express. Photographs © 1996 Bob Cole.

to identify each mall (by giving it a name and sometimes a theme), malls are notoriously anonymous, perhaps because, as Sorkin (1992) points out, consumer capitalism demands sameness behind the variety. The mall is replicable so that one in Portland, Oregon, is indistinguishable from one in Orlando, Florida, and remarkably similar to one in Berlin or Sydney. Their replicability enables malls to detach themselves from their surroundings and become free-floating, hypermediated experiences. They share this quality of detachment with other high-technology spaces, such as airports, supermarkets, and multiplex movie theaters (when these are not already incorporated into malls). All such spaces are examples of what the anthropologist Marc Augé (1995) has called "non-places," by which he means "spaces which are not themselves anthropological places."

Augé contends that in "supermodernity . . . [a] dense network of means of transport which are also inhabited spaces is developing; where the habitué of supermarkets, slot machines and credit cards communicates wordlessly, through gestures, with an abstract, unmediated commerce." For Augé, these nonplaces are not metaphorical, but can be measured and quantified "by totaling all the air, rail and motorway routes, the mobile cabins called 'means of transport' (aircraft, trains and road vehicles), the airports and railway stations, hotel chains, leisure parks, large retail outlets, and finally the complex skein of cable and wireless networks that mobilize extraterrestrial space" (77). Nonplaces, such as theme parks and malls, function as public places only during designated hours of operation. There is nothing as eerie as an airport at three o'clock in the morning, or a theme park after closing hours, when the careful grids of railings and ropes that during the day serve to shepherd thousands of visitors to ticket counters or roller coasters stand completely empty. Such spaces then seem drained of meaning. A good example is the plaza beyond the outfield walls of Atlanta's newly constructed baseball park, Turner Field (fig. 10.4). This plaza has been designed to have the feel and function of a town square, but it is available only to ticketholders and open only on game days. Most public spaces—think of market streets such as Strøget in Copenhagen and the French Quarter in New Orleans—are deserted for some hours during the night and early morning. However, after-hours establishments attest to the life of such urban spaces long after the shops have closed. Many people live in the French Quarter or on and off Strøget, whereas nobody lives at Turner Field or in Disney World (although vacationers may lodge there for a week at a time). The Turner Field plaza has no

Figure 10.4 Turner Field. (*top*) The plaza. (*bottom*) The Chop House. (*opposite*) Arcade games. © 1997 The Atlanta Braves. All rights reserved. Used by permission.

connection to the inhabitants of the surrounding, economically depressed area, and Disney World was built on a swamp with a substantial buffer to separate it from the city of Orlando (in contrast to the early parks on Coney Island, which were accessible by public transit and functioned as extensions of New York City).

Augé further characterizes nonplaces as sites for experiencing the reality of mediation: "Frequentation of non-places today provides an experience—without real historical precedent—of solitary individuality combined with non-human mediation (all it takes is a notice or

a screen) between the individual and the public authority" (117). What the individual experiences in these mediated encounters is the hyper-mediacy of these nonplaces, which are defined not by their associations with local history or even with the ground on which they are built, but primarily by the reality of the media they contain. Augé continues: "The real non-places of supermodernity—the ones we inhabit when we are driving down the motorway, wandering through the supermarket or sitting in an airport lounge waiting for the next flight to London or Marseilles—have the peculiarity that they are defined partly by the words and texts they offer us" (96). Increasingly, these mediated spaces are also defined by video and audio as pure perceptual experiences, expressions of the enjoyment of media.

To Augé's list of nonplaces we would add cyberspace itself: the Internet and other manifestations of networked digital media. Cyberspace is not, as some assert, a parallel universe. It is not a place of escape from contemporary society, or indeed from the physical world. It is rather a nonplace, with many of the same characteristics as other highly mediated nonplaces. Cyberspace is a shopping mall in the ether; it fits smoothly into our contemporary networks of transportation, communication, and economic exchange. Nevertheless, many enthusiasts insist on the separateness and uniqueness of cyberspace. John Perry Barlow's "Declaration of Independence for Cyberspace," which circulated in 1996 during the controversy over government censorship of the Internet, begins: "Governments of the Industrial World, you weary giants of flesh and steel, I come from Cyberspace, the new home of Mind. On behalf of the future, I ask you of the past to leave us alone. You are not welcome among us. You have no sovereignty where we gather" (http://www.eff.org/pub/Publications/John_Perry_Barlow/barlow_0296. declaration January 13, 1998). If they have no sovereignty, it is because cyberspace is a nonplace, although Barlow would not accept this characterization, and in any case the "giants of flesh and steel" already govern quite successfully any number of nonplaces. Barlow's denial that the Internet is part of traditional history and society is echoed, with less bloated rhetoric, by many other writers, for whom cyberspace has become a theological concept.

THE THEOLOGY OF CYBERSPACE

In fifteenth- and sixteenth-century Italian religious paintings, the landscape is represented as a subordinate, almost decorative element in relation to the larger religious themes. Both painters, who perfected the Albertian window, and their audience viewed the landscapes through windows or doors, so that for them nature was framed by contemporary architecture. Such paintings often set the scene in an interior, not because the story demanded it, but as a way of symbolizing and containing their theological message. In these paintings, what we regard as the natural world was subordinated to the religious, and that subordination was expressed through the Italian "windowed" style. The subordination of nature began to give way as early as the seventeenth century, in later Italian painting and especially in Dutch landscapes. And since the nineteenth century, when nature for the most part had replaced God and the church as the largest context for making sense of human actions and purposes, the windows of the Italian Renaissance have not been needed as a frame. On the computer screen, however, the windows have returned: everything in this world (and, as the Mars Pathfinder mission demonstrated in 1997, beyond this world as well) is made visible to us through windows, which we can click on and enter in a more literal way than one could enter the windowed spaces of Italian paintings. Furthermore, for enthusiasts at least, cyberspace is bidding to replace nature as the largest interpretive context. As Marcos Novak (1991) puts it: "Cyberspace involves a reversal of the current mode of interaction with computerized information. At present such information is external to us. The idea of cyberspace subverts that relation; we are now within information. In order to do so we ourselves must be reduced to bits, represented in the system, and in the process become information anew" (225). Just as, in early religious paintings, nature was initially separate from us and then became the predominant context for understanding our world and our actions, so "the idea of cyberspace" transforms information from something separate and contained within our computers to a space we can inhabit. The current development of the visual and conceptual space of the computer screen thus mirrors the development of the space of the canvas in the history of Western painting. We inhabit cyberspace just as previous generations inhabited nature, or even earlier generations lived in a theocentric world. For Novak, Benedikt, and others, the master narrative of our culture is no longer the story of God's relation to us or of our relation to nature, but of our relation to information technologies. It is a theology of cyberspace.

When William Gibson invented the term in his novel *Neuromancer* (1986), he described cyberspace as "a consensual hallucination experienced daily by billions of legitimate operators in every nation . . . a graphic representation of data abstracted from the banks of every computer in the human system. Unthinkable complexity. Lines of light ranged in the nonspace of the mind, clusters and constellations of data. Like city lights receding" (52). For Gibson, cyberspace consisted of the network of all computer and information processing systems on the earth or in orbit. When hackers "jacked in" using a headset, not unlike the wire in *Strange Days,* they could see and feel their way through this electronic network. The passing information had colors and shapes, and the network itself defined a space through which they could move. Gibson's definition of cyberspace as a combination of networking and virtual reality, a space in both a metaphorical and a visual sense, has become paradigmatic for others (such as Novak, David Tomas, and Benedikt himself) in their observations about cyberspace. Tomas (1991) indeed speaks of "a parallel world of potential workspaces" (35); Benedikt (1991) of a "globally networked . . . 'virtual' reality . . . made up of data, of pure information" (122–123). For cyberspace enthusiasts, there are two worlds: "the sensorial world of the organically human" and the digitized, pure, immaterial world of cyberspace. Benedikt thinks of the relation between these two worlds as an evolving process of dematerialization: "And cyberspace, we might now see, is nothing more, or less, than the latest stage in the evolution of [Sir Karl Popper's] *World 3,* with the ballast of materiality cast away—cast away again, and perhaps finally." Although Benedikt immediately qualifies this statement, insisting that cyberspace or virtual reality will never replace "'real reality,'" he nonetheless conceives of these as two distinct, autonomous realms (4). Proponents of cyberspace seem to be replaying the logic of transcendence at the heart of Christianity, as when Benedikt, sounding very much like a revivalist preacher reminding us not to ignore the care of our spirit while caught up in the bodily snares of this world, implores us to take care of cyberspace: "The design of cyberspace is, after all, the design of another life-world, a parallel universe, offering the intoxicating prospect of actually fulfilling—with a technology very nearly achieved—a dream thousands of years old: the dream of transcending the physical world, fully alive, at will, to dwell in some Beyond—to be empowered or enlightened there, alone or with others, and to return" (131).

This dream of transcendence is so compelling that its advocates will sometimes ignore even the most obvious material limitations of cyberspace. For example, Michael Heim (1991) suggests that "the computer network appears as a godsend in providing forums for people to gather in surprisingly personal proximity—especially considering today's limited bandwidths—without the physical limitations of geography, time zones, or conspicuous social status" (73). Yet precisely the opposite is true. The people are not in personal proximity; furthermore, geography, time zones, and social status are indeed limitations or rather characteristics of computer networks. Where we are located on earth (in what kind of urban or rural setting, in an industrialized or developing country) will determine how and whether we can connect to the Internet at all. The institutionalized system of time keeping affects every phase of "time-stamped" Internet communications. Finally, the conspicuous social status of a postindustrial, computer-owning, global citizen is as much a part of the Internet as are routers and protocols. Cyberspace exists in a tightly defined network of computers, economic status, and considerations of time and space. It is only within this network that one can enjoy what Heim describes as the erotic experience of cyberspace, or what Benedikt characterizes as transcendence. The apparent rejection of the material world and the human body by cyberspace enthusiasts (and we shall later argue that the rejection can only be apparent) has called forth serious criticism from such feminist and cultural studies scholars as Donna Haraway, Anne Balsamo, and Allucquère Rosanne Stone.

In matters pertaining to the theology of cyberspace, we must declare ourselves agnostics. We do not believe that cyberspace is an immaterial world, but that it is very much a part of our contemporary world and that it is constituted through a series of remediations. As a digital network, cyberspace remediates the electric communications networks of the past 150 years, the telegraph and the telephone; as virtual reality, it remediates the visual spaces of painting, film, and television; and as a social space, it remediates such historical places as cities and parks and such nonplaces as theme parks and shopping malls. Like other contemporary mediated spaces, cyberspace refashions and extends earlier media, which are themselves embedded in material and social environments.

Television

11

distinguished television from film on technological grounds. Stanley Cavell (1986) too commented on the ontological differences between film and television. As Sandy Flitterman-Lewis (1992) put it,

Films are seen in large, silent, darkened theaters, where intense light beams are projected from behind toward luminous surfaces in front. There is an enforced and anonymous collectivity of the audience because, for any screening, all viewers are physically present at the same time in the relatively enclosed space of the theater. In contrast to this cocoonlike, enveloping situation is the fragmentary, dispersed, and varied nature of television reception. The darkness is dissolved, the anonymity removed. (217)

In the past, the division between film and television was clear. While we view film in a public space in the company of strangers who join us in constituting the audience, we usually watch or monitor the television in private spaces—our own home or a friend's. Furthermore, unlike film, television functions in a practical way within our domestic economy. Film offers us a world elsewhere, an opportunity temporarily to set aside our cultural, personal, and economic circumstances, while television offers us a means of structuring those circumstances on a daily basis. As usual, new technologies and practices are working to confuse these classic differences. VCRs make it possible to monitor our films at home, while bars and some restaurants offer television to their patrons and the lobbies of movie theaters are now filled with television monitors screening coming attractions. Nevertheless, as a cultural idea, the film has still managed to remain distinct from television.

Television acknowledges its mediation more explicitly and readily than film does, and one reason may indeed be technical. Despite its interest in a kind of social or ideological realism, television is not as capable of photorealism as are film, photography, and now computer graphics (Fiske 1987, 21–36). McLuhan and Williams, media critics with very different agendas, have both suggested that the poorer resolution or different lighting robs television of visual depth (McLuhan 1964, 268–294; Williams 1975, 62). Video technology tends to flatten the image, so that there is less opportunity to develop deep and convincing linear perspectives. The television broadcast protocols have until now offered the viewer much less visual information than a photograph or a film. McLuhan made much of the television's low resolution, calling the televised image "a flat two-dimensional mosaic" (273). Referring to the NTSC standard image, still broadcast in the

1990s, McLuhan went on to wonder "whether all this would change if technology stepped up the character of the TV image to movie data level" (273). His conclusion—that high-resolution television would no longer be television at all—illustrates one of the dangers of McLuhan's technological determinism, which depends on seeing as causes the details of a technology that may well change. ⊘ **p. 75** In any case, as we are now beginning to experience digital and high-definition television (HDTV), we can appreciate McLuhan's insight without accepting his determinism. It seems fair to say that the flatness and coarseness of the traditional televised image did make it harder to remediate the perspective techniques of photography and film and that perceptual transparency has therefore been a less successful strategy for television than for these other media.

STYLES OF TELEVISUAL REMEDIATION

Even if television has been less fully committed to photo- or filmic realism, it nevertheless has its transparent styles. Popular culture in the United States seems intuitively to divide television according to its logic of remediation. Transparency is the style favored by dramas, soap operas, daytime talk shows, and certain "real-life" programs, while hypermediacy is the style of most news and sports programming, situation comedies, special events such as beauty pageants, and commercials. Whether transparent or hypermediated, all television programs present the experience of watching television as itself authentic and immediate. Even when television acknowledges itself as a medium, it is committed to the pursuit of the immediate to a degree that film and earlier technologies are not. Because of the structure of financing, television is even more immediately responsive than film to what advertisers and producers perceive as cultural demands. It is as if television programs need to win the moment-by-moment approval of their large, popular audiences, to evoke a set of rapid and predictable emotional responses: television must pursue immediacy as authentic emotion, as exemplified most plainly in the "heartwarming" drama.

Television's claim to superiority over film, photography, and earlier visual media is that a television broadcast can be "live" (cf. Feuer 1983, 12–22). As Flitterman-Lewis (1992) puts it, "a film is always distanced from us in time (whatever we see on the screen has already occurred at a time when we weren't there), whereas television, with its capacity to record and display images simultaneously with our viewing, offers a quality of presentness, of 'here and now' as distinct from the

cinema's 'there and then.' It is television's peculiar form of presentness—its implicit claim to be live—that founds the impression of immediacy" (218). Television monitors events and reports (or at least
seems to report) changes immediately. Monitoring, the earliest form
of television, remains its paradigm (cf. Cavell 1986). Although a vast
network of technical devices and economic and social forces typically
intervenes between the origin and delivery of the image, we still behave
toward television as if it were a direct channel between ourselves and
the event. We even use the term *channel* to designate the signal delivered on one frequency. At times when it cannot conceal that this network stands between us and the event, television is ready to adopt
another strategy and insist that it is itself the event and so, by definition, immediate. And because it asserts itself as a medium, television
has also been less reluctant than film to accept digital technologies that
may enhance its mediated status. Television seems willing to entertain
a wider range of visual and cultural styles and to remediate other media
more vigorously and more frankly than popular film. If this was true of
television even in the 1950s and 1960s, digital technology has now
extended the range of this established medium still further into the
hypermediated. Television has enthusiastically received computer
graphics and digital editing and is deploying them in the service of
both transparency and hypermediacy.

In the case of dramatic series and "made-for-TV" movies, the
uses of digital media are very similar to those in Hollywood films. The
aim is usually to create special effects through digital compositing in
such a way that the viewer cannot detect the presence of the computer.
The need to save money and time is more pressing in television than in
film, and so digital technology is used increasingly to fashion or alter
scenes that would be too costly to shoot with the appropriate number
of actors, location, time of day, and so on. Instead of a whole company
of men marching across a field, a live-action shot may include only a
handful of marchers, which the digital compositor will replicate to fill
out the company. The effect is spoiled if the viewer notices that there
are really only six men appearing repeatedly across the screen. No
viewer can object to digital compositing as dishonest in the context of
fiction. The claim to the real here is not based on events that "really
happened," but, as with film, on the authenticity of the emotions
that the images provide the viewer and on the transparency of the
mediation.

TELEVISION NEWS

News and information shows are a different matter because their claim to immediacy *is* based on the shared belief that they are presenting what "really happened." The insistence on the liveness of the action is what gives television news its special claim among journalistic media. (By contrast, analysis, especially political analysis, is regarded as inappropriate for television—almost a violation. It remains the province of print journalism, ostensibly because television networks are not allowed to play political favorites, but in fact because a consistent and prolonged point of view required for analysis or reflection is incompatible with televisual immediacy.) Nevertheless, television news and information shows are increasingly willing to use digital technology in the service of hypermediacy without giving up their claim to be live. In commercials, news shows, and sports broadcasts, television is borrowing the windowed and multimediated look of the computer screen. Paradoxically, the windowed style is most evident in shows that purport to offer us a transparent view of real-time events. Because news programs aim to provide viewers with as much information as possible in the shortest possible time, they tend to fill up the screen with visible evidence of the power of television to gather events. This leads to what we might call the "CNN look," in which the televised image of the newscaster is coordinated with a series of graphics and explanatory captions, until the broadcast begins to resemble a web site or multimedia application.

Although the presence of acknowledged digital media makes the televised view less transparent, it does not seem to lessen the sense of immediacy. CNN is known for its "up-to-the-minute" coverage of wars, crimes, and natural disasters. The newscasters often remind us that the images are coming live from some disaster site, even though what the viewer sees is a multimediated screen in which the live feed is confined to one window. (The highly mediated and orchestrated coverage of the Persian Gulf War by CNN and the other networks is an example that has been infinitely studied; for example, in Jeffords's and Rabinowitz's *Seeing Through the Media.*) The borders of these windows can mark abrupt transitions from one logic to the other, as they do in figure 11.1. This discussion between a news anchor in Washington, D.C., and a reporter in Aspen, Colorado, seems to be taking place in cyberspace: each subject is framed with identifying text as if their images were part of a multimedia presentation. We can see the effect of twenty years of the Internet and computer graphics by comparing this

recent screen from 1998 to an "air check" from the first days of CNN news in 1980 (fig. 11.2). In the early air check, the newscaster occupies a space that we recognize as part of our world; the windowed style is still years away, and the only text on the screen is the sheaf of papers he holds in his hands. Today, CNN still insists on the immediacy and timeliness of the report itself, and the viewer seems to agree. However, televised immediacy is no longer characterized by a unified, transparent screen.

Television accommodates this visible multiplicity more easily than film. Other than the use of subtitles, traditional film avoids combining words and images in the same frame, except where the presence of words can be explained within the fictional world, as with road signs or letters that characters may read. Television news and information broadcasts seem to need no such excuse. However, even on television, there remain pockets of resistance to hypermediacy—for example, in the coverage of some sports such as baseball. The screen that baseball fans see looks more or less as it did thirty years ago, with the conventional, transparent shots of the batter from center field, or the pitcher from behind the plate or from the first- or third-base lines. Interestingly, such old-fashioned coverage is more likely to be found in local or regional-based networks like TBS in Atlanta or WGN in Chicago, although even these stations provide instant replays and flash statistics

on the screen underneath each batter. The national coverage of baseball by Fox or ESPN, not limited to promoting an enduring identification with a particular team, has introduced further enhancements, including split screens, an overlay of the score and situation in the upper-left-hand corner of the screen, more textual and graphic overlays (such as a color graphic indicating a hitter's "hot" and "cold" zones), pregame interviews inserted in small windows on screen, and even the "catcher-cam" (a camera attached to the catcher's mask) used by Fox in covering the 1997 All-Star Game.

None of these digital interventions is felt to disturb the liveness of the broadcast, even though the viewer can no longer pretend that what she is seeing is the single point of view that she might occupy if she were sitting in the stadium. Indeed, as the catcher-cam suggests, the aim of these multiple mediations is to provide greater immediacy. (A camera attached to the catcher's mask would seem to provide an authentic, first-person point of view of the game. However, just as with the overuse of the subjective camera in some Hollywood films, the effect is to call our attention to the medium itself.) Ironically, Fox's or ESPN's complicated television screen reflects what the viewer would now experience in the stadium, which itself has become a multimedia space, with huge screens that present statistics, "human-interest" images, and re-plays. Both at home and in the stadium, the viewer is experiencing the reality of media. And all of these ricocheting remediations apparently do nothing to damage the authenticity of sporting events, around which sportscasters continue to weave sentimental narratives. The coverage of the Olympics, the most popular television program on earth, shows just how far television can go in combining elaborate technology with naive stories of struggle and victory.

There are other facets to news and information on television in which transparency continues to dominate. In some local news and sports broadcasts, for example, there is a greater emphasis on traditional live reporting—a news reporter talking to the camera while standing at the scene of an event—perhaps simply because there are fewer resources for sophisticated digital interventions. Such local broadcasts are often called "eye-witness news," where the reporters and the camera offer themselves as the viewer's eyes on the world. Here the television camera does function as a point-of-view technology, in the tradition of painting, photography, and film. There is also the genre of pseudo-documentary that promises authenticity through transparency: cameras follow police while they make dangerous arrests or are placed on the helmets of race car drivers or skydivers. These programs, in fact, use all the techniques of documentary filmmaking to cull a narrative out of the apparent chaos of the events they present. They also rely heavily on the subjective camera. Although they are recorded and edited, they borrow the sense of immediacy that live television evokes. In such cases, as in narrative films, to acknowledge the presence of digital technology would be the wrong logic for this genre.

The Immediacy of Commercial Television

One genre that we have not yet discussed is the one often considered quintessential to television: the commercial. The televised commercial is an obvious remediation of advertising in print and especially on the radio. As Mimi White (1992) and many others have recognized, television commercials are not merely the means of financing particular broadcasts. In the United States, and increasingly in Europe and elsewhere, commercial advertising helps to define television as a medium. Once again, every medium is a network of economic, social, and cultural as well as technical elements, and the network of relations that constitute American television is most clearly visible in the commercial.

These commercials can be (fairly) transparent or hypermediated, but in either case they mimic the narrative structure of other television genres (Kozloff 1992, 68–69). Like the other genres, commercials are vigorous in their pursuit of immediacy. In a matter of seconds, a commercial must seize the viewer with its message that a particular product or service should be bought. The transparent commercials usually want to evoke sympathetic feelings in the viewer (security, warmth, love—or sometimes their opposites), to validate these feelings as authentic, and to associate them with the product. A commercial for a long-distance phone service shows a grandmother in a loving conversation with her distant grandson and suggests that long-distance "brings people together." Hypermediated commercials, however, may acknowledge the fact that they are trying to sell something and appeal to the viewer's perceived sense of sophistication by offering her a video experience to enjoy and to associate with the product. Both transparent and hypermediated commercials must address the viewer either directly or by creating a fictional proxy. As Allen (1992) suggests, the point is "to give the viewer at home an image of himself or herself on screen and to make sure the viewer knows that he or she is the person to whom the show (and its accompanying commercials) is offered. . . . By simulating face-to-face exchanges, television attempts to 'de-mediate' our relationship with it" (125). Commercial television turns immediacy itself into a commodity.

On the other hand, a commercial is no simulacrum. Its force is lost unless the viewer connects it with the product itself and feels an urge to buy. "Every commercial is an implicit unanswered question— 'Will you buy?'—that calls for an action the commercial text cannot provide, because only real viewers can buy the very real commodities the commercials advertise" (Allen 1992, 125). The video commercial, the product, and the practices of buying and selling form themselves into a network in which each element relates to and completes the others. Perhaps more than any other television genre, the commercial insists on the reality of television— not just its power as a medium, but its place in our physical and social world. When the viewer goes to a supermarket, she will see products labeled "as seen on TV," as if the presence of the commercial validates the product. The most intriguing form of advertising now, the infomercial, is particularly insistent on connecting the product to the world. It combines various techniques from television and film documentary with the traditional commercial, and, by its length and frank acknowledgment of its intention to sell, it further insists on the inseparability of the message and the product. Computer graphics and digital technology have so far done little to change this form, but they can contribute to the sense of authenticity and immediacy through the same techniques (text and graphics integrated with video) that we see in television news broadcasts.

Baudrillard (1983) has contended that (American) television is preoccupied with itself as a medium and only pretends to be offering events as they happen: that television is a cultural device for covering up the absence of the real. The shock value of Baudrillard's claim rests on an old-fashioned premise that there should be a strict separation between the medium and the reality and that therefore media should be transparent to reality. Baudrillard expects us still to believe that the Renaissance logic of transparency is the norm from which our culture has diverged. For our culture, however, the logic of hypermediacy is at least as compelling. Just as reality and mediation have become inseparable off-screen, so hypermediacy has become the formal mark of liveness on television. Like other media, television is now simply part of the reality. Television sets are real objects in the physical world and in fact are growing larger with projection television and more physically encompassing with "surround-sound" speakers. Where the aim of film is to make us briefly forget the world outside the theater, the aim of television is to remind us of and to show us the world we inhabit.

As sociologists have recognized, television viewing has woven itself into our social and familial lives. Because "television viewing constitutes a large temporal part of our lives," argues Larry Grossberg (1987), "we must note its integration into the mundanities of everyday life, and simultaneously, its constant interruption by, and continuity with, our other daily routines" (35). Jan-Uwe Rogge (1989) contends that the "general ubiquity" of media like television "causes them to be allocated certain functions in people's everyday lives. The media form a part of the family system, a part many can no longer imagine living without" (169). In other words, "viewers experience themselves as being 'socialized,' as belonging to a kind of electronically constituted society whenever and as long as they watch television" (Rath 1989, 89). Like ubiquitous computing and the World Wide Web, but unlike film and virtual reality, television confronts us with the reality of mediation as it monitors and reforms the world and the lives and practices of its inhabitants. ◈ **p. 58** Just as it remediates film or other media, television remediates the real.

The World Wide Web

12

The World Wide Web has already passed through several stages, each of which refashions some earlier media. The Web today is eclectic and inclusive and continues to borrow from and remediate almost any visual and verbal medium we can name. What is constantly changing is the ratio among the media that the Web favors for its remediations; what remains the same is the promise of immediacy through the flexibility and liveness of the Web's networked communication. The liveness of the Web is a refashioned version of the liveness of broadcast television. ▷ **p. 187**

TEXT AND GRAPHIC DESIGN

The Internet itself, as a communications system and as a cultural symbol, remediates the telegraph. We still picture the Internet as a reticule of electric lines covering the industrialized world, as the telegraph first did in the nineteenth century, even though the Internet today consists of a variety of data links, including lines above ground, buried cables, and microwave and satellite links. Prior to the World Wide Web, the services of the Internet (such as email and simple file transfer) refashioned principally alphabetic media (the book, the letter, the technical report). Although it was possible to transmit digital graphics, most users were limited to ASCII text. And because the Internet could not pretend to offer the range of materials available in print, it had to rely on speed of communication as the only advantage in its remediation. This speed was most telling in electronic mail, by far the most popular use of the Internet even into the early 1990s.

In its obscure first years, the Web too remediated only textual communication. A CERN physicist, Tims Berners-Lee, proposed the

Figure 12.1 The Lynx text-only presentation of the home page of the School of Literature, Communication, and Culture at the Georgia Institute of Technology. http://www.lcc.gatech.edu January 25, 1998.

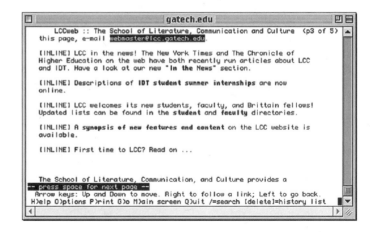

World Wide Web hypertext service so that scientists could more readily share their papers and numerical data. The earliest browsers, such as Lynx, presented only text on web pages (fig. 12.1). However, in 1993, Marc Andreessen and colleagues at the University of Illinois created the first graphical browser, the forerunner of Netscape, which permitted static images to appear along with text on the page (fig. 12.2). (Hafner and Lyon 1996, 257–258, 263). This apparently minor addition had two momentous consequences. First, the Web began to engage a much larger audience of users, including most academics and researchers, who were already using email, and soon a large fraction of technically literate people throughout the industrialized world. Without graphics on the World Wide Web, there would not now be tens of millions of Internet users, nor would there be much interest from the business community. The second consequence, related to the first, was that the World Wide Web could now refashion a larger class of earlier media. In addition to the letter and the scientific report, it could now remediate the magazine, the newspaper, and graphic advertising. Internet magazines and news services became popular and important genres. The tradition to which web designers now looked for inspiration was graphic design for print, and the principles of web page design became similar to those for laying out magazine articles, advertisements, and title pages (fig. 12.3, plate 16). Even the differences, such as the smaller space and poorer resolution of the computer screen, were analyzed in a vocabulary provided by graphic design.

Graphic designers brought to the Web their obsession with visual perfection, which expressed itself in this new medium as a need to

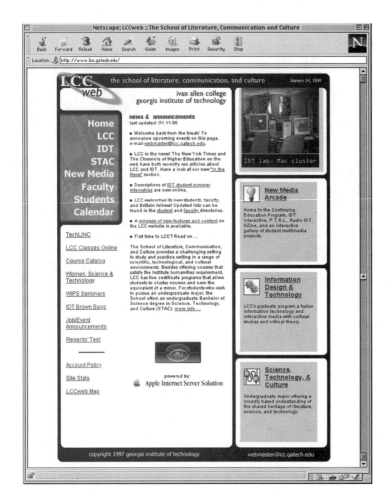

control the placement and color of every pixel on the user's screen. (This obsession was not shared by the computer programmers who built the first generation of web sites and browsers. They placed a higher value on user control and customization.) As always, these remediations combined respect and rivalry. While it was clear that the computer screen could not compete with the printed page in precision, the Web did have in its favor speed of delivery and point-and-click interactivity. At the same time, as the numbers of both servers (information sources) and clients (the audience) continued to grow, the Web became an increasingly important remediator of all sorts of printed information. It began to resemble a conventional public library in the scope of its materials,

Figure 12.3 Graphic design on the Web: the *Creating Killer Web Sites* splash (opening) screen. http://www.killersites.com January 28, 1998. © 1998 David Siegel. Used by permission.

while public libraries themselves were expanding their definition of appropriate materials and even including Internet terminals in reading rooms.

Traditional graphic design could not account for moving images, so the Internet and World Wide Web necessarily passed into a new phase when they began to deliver animation, fuller interactivity, and digital video and audio. The old remediations were not abandoned. The Web still refashions the personal letter, the book, and the magazine, but now it also refashions and reforms CD-ROM or DVD multimedia, radio, film, and television. It rivals all these forms by promising greater immediacy and by recontextualizing them in the encompassing electronic environment of cyberspace.

THE VARIETY OF REMEDIATIONS ON THE WORLD WIDE WEB

There are a number of possible strategies for remediation, from respectful to radical, and designers for the World Wide Web have adopted each of these strategies at various times. ▷ **p. 44** There have been and remain many web sites that highlight other media without any apparent critique. This respectful attitude is most common in remediations of more venerable media: the printed book, static graphics, paintings, and photographs. The purpose of Project Gutenberg is to collect pure verbal versions of "classic" texts; the site adds little in the way of graphic orna-

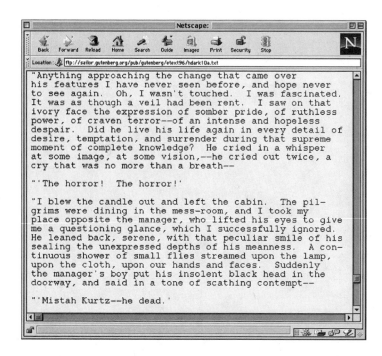

Text shown in the browser window:

```
"Anything approaching the change that came over
his features I have never seen before, and hope never
to see again.  Oh, I wasn't touched.  I was fascinated.
It was as though a veil had been rent.  I saw on that
ivory face the expression of somber pride, of ruthless
power, of craven terror--of an intense and hopeless
despair.  Did he live his life again in every detail of
desire, temptation, and surrender during that supreme
moment of complete knowledge?  He cried in a whisper
at some image, at some vision,--he cried out twice, a
cry that was no more than a breath--

"'The horror!  The horror!'

"I blew the candle out and left the cabin.  The pil-
grims were dining in the mess-room, and I took my
place opposite the manager, who lifted his eyes to give
me a questioning glance, which I successfully ignored.
He leaned back, serene, with that peculiar smile of his
sealing the unexpressed depths of his meanness.  A con-
tinuous shower of small flies streamed upon the lamp,
upon the cloth, upon our hands and faces.  Suddenly
the manager's boy put his insolent black head in the
doorway, and said in a tone of scathing contempt--

"'Mistah Kurtz--he dead.'
```

mentation, so as not to distract from the alphabetic texts themselves (fig. 12.4). Its editor, Michael Hart, has called the computer a "Replicator Technology," because it can reproduce texts infinitely and without adding errors (http://www.promo.net/pg/history.html January 13, 1998). Hart's replication is nothing other than respectful remediation. CETH—the Center for Electronic Texts in the Humanities—is another example of respectful remediation (http://www.ceth.rutgers.edu/ January 13, 1998). Such textual databases in fact preceded the introduction of the Web and at first relied on earlier services of the Internet or even digital tape to achieve their respectful remediations of the book. We can also point to the web site for the American Memory Project of the Library of Congress (http://lcweb2.loc.gov/amhome.html January 13, 1998), which preserves documents, prints, and early photographs, as well as some early films and sound recordings (fig. 12.5). And there are many virtual museums and art galleries that offer a sampling of digitized images, often laid out in some arrangement that reflects the physical space of the building itself.

Perhaps developers of these web sites and our popular culture at large are inclined to be respectful precisely because these media are

Figure 12.5 A Civil War photograph: *Atlanta, Ga. Trout House, Masonic Hall, and Federal encampment on Decatur Street.* Library of Congress: American Memory. http://lcweb2.loc.gov/ammem/. © Library of Congress, Prints & Photographs Division.

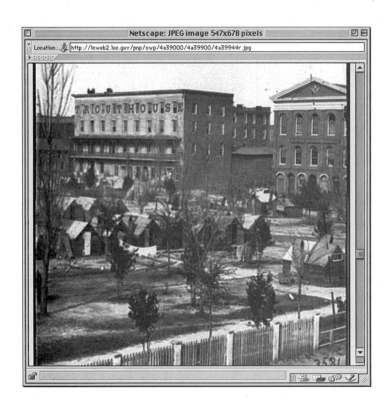

regarded as played out and therefore not likely to threaten the new digital media. In reproducing classic texts made for print or oil paintings hanging on a museum wall, the Web can fulfill an archival function without giving up its own claim to being revolutionary. Web designers feel less need to compete with "classic" authors or photographers because these modes of representation already seem complete. There are also film archives, as in the American Memory Project, although the Web's relationship to film is more complicated and contentious.

The remediation of print is by no means sacrosanct in this new medium. Web newspapers, magazines, and encyclopedias, for example, do seek to improve on the printed versions. Thus, the encyclopedia in CD-ROM, DVD, or Web form makes predictable claims to both transparency and hypermediacy. All electronic encyclopedias are hypermediated and can claim to move the reader to desired information more efficiently by means of string searches or by hyperlinks. This hypermediacy is the main improvement offered by most web encyclopedias—for example, by the Britannica Online, which, although it

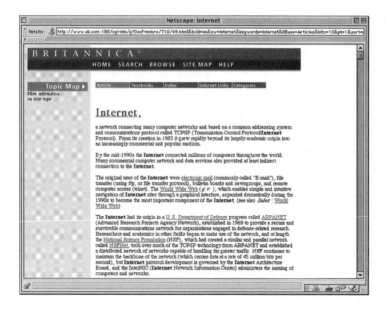

Figure 12.6 A page from the Britannica web site. Reprinted with permission from *Britannica Online*, Version 98.1.1. © 1997 by Encyclopedia Britannica, Inc.

contains some video, is primarily a collection of textual articles with static graphics (fig. 12.6). The CD-ROM or DVD encyclopedias, however, promise a new transparency through the animation, video, and audio that cannot appear in a printed version. ⊳ **p. 46** The user can hear Martin Luther King's voice or the cry of a particular exotic bird; she can see digitized video of a volcanic eruption or the first landing on the moon. The claim here is that the electronic encyclopedia can bring her closer to the event by offering such transparent media instead of mere prose. Such multimedia encyclopedias are also beginning to appear on the Web.

Web and Internet applications refashion the newer perceptual media of radio, television, and telephone more aggressively than they refashion print. With radio and television, the claim is not that the Internet provides a new transparency, although the quality of the audio (if not video) is already approaching the level that broadcasting or cable can provide. However, on the Internet, the listener has greater control over her listening or viewing experience of radio. It is an immediacy that she achieves through the hypermediacy of the windowed interface. She now listens to Internet radio with a mouse in one hand while she looks at a web page; she reads rubrics as she listens and may change the order of the materials by clicking on the links provided. Similar interfaces for Internet television already exist and will no doubt flourish as soon as the bandwidth to the home can handle full-screen, full-motion images. With the Internet phone services, more senses come into play, as the user makes, retrieves, and modifies calls through a graphical user interface. The main claim of improvement, however, is economic: the Internet phone is cheaper to use for long-distance calls.

WEB CAMERAS

Like other digital media, the Web may radically remediate its predecessors while failing to acknowledge them at all. The so-called web cameras only occasionally acknowledge their cultural role as "television only better." Apparently frivolous, web cameras are in fact deeply revealing of the nature of the Web as a remediator. Trained on some corner of the world—a hamster in a cage, a coffee machine, or the traffic on an expressway—web cameras take up the monitoring function of television and video. Broadcast television and closed-circuit video still perform this cultural task both publicly and privately. Security cameras guard the interior and exterior of buildings and private homes, while we have come to expect that news networks such as CNN will provide us with a constant video stream for any important natural or human disaster. ◁ **p. 189** Television monitors the commonplace as well as the disastrous; it both transforms the commonplace into an event (the Weather Channel) and makes the disastrous commonplace (with its endless coverage of developing tropical storms or forest fires).

Now the Web and related services on the Internet have begun to supplement and rival broadcast television in this role. Because streaming video on the Web is relatively cheap, we can now afford to monitor quotidian events more closely than ever. And, as always, the Internet can offer its user an interactivity that is not available with conventional broadcast television. At some sites the visitor can even adjust the camera's view herself.

In comparison with the viewing of film, the monitoring function of television is relatively private, since we watch television in our living room rather than in a public place. ◁ **p. 185** An indication of this difference is the way in which the VCR turns film into television. Watching a film amid the distractions and conversations of the living room often becomes an experience of casual monitoring rather than intense viewing. Yet the World Wide Web offers an even more private experience than television, because the individual browser is often alone with her machine, and in any case only one person can conduct the interaction. Web cameras are in some ways better monitors than televi-

sion, and indeed there are even web sites that allow the viewer to monitor television shows as they progress. Web cameras are now often in stop
motion, but full-motion video eventually will put the Web in direct
competition with broadcast and cable television (Reid 1997).

Web cameras would seem to operate under the logic of transparency, as each provides an unedited stream of images that makes some
part of the physical world transparent to the Internet. Many cameras
are pointed at nature sites such as mountains and beaches, despite the
fact that, except for the daily changes in lighting and seasonal changes
in the weather, there are few changes to monitor. The function of these
nature cameras is to put the viewer in touch with the exotic or the
remote, a service performed by photography and film in the last hundred years. Thus, a series of "robot cameras" on Maui track the conditions in paradise at sixty-minute intervals (fig. 12.7), while another
camera takes the viewer to the perpetually frozen Mawson Station in
Antarctica (fig. 12.8). In 1997, when the Mars Pathfinder became the
first spacecraft to land on another planet after the widespread deploy-
ment of the Web, the site operated by the Jet Propulsion Laboratory
became the world's most distant and exotic web camera (fig. 12.9). The
site received millions of "hits" in the first days after the landing, even
though there was nothing to see but a rocky desert and an undifferenti-

Figure 12.8 A web camera from Mawson Station in Antarctica. http://www.antdiv.gov.au/aad/exop/sfo/mawson/video.html January 24, 1998 © Commonwealth of Australia, Australian Antarctic Division. Used by permission.

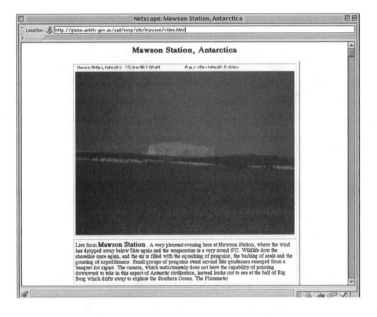

Figure 12.9 The Mars Pathfinder web site. http://mpfwww.jpl.nasa.gov. © 1998, NASA Jet Propulsion Laboratory. All rights reserved. Used by permission.

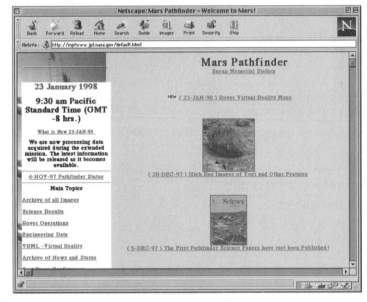

Figure 12.10 A panoramic view by the Miami Beach Cam. http://video-monitoring.com January 24, 1998. © 1997, Erdman Video Systems, Inc. Used by permission.

ated sky. The only movement was made by the spacecraft's own automated rover, as it raced across the surface of the planet at speeds of less than two feet per minute taking pictures and measurements of the rocks and soil. For most of the public, who have no knowledge of geology, the fascination could only have been with the reality of media ⊗ **p. 58**: the fact that scientists had succeeded in putting several cameras on Mars. What the scientists then asked us to watch—and we responded enthusiastically—were these media in operation.

Web cameras reveal again our fascination with media. What other motive can there be for transmitting around the world an endless stream of images of one's goldfish? Such a site serves no imaginable practical or aesthetic purpose; the designer can only be demonstrating to herself and to us the monitoring function of the Internet. Once again, transparent immediacy passes into hypermediacy, for if these web cameras make part of the physical world available, they also mediate that corner of the physical world by bringing it into cyberspace. They make Maui, Antarctica, and Mars nodes on the Internet. Many of these sites explore the aesthetic of hypermediacy by multiplying the camera images on one page. They may present several images by the same camera taken over time; they may build a panorama from the images of several closely aligned cameras (fig. 12.10); or they may simply present unrelated images. One site lets the browser make her own web jukebox by

Figure 12.11 Guinea Pig Television. http://www.olywa.net/jandrews/beta.htm January 24, 1998. © 1995–1998 Scenic Eastside Hill/OinkerNet. All rights reserved. Used by permission.

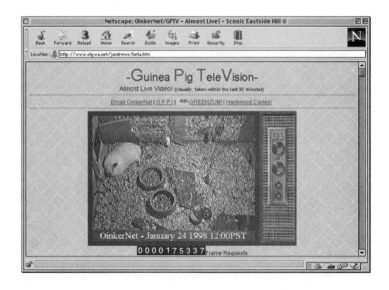

placing any three cameras side by side (fig. I.6). These techniques make us conscious of each web camera as a mediating technology. The "Guinea Pig Television" site goes further in playfully acknowledging the Web's remediation of television, because the designer has put the animals on view inside the graphic frame of a television set (fig. 12.11).

Many web cameras are trained on built environments rather than natural ones: city squares, highways, college dorms, and doughnut shops. These sites have their agenda in remediating our social spaces and in defining their oscillations between transparency and hypermediacy. We will limit ourselves to one example: a site from the Netherlands that purports to be a view of the red-light district in Amsterdam (fig. 12.12). Here the prostitutes put the shade up when they are available and pull it down when they are with a customer. As the site monitors the shade, it enacts the two logics of remediation. When the shade is up, the window becomes transparent, and the web image expresses quite literally the viewer's desire for sexual as well as visual immediacy. ⊘ **p. 78** When the shade is down, the viewer can examine only the window itself and consider what may be going on inside. The image becomes a representation of the desire for immediacy, which the web site produces, thwarts, and then reproduces.

THE HETEROGENEITY OF THE WEB
The ultimate ambition of the Web designer seems to be to integrate and absorb all other media. Even in the cases of respectful remediation,

the user may be left to wonder why she ever needs to return to the original medium. When all classic texts finally become available online, why return to the printed library? On the other hand, there are economic and cultural forces that work against the designer's desire to absorb everything into the Web. Museums in need of physical patrons may post only a small number of items on their web sites, and the text may point out that the reproductions on the Web cannot do justice to the originals. Many organizations develop web sites whose role is to complement other media products they own. Newspapers and television networks maintain extensive sites, but surely have no plans to discontinue their printed papers or televised broadcasts, although they may start wholly new ventures on the Web (Reid 1997). Instead, their earlier and newer media both rival and support each other. CNN's web pages contain audio and video clips from the same feeds available to their television network; the front page and the web site of *USA Today* are similar in style and content (fig. 1.6 and 1.7); and so on.

The hybrid and inclusive character of the Web does not make it any easier for our legal and legislative institutions to control this new technology; they would prefer to understand the Web by simple analogy to one earlier medium. The controversy over the censorship of the World Wide Web in the United States has really been a debate over the appropriate analogy: is the Web a new kind of television, newspaper, or indeed a virtual street corner? In striking down the Communications Decency Act in 1997, the Supreme Court decided that the Internet deserved the freedom of expression accorded to print rather than television. American television is censored for sexual content, ostensibly because it is so accessible to children, but in fact because of its assumed immediacy. In its ruling, the Court was endorsing the unstated assumption that visual media are more immediate than words and that visual pornography is therefore more threatening than verbal. The justices accepted the notion that the Internet is essentially a verbal medium with some pictures—a characterization that was only partly true in 1997 and is becoming less accurate as streaming audio and video, Java applets, and VRML proliferate. If the Internet and the Web remained as they were in the mid-1990s, then the decision striking down the Communications Decency Act could have been the last judicial word. But the increasing remediation of television on the Internet will likely mean a continued debate. It will be interesting to see whether legislatures and courts continue to regard the Internet as a book as it comes to look more and more like television—and as television comes to look more and more like it. The powerful cultural forces that fear the immediacy of the image can only become more alarmed. On the other hand, the Internet is not comfortable with the logic of transparency, and so pornography on the Internet will always oscillate between visual immediacy and the irony and self-referentiality of the Amsterdam web camera.

The cultural expectation that the Web remediate all earlier media means that the web interface can never be completely transparent. The strategy that dominates on the Web is hypermediacy, attaining the real by filling each window with widgets and filling the screen with windows. Hypermediacy is also the predominant strategy of broadcast television. Insofar as the Web is like television, it is committed to monitoring the real and the quotidian. Indeed, while television may still (barely) distinguish between the physical reality and its mediated presentation, the Web is even more aggressive in breaking down that barrier and insisting on the reality of mediation itself. Everything, from the snow fields of Antarctica to the deserts of Mars, finds its way on to the Web.

Ubiquitous Computing

13

Ubiquitous computing is virtual reality's opposite number. In virtual reality, the computer interface is erased, and all we see is what the computer places before our eyes. ▷ **p. 21** Ubiquitous computing, on the other hand, turns our whole world into a computer interface. So, while virtual reality refashions the immersive qualities of Hollywood film ▷ **p. 163**, ubiquitous computing appeals to us as a kind of interactive television that monitors and rearranges our physical world.

TELEPRESENCE AND AUGMENTED REALITY

If there were such thing as a "typical" virtual reality application, it would be the architectural walk-through, a three-dimensional model of a building with corridors and rooms. A residential architect might do this in order to give a sense of her design to a client who cannot visualize the house from blueprints; a student architect might build a walk-through and then discuss specific visual problems with a teacher. In such applications, the virtual reality is complete in itself. It is, in fact, Baudrillard's simulacrum, bearing no necessary resemblance to anything that exists in the physical world. Ironically, the apparent immediacy of such a virtual reality comes from its total opacity. The eyepieces of the headset block out the world of light, and for this very reason, the person wearing the headset becomes blind in the physical world and needs help to find her seat or to adjust her position (fig. I.2). ▷ **p. 161** The purpose of this opacity to the physical world is to provide the user with a perfectly transparent world generated by the computer.

In addition to these opaque systems, however, there are hybrid technologies for *augmented reality* and *telepresence.* They have in common with full virtual reality that they place computer graphics or video before the user's eyes and that they often track her head or body movements to control the graphic displays. On the other hand, telepresence and augmented reality call forth their own, more complicated remediations. Telepresence systems use video signals and computer graphics to place the user at a remote or inaccessible location. A robot with video cameras might be sent into a nuclear power plant after an accident, where the radiation levels are too high for human workers, and signals from the camera might be channeled to a worker who is a safe distance from the plant. The worker could then explore the damage by moving the robot and perhaps even grasp objects with a remote arm. In this case, the images are not computer generated, as they are in the architectural walk-through, but are instead provided from the world of light through digital video. These telepresence systems are related to the robots that now operate in all sorts of environments, from the oceans to outer space. They can also be regarded as higher-tech versions of the security and surveillance cameras that are now ubiquitous. Whenever they rely on live (or even delayed) video, telepresence systems are clearly remediating the monitoring function of broadcast television and closed-circuit video.

Medical telepresence and teleoperators take the doctor or technician to a location within a patient's body, and they may also radically change the scale of one's vision and manipulation. Instead of using a conventional endoscope, telepresence allows a doctor to fly through a computer reconstruction of the patient's insides, as if the doctor had herself shrunk to the size of the endoscope's probe (Satava and Robb 1997). This voyage through the body is itself an obvious remediation of science fiction films such as *Fantastic Voyage* (1966), where a team of researchers and their submarine (!) are shrunk to fit into a man's bloodstream. Figure 13.1 (plate 17) shows an experimental teleoperation system, in which the operator at the left is controlling a microsurgical robot that cuts into the patient's (or in this prototype a mannequin's) cornea (Hunter et al. 1993). In this hypermediated environment, the operator is surrounded by live and computer-enhanced video images and manipulates the patient through the images and feedback provided by the telerobot.

Telepresence can thus define a relationship between the medium and the physical world different from that of virtual reality. While virtual reality would replace the physical world with a simulacrum, telepresence brings the physical world into the virtual environment (and vice versa). While virtual reality abandons the world, telepresence insists that computer-mediated signals and real-time track-

Figure 13.1 A telepresence application: a microsurgical robot. *Presence,* Cover 2,4 (Fall, 1993): MIT Press. Image by Tilemachos D. Doukoglou and Serge R. Lafontaine. Used by permission.

ing devices are part of the physical world and can join with human operators in affecting their environment. The interface of a telepresence system is highly mediated and yet is supposed to be transparent, in the sense that it should transmit a view to the human operator and allow the operator to interact "naturally" with what she sees. For that reason, telepresence becomes more difficult over large distances. The robot explorers on Mars are too far away to allow a human operator to steer them directly. The Mars Pathfinder is a system in which the human operator's presence is highly limited and mediated. ▷ **p. 205**

In many hybrid systems for augmented reality, the user may wear special glasses or a headset that is not entirely opaque to the world of light. The user can see the physical world, but the headset can also display computer graphics over part or all of the field of view. Instead of blocking out the world, the computer writes over the world and therefore comments on and (in some cases literally) colors what the user sees. Boeing, for example, has tested a system in which the worker wears a headset while connecting the hundreds of miles of wiring in their commercial aircraft: one eye sees normally, while the other is covered by a monocular eyepiece. When the worker looks at a formboard carrying hundreds of wires, the computer determines exactly where she is looking and can display in the eyepiece an assembly diagram and parts lists drawn from a database (see Nash 1997). Such a display of free-floating text and images could not have been conceived prior to the windowed style in desktop computers of the 1980s. Meanwhile, doctors too use a sort of augmented reality to perform microsurgery—to reach into and alter inaccessible areas of the patient's body. Even artists have experimented with augmented reality to create installations in which the user walks through a real space but sees shapes and colors overlaid at the artist's discretion. ▷ **p. 143**

Ironically—and we can now appreciate the irony—neither augmented reality nor telepresence can make the same claim to transparency as the claim made by complete, and therefore opaque, virtual reality. Augmented reality remediates not perspective painting, but rather the windowed style of the desktop interface. In laying icons, texts, and images over visible objects in the world, augmented reality frankly admits that it is a digital medium interposing itself between the viewer and an apparently simple and unitary physical world. Augmented reality is hypermediated, for it makes the user aware of computer graphics as medium, even if the goal is to keep the graphics and the external object in close registration. In this sense, augmented reality is the opposite of telepresence, although, like telepresence, augmented reality celebrates the reality of its own mediation, the power of computer graphics to act as objects in and therefore to affect the world.

THE HYPERMEDIACY OF UBIQUITOUS COMPUTING

Enthusiasts for digital technology in general and virtual reality in particular are fond of a form of naive storytelling to convey their vision. John Tiffin's and Lalita Rajasingham's *In Search of the Classroom* (1995) offers such a narrative, in which Shirley, a high school student, goes through her day wearing her helmet and visiting various impossible places in virtual reality. In narratives of pure transparency like this one, there is eventually a rupture. If the story goes on long enough, Shirley is certain to come upon a television, a movie screen, or even a desktop computer represented inside the virtual reality, an acknowledgment that media are among the objects that make up our world. If the virtual space reflects our world, then it will also have computers, televisions, radios, books, newspapers, and so on. Yet there is an irony of self-reference. If virtual reality is about stepping through the medium into unmediated reality, then why does the virtual world need computers? Moreover, once we let computers and other media into the space, what is to keep them from multiplying so that the user can consult them at any time for any purpose? The question becomes: If we can have computers everywhere, why do we need virtual reality?

Figure 13.2 Classroom 2000: an experiment in ubiquitous computing for education. Courtesy of Professor Gregory Abowd, GVU Center, Georgia Institute of Technology. Photo by Richard Grusin.

Ubiquitous computing, first developed by Mark Weiser and others at Xerox PARC (Want et al. 1995), is just such a vision— of virtual reality turned inside out. Where virtual reality invites the user to become part of a world beyond mediation, ubiquitous computing offers the user a world in which everything is a medium, because everything is or contains a computing device. In Classroom 2000, for example, at the Georgia Institute of Technology, the mediation of the educational environment is frankly acknowledged. Everything the instructor says and does is recorded on digital video and made available for the students to examine after class. The students themselves have hand-held computers so that they can record their own notes and questions, which are synchronized with the classroom discussion. Even the whiteboards are computer screens that capture what the instructor writes, which is later transmitted to a web site (fig. 13.2).

Enthusiasts for ubiquitous computing envision environments in which our data files, applications, and preferences follow us automatically from computer to computer as we move around our workplace. Devices that are now "dumb," such as windows, doors, and refrigerators, become "smart," communicating with us and with one another and anticipating our needs. Indeed, we can see the excesses of ubiquitous computing most clearly in proposals for the "house of the future," which is really very much the house of the past—a vision of superautomation of household tasks from the 1950s, but with the addition of microchips everywhere. Ubiquitous computing is an attempt to reform reality by making technological objects conform to human needs and wishes: windows that open at bedtime because we like to sleep in the fresh air, refrigerators that notify us when we are low on milk, computers that download program updates before we ask for them, and so on. In one sense such a reform would be nothing new because we have always defined and constructed technologies to conform to and carry out our cultural preferences. ⊙ **p. 59** What is new, perhaps, is the overt expression of these choices and often the technological overkill involved. This overkill is almost animistic, because by injecting media into every imaginable device, ubiquitous computing brings these devices to a kind of artificial life. Ubiquitous computing is an extreme form of hypermediacy.

Systems for ubiquitous computing also carry with them the possibility of total surveillance: the computers track us and each other as they continually readjust our environment to meet our anticipated needs. Some enthusiasts also imagine a vast industry of (often preposterous) wearable computers: watches, hats, belts, and shoes that entertain or inform us. Finally, there are the evangelists for "nanomachines," microscopic devices placed throughout the environment, even inside our bodies for medical purposes. These reformers are all remediators of reality, who want to turn our physical world into a place where everything mediates something else.

By the standards of a generation ago, we have already achieved ubiquitous computing. In the 1950s and 1960s, computers were large and very expensive devices locked in climate-controlled rooms and tended by a class of specialists. Today, tens of millions of computers are busy remediating the real. Already there are wearable devices that will help us to achieve the immediacy of sex, if we are prepared to turn our bodies into media. The digital artist David Rokeby (1995) writes: "In France, a few years ago, I encountered an intriguing device called Le Flashing. It was a tiny radio transceiver in the shape of a wearable pin that had a light-emitting diode on the front. The device could be set to transmit and receive on a variety of wavelengths. The wearer selected personal wavelengths from a range representing a variety of sexual preferences. When two people with corresponding frequencies came within a few feet of each other, the diodes on each device would begin to flash" (142). Le Flashing would produce immediacy through hypermediacy, for the pin is a gimmicky medium that calls attention to itself. (It is appropriate, too, that hypermediacy is associated here with polymorphous sexual practices.) ⊙ **p. 84** Nevertheless, the visions of ubiquitous

The Starfire Desk-Sized Computer

Mail, calendar, family pictures

Information space

Documents

Mouse

Video-conference windows

Still some paper-based work being done ...

Figure 13.3 Julie at her cyberdesk: a scenario in ubiquitous computing for business from *Starfire: A Vision of Future Computing*. Video. © 1997, Sun Microsystems, Inc. Used by permission.

computing remain utopian and futuristic, which is not to say that they are free of capitalist impulses. There have been a number of films (such as Apple's *Knowledge Navigator* and Sun's *Starfire*) that present equally utopian, corporate visions of ubiquitous computing (fig. 13.3).

Ubiquitous computing reverses virtual reality in another important way. In reforming reality, the ubiquitous enthusiasts seem to want to avoid the shifts of perspective that characterize virtual reality. The question of the subject does not need to arise, because with ubiquitous computing, we do not have to occupy different points of view. Instead, we stay put figuratively and even literally, while the computers bustle around—opening files, opening windows, switching cameras and sound systems on and off—to suit our needs. Instead of virtual reality, ubiquitous computing is genealogically related to the television and even the Internet. Like television and the Web, ubiquitous computing would be a network of mediating machines that span the world and enter into our daily lives. Like television and the Web, ubiquitous computing means the constant monitoring of the quotidian. ⊘ **p. 204** Ubiquitous computing is not satisfied with mere monitoring; it wants to affect what it monitors—hence teleoperation. Ubiquitous computing therefore insists even more aggressively on the reality of media in our social and physical world. ⊘ **p. 58**

In March 1997 the editors of *Wired* magazine, Kevin Kelly and Gary Wolf, announced in their typical enthusiastic style the death of the graphical Web browser, which at the date of publication was almost exactly four years old, and the convergence of electronic media to a new paradigm of "push" technology. With the help of the vocabulary that we have developed (*transparency, immediacy, hypermediacy,* and *remediation*), we are now in a position to understand the rhetoric of the manifestos and the critiques that surround new media—the rhetoric, for example, of the opening paragraphs of the *Wired* article:*

> *The Web browser itself is about to croak. And good riddance. In its place . . . broader and deeper new interfaces for electronic media are being born. . . . What they share are ways to move seamlessly between media you steer (interactive) and media that steer you (passive). . . . The new interfaces work with existing media, such as TV, yet they also work on hyperlinked text. But most important, they work on the emerging universe of networked media that are spreading across the telecosm. As everything gets wired, media of all kinds are moving to the decentralized matrix known as the Net. While the traditional forms—broadcast, print—show few signs of vanishing, the Net is being invaded by new media species.*

Wired prefers the logic of hypermediacy to the logic of transparency. We can see hypermediacy in the page layout of the magazine, and

[The excerpts in this chapter are taken from the article "Kill Your Browser" in the March, 1997 number of Wired. The article was written by Kevin Kelly, Gary Wolf, and the other editors. © 1997–1998 Wired Magazine Group, Inc. All rights reserved. Reprinted by permission.]

we can read it in the prose, which is both urgent and self-conscious. To suggest that everything will "get wired" is to suppose that we will take pleasure in becoming a highly mediated world. The *Wired* editors believe in the reality of media, and they imply that media themselves are as natural as the physical universe. They are predicting no mere social revolution. For them, digital technology has the force of nature: cyberspace (or the telecosm) is undergoing a kind of big bang. They will later suggest that, instead of exploding, all the various media of cyberspace are converging, as if they were being pulled together by a force as ineluctable as gravity. The editors evoke digital technology itself as the agent of change and are not concerned with exploring media as social, cultural, technical hybrids. However, they do recognize the heterogeneity of our current moment: traditional media will continue to exist alongside the new networked forms.

> *Networked communications need interfaces that hop across nodes, exploiting the unique character of distributed communications. Technology that, say, follows you into the next taxi you ride, gently prodding you to visit the local aquarium, all the while keeping you up-to-date on your favorite basketball team's game in progress. Another device might chime on your wrist, letting you know that the route home is congested with traffic, and flashing the address of a restaurant where you can eat cut-rate sushi while waiting it out. At home on your computer, the same system will run soothing screensavers underneath regular news flashes, all the while keeping track, in one corner, of press releases from companies whose stocks you own. With frequent commercial messages, of course.*

This technology of "distributed communications" sounds very much like ubiquitous computing. Here is the Internet reaching out into the world to inform and reform taxis and restaurants into sites for new media. The monitoring function that the Internet inherits from television has now become ubiquitous—in the sense that it can both monitor everywhere and deliver its reports anywhere. At the same time, a bourgeois, utopian narrative is beginning to emerge: "you" seem to be a well-to-do urbanite who follows basketball, eats sushi, rides in taxis, and has a stock portfolio. The economic aspect of the media hybrid enters the narrative without fanfare. It is not just that you will need money to enjoy the benefits of ubiquitous networking; the information that the network monitors and delivers on stock reports and sushi bars will be of use only if you can afford to buy stocks and eat in restaurants. And commercial messages are "of course" part of the flow.

[In place of the Web browser] a new medium is arising, surging across the Web in the preferred, many-to-many way: anything flows from any-one to anyone—from anywhere to anywhere—anytime. In other words, a true network like the telephone system, rather than a radiating system like radio or TV. This new medium doesn't wait for clicks. It doesn't need computers. It means personalized experiences not bound by a page— think of a how-to origami video channel or a 3-D furry-muckers VR space. It means information that cascades, not just through a PC, but across all forms of communication devices—headlines sent to a pager or a traffic map popping up on a cellular phone. And it means content that will not hesitate to find you—whether you've clicked on something re-cently or not.

We are still in a hypermediated environment, and yet we seem to be confronted by one all-encompassing medium rather than many— one whose characteristics are openness to and transparency for all the participants. And it is almost as if the medium transcends any particu-lar technology; it needs no computer. Instead, information cascades from device to device, seeking you out. The unimpeded flow is what matters. But flow is a familiar concept applied to television as much as the Internet. Again here an organic metaphor is mixed with references to technology to create an aura of naturalness and inevitability.

It means, in short, a more full-bodied experience that combines many of the traits of networks with those of broadcast.

"Experience" is the measure of this new medium, which we rec-ognize as the claim to immediacy made by every attempt at remedia-tion. In this case, it is the promise of immediacy that combines the characteristics of the Internet with those of television and radio. Televi-sion offers immediacy through its stream of "live" images or sounds. This stream puts the viewer in contact with the world. As it converges with television, the Internet makes much the same offer but with the added value of interactivity. Now the user can choose which portion of the world to monitor by turning on one or more video, audio, or textual streams. Or the reverse: the various streams will monitor her.

The buzz phrase for this convergence is "push media." Content is pushed to you, in contrast to the invitational pull you make when you click on the Web. The push can be gentle, in-your-face, intermittent, in the back-ground, or always on. . . . At first glance all this looks a lot like the revenge of TV. . . . But when the Wall Street Journal *trumpeted the arrival of push media by declaring that the Internet "has been a medium in search of a viable business model. Now it has found one: television," it got the story almost entirely wrong. The new networked media do borrow ideas from television, but the new media landscape will look nothing like TV as we know it. And indeed, it will transform TV in the process.*

In fact, both *Wired* and the *Wall Street Journal* have it partly right. Convergence is remediation under another name, and the remediation is mutual: the Internet refashions television even as television refashions the Internet. The *Wired* editors are right that the business world wants to understand remediation only in one direction, as the reforming of the Internet into television. The reason is that the business world understands television and its mechanisms for the economic control of its audience. The Internet, at least the World Wide Web, is a new and potentially unruly medium that gives its audience more choices over the content presented. For the readers of the *Wall Street Journal,* convergence should restore the previous status quo; it should channel innovation along economically entrenched and socially familiar lines. The claim that push technology is radically new should simply be part of the marketing strategy. The editors of *Wired* must claim to be more savvy than the editors of the *Wall Street Journal,* but their rhetoric of revolution exaggerates the differences between the World Wide Web, television, and the new, converged form and therefore causes them to underestimate the power of television to remediate the Web. Not only will the new media landscape look like television as we know it, but television will come to look more and more like new media.

Convergence is the mutual remediation of at least three important technologies—telephone, television, and computer—each of which is a hybrid of technical, social, and economic practice and each of which offers its own path to immediacy. The telephone offers the immediacy of the voice or the interchange of voices in real time. Television is a point-of-view technology that promises immediacy through its insistent real-time monitoring of the world. The computer's promise of immediacy comes through the combination of three-dimensional graphics, automatic (programmed) action, and an interactivity that television cannot match. As they come together, each of these technologies is trying to absorb the others and promote its own version of immediacy. In our visual culture, promoters of the telephone have perhaps the least convincing case, but they will argue that convergence is about authenticity of communication, about "people talking to people." Supporters of the computer rely on its traditional role as an information processor and suggest that the new, converged technology should focus on providing more verbal and visual information at the user's request. For the television supporters, probably the most numerous, the principal use of the new technology should be to push entertainment, information, and commercials to the willing user.

Yet the double logic of remediation suggests that in our heterogeneous culture, no one technology is likely to eliminate the others. In addition to enhanced televisions, we will (and already do) have multimedia computers that can present and manipulate video images. We will have inexpensive computers designed to get most of their information and applications from a network. Convergence is often misunderstood to mean a single solution, but in fact, as these technologies appear, they remediate each other in various ways and in various ratios to produce different devices and practices. Convergence means greater diversity for digital technologies in our culture. It may always be true that, by bringing two or more technologies together, remediation multiplies the possibilities. For the remediation at least spawns one new technique while leaving the two others available for cultural use. Sometimes the editors of *Wired* appear to understand the heterogeneity of new media, but sometimes they can hardly resist the attraction of the unified and homogeneous.

> *The Web is a wonderful library, but a library nonetheless. On the other hand the new networked media—part instructional and part entertainment—are not archival, but immersive. The image to hold in mind is an amusement park, full of experiences and information coming at you in many forms, some scripted, some serendipitous. It may be intense, it may be ambient, but it always assumes you are available.*

The Web is rejected here because it remediates the culture of the printed book. Despite their support for the heterogeneity of the Web, the editors cannot be enthusiastic about a technology that is not primarily perceptual. The book (and the World Wide Web as book) cannot compete in immediacy with the experiences offered by visual media. In the claim that new media should not be merely archival but immersive, the rhetoric of virtual reality finally enters in, with its promise of the immediacy of experience through transparency. But the editors' vision here is mixed, and the immersion that they seem to have had in mind is rather like the immersion experienced by the hackers in William Gibson's *Neuromancer.* They perceive data in cyberspace synaesthetically as lights, shapes, and colors. An amusement park like Disney World is hypermediated; it offers sensory overload and places side by side a series of visible remediations of film and television. Like television and the World Wide Web, the amusement park insists on the reality of media: at Disney World the cartoon characters are larger than life-size and walk around the park hugging children.

> *Push media arrive automatically—on your desktop, in your email, via your pager. You won't choose whether to turn them on, only whether to turn them off. And there will be many incentives not to. . . . Push media are "always on." And there are human agents behind the scenes, working overtime to keep the content always on target, always on top of things, always seeking you out.*

We recognize here the traditional appeal to the automatic, a tradition that extends back to photography. Push media function without immediate human intervention, and yet in this vision, at least there are human agents behind the curtain, manipulating the images to give them the appearance of spontaneity and freshness. These human agents seem to perform a role similar to that of the traditional photographer, who composes the scene and then hands control over to the mechanism.

> *The promise of push-pull media is to marry the programming experience of television with two key yearnings: navigating information and experience, and connecting to other people.*

The programming experience of television is the experience of an endless stream of images (refreshed thirty times per second) monitoring the world for the viewer. Navigating information and experience is the hypermediacy of the World Wide Web, in which the user is constantly reminded of the interface as she selects and follows the links. Finally, the promise of "connecting to other people" suggests transparency—breaking through the medium to achieve human contact. In the double logic of remediation, the desire for transparent immediacy is seldom abandoned, even by those most committed to and fascinated with hypermediacy.

We have now looked at the process of remediation in a variety of contemporary media. In each case we have seen the user or the viewer enter into a twofold relationship with the medium. On the one hand, she seeks immediacy of the real in the denial of mediation. On the other, she seeks that immediacy through the acknowledgment and multiplication of media. In this concluding part, we pursue the reflexive relationship between user and medium by examining some consequences of the remediating power of digital media for our culture's definitions of the self.

The Remediated Self

15

As so many media critics have recognized, we see ourselves today in and through our available media. When we look at a traditional photograph or a perspective painting, we understand ourselves as the reconstituted station point of the artist or the photographer. When we watch a film or a television broadcast, we become the changing point of view of the camera. When we put on the virtual reality helmet, we are the focus of an elaborate technology for real-time, three-dimensional graphics and motion tracking. This is not to say that our identity is fully determined by media, but rather that we employ media as vehicles for defining both personal and cultural identity. As these media become simultaneously technical analogs and social expressions of our identity, we become simultaneously both the subject and object of contemporary media. We are that which the film or television camera is trained on, and at the same time we are the camera itself. This is not an entirely new phenomenon. Older, verbal media continue to serve this function of identification as well. We continue to define ourselves through characterizations in popular written fiction and in news, fashion, and leisure magazines—to identify with the voices in which those written narratives are told. New media offer new opportunities for self-definition, for now we can identify with the vivid graphics and digitized videos of computer games as well as the swooping perspective of virtual reality systems and digitally generated film and television logos. We can define ourselves through the converging communication technologies of the telephone and the Internet.

Whenever our identity is mediated in this way, it is also remediated, because we always understand a particular medium in relation to other past and present media. When we watch the filmed adaptation of a novel, we bring to the film a notion of self appropriate to voiced prose. When we participate in virtual reality, our digital point of view is understood as a remediation of the point of view that we have occupied for decades in film and television and for centuries in photographs and paintings. When we run a multimedia program on our desktop computer, each windowed space (containing prose, static graphics, audio, or video) offers a different mediation of the subject, and our experience is the remediation of these differences. Because we understand media through the ways in which they challenge and reform other media, we understand our mediated selves as reformed versions of earlier mediated selves.

Accordingly, there are two versions of the contemporary mediated self that correspond to the two logics of remediation. When we are faced with media that operate primarily under the logic of transparent immediacy (virtual reality and three-dimensional computer graphics), we see ourselves as a point of view immersed in an apparently seamless visual environment. In a virtual environment, we have the freedom to alter our selves by altering our point of view and to empathize with others by occupying their point of view—techniques pioneered in film and now extended and intensified in digital media. At the same time, the logic of hypermediacy, expressed in digital multimedia and networked environments, suggests a definition of self whose key quality is not so much "being immersed" as "being interrelated or connected." The hypermediated self is a network of affiliations, which are constantly shifting. It is the self of newsgroups and email, which may sometimes threaten to overwhelm the user by their sheer numbers but do not exactly immerse her.

This networked self is constantly making and breaking connections, declaring allegiances and interests and then renouncing them—participating in a video conference while sorting through email or word processing at the same time. Unlike the user of virtual reality, who shuts herself off from physical space by putting on a head-mounted display, the networked self may lead simultaneous lives in cyberspace and in her physical office. The remediated self is also evident in "virtual communities" on the Internet, in which individuals stake out and occupy verbal and visual points of view through textual and graphic manifestations, but at the same time constitute their collective identities as a network of affiliations among these mediated selves. The virtual community is the community as both subject and object of the process of remediation; it remediates the notion of community as defined in and through such earlier media as telegraph, telephone, radio, and television.

But just as the two logics are alternate strategies for achieving the same goal of the real or authentic experience, so these two definitions of the self are complementary rather than contradictory.[1] Both definitions assume that the authentic self can be achieved through the appropriate digital media, which are themselves both transparent and hypermediated. Just as hypermediacy encompasses and complicates transparent immediacy, the hypermediated or networked self encompasses and multiplies the self of virtual reality. The networked self is made up both of that self that is doing the networking and the various selves that are presented on the network.

This remediated self reminds us of the analysis of the "empirical self" by the American pragmatist William James, whose monumental *Psychology* (1890) was written at a moment when the emergence and expansion of telegraph networks were producing a reconfiguration of notions of self not unlike that which has accompanied the growth of the Internet.[2] For James, this empirical self is *"the sum total of all that {a man} CAN call his"* (291), and that sum has material, social, and spiritual constituents. The material self includes (from innermost to outermost) the body, clothes, family, and home (292–293). The social self is described as "the recognition which [a man] gets from his mates," so that "properly speaking, *a man has as many social selves as there are individuals who recognize him* and carry an image of him in their mind" (293–294). The spiritual self is more elusive, but James variously identifies it as "the most enduring and intimate part of the self, that which we most verily seem to be" (296); as "a sort of innermost centre within the circle, of sanctuary within the citadel, constituted by the subjective life as a whole" (297); as "the *active* element in all consciousness" (297); and as the "part of the Self [that] is *felt*," that "which is as fully present at any moment of consciousness in which it *is* present, as in a whole lifetime of such moments" (298–299).

James's account of the various aspects of the self is in some ways remarkably contemporary and has a curious resonance with the networked self of digital technology. James's spiritual self is like the part of the networked self that does the networking; it actively makes affiliations and associations. This active self works through various media. As James's self is manifested through clothes, home, and familial and social relations, the networked self is manifested through the affiliations it makes among digital media. The form these affiliations take,

1. Sherry Turkle has explored how computers in general and the Internet in particular affect contemporary notions of identity in *The Second Self* and, more recently, *Life on the Screen*.

2. This period of "electric communication" is described by Carolyn Marvin in *When Old Technologies Were New*.

and thus the form our networked selves take, is constrained by the formal qualities of the particular media through which they are expressed. To say, for example, that the self is expressed in its email affiliations is not to say that the self is disembodied but that it is embodied in a particular mediated form (as electronic text, with a return address, a user ID, a signature, and so forth). The same is true of all the mediated expressions of the networked self: the self that participates in a video conference is embodied as a video and audio image within the available digital video technologies; the self that surfs the Web is embodied in its IP address, its web browser, and its plug-ins; and so on. James's account of the self illuminates to a different degree the self that does the networking or the self of virtual reality as well. Both of these remediated selves are felt as the more active elements of consciousness. And even the self of virtual reality has its material and social aspects as well, most obviously in the VR rig that figures even in the futuristic wire of *Strange Days* or in the network of social relations through which one has access to the VR experience and by means of which one navigates within a virtual reality application.

MEDIATION AND THE PRESENCE OF THE SELF

The desire to express one's self through (artistic) media is a hallmark of romanticism and long predates the development of digital media. The philosopher Stanley Cavell (1979) has noted how the desire for self-expression came out of the desire for the real: "What [traditional] painting wanted, in wanting a connection with reality, was a sense of *presentness*—not exactly a conviction of the world's presence to us, but of our presence to it. At some point the unhinging of our consciousness from the world interposed our subjectivity between us and our presentness to the world. Then our subjectivity became what is present to us, individuality became isolation. The route to conviction in reality was through the acknowledgement of the endless presense of self" (22). As Cavell goes on to point out, the strategy for achieving this unmediated relationship shifted with romanticism from an emphasis on the world as object (mimesis) to the viewer as subject (expression): "To speak of our subjectivity as the route back to our conviction in reality is to speak of romanticism" (22). If the Enlightenment subject was content to stand and gaze through the window frame, the romantic subject wanted to get closer. And if in turn the romantic was convinced that it was the self's responsibility and was within the self's power to undertake an active search for reality, modernism went further in espousing the "end-less presence of the self" to itself.

In their current efforts to achieve self-presence, creators of digital media have adopted both romantic and modernist strategies. When a viewer examines a linear-perspective painting, there remains a critical visual distance; the window frame separates the subject from the objects of representation. There are two ways to reduce this distance and so to heighten the sense of immediacy: either the viewer can pass through the window into the represented world, or the objects of representation can come up to or even through the window and surround the viewer. Digital media have experimented with both of these strategies. Virtual reality adopts the romanticism of the first. It allows the viewer to pass through Alberti's window in an active search for reality to examine and in some cases even to manipulate the objects of representation. ▷ **p. 21** Although this move may have been implicit in illusionistic painting, realistic photography, film, and television, virtual reality enthusiasts insist that something new has happened, when the move through Alberti's window becomes explicit and operational.

The second, more modernist strategy has been adopted by ubiquitous computing and by hypermedia in general: the subject stays where she is, and instead the objects of representation come to her to be appreciated individually. ▷ **p. 212** In hypermedia applications, the objects press themselves against Alberti's window and divide it into numerous panes or frames that compete for the subject's attention; in ubiquitous computing, the applications embody themselves as separate machines and appliances and are distributed throughout the environment. The goal is still immediacy through contact, but now the immediacy is achieved when the user recognizes the multiple and mediated character of the objects before her.

The definition of the subject is similar in either case. In three-dimensional computer graphics, the subject is defined by the perspectives that she occupies in the virtual space. In this respect, she is like the Enlightenment subject who was also defined by the station point that he took up in front of the canvas or more generally by the verbal and visual points of view that he held in his relations with the world. But in her quest for immediacy, the subject in virtual space is not satisfied with a single point of view; instead, she seeks out the positions of other participants and objects in that space. She understands herself as a potentially rapid succession of points of view, as a series of immediate experiences derived from those points of view. In the same way in hypermedia, she is defined as a succession of relationships with various applications or media. She oscillates between media—moves from window to window, from application to application—and her identity is constituted by those oscillations. In the first case, the subject is assured of her existence by the ability to occupy points of view, while in the second she is assured by her multiplication and remediation in the various media or media forms that surround her.

But why is this second, hypermediated self necessary at all? The desire for immediacy would appear to be fulfilled by the transparent technologies of straight photography, live television, and three-dimensional, immersive computer graphics. Such transparent technologies, however, cannot satisfy that desire because they do not succeed in fully denying mediation. Each of them ends up defining itself with reference to other technologies, so that the viewer never sustains that elusive state in which the objects of representation are felt to be fully present. Our culture tries this frontal assault on the problem of representation with almost every new technology and repeatedly with the familiar technologies. When that strategy fails, a contrary strategy emerges, in which we become fascinated with the act of mediation itself.[3]

3. This psychological economy of remediation, in which the desire for immediacy cannot be fulfilled by transparent media and must therefore be supplemented by technologies of hypermediacy, is analogous to the Lacanian critique of desire as summarized by Slavoj Žižek (1993): "Desire is constituted by 'symbolic castration,' the original loss of the *thing;* the void of this loss is filled out by *objet petit a,* the fantasy object; this loss occurs on account of our being 'embedded' in the symbolic universe which derails the 'natural' circuit of our needs" (3). The double logic of remediation recapitulates this Lacanian psychic economy.

When transparent media fail to satisfy us, opaque (hypermediated) media become necessary to our experience of ourselves. If immediacy were possible, if the self could become one with the objects of mediation, then media would not need to enter into the definition of self at all. We could then be just subjects in the world. But that utopian state is certainly not available to us today, when media are as much a part of our world as any other natural and technical objects. Whenever we engage ourselves with visual or verbal media, we become aware not only of the objects of representation but also of the media themselves. Instead of trying to be in the presence of the objects of representation, we then define immediacy as being in the presence of media. This fascination with media works as the sublimation of the initial desire for immediacy that Cavell identified as central to the Western tradition: the desire to be immediately present to oneself.

THE REMEDIATION OF THE BODY

We have already considered the possibility that the desire for immediacy, at least as expressed in the visual technologies of transparency, might itself be an exclusively male desire. ◑ **p. 78** We now need to consider whether the self defined by that desire is also gendered. Feminist theorist Evelyn Fox Keller and others have argued that the Western, male gaze is abstracted and disembodied; furthermore, many theorists reject Cartesian dualism with its notion that the self can be defined in the absence of the body (Keller and Grontkowski 1996; Stone 1991; Hayles 1993, 1995; Balsamo 1996; Haraway 1991). For our purposes here, the denial of mediation in transparent technologies—the attempt to get past the medium to the unmediated real—may also reflect the denial or subordination of the body in Western definitions of the self.

Recent feminist theory has insisted not only on the embodiment or materiality of the self but also on the increasingly complicated relationship between the body and technology in contemporary culture. Donna Haraway's influential cyborg is the body as remediated by various contemporary technologies of representation. Following Haraway, many others have shown how the body itself functions as a medium: through traditional means such as choice of clothing and jewelry, as well as more radical ones such as cosmetic surgery, bodybuilding, and body piercing. Clothing and jewelry treat the body as a medium in the sense that the body becomes the material ground that carries or bears expressive decoration; such decoration appears to respect the boundary between the body and the world. However, as Haraway and others remind us, our contemporary culture delights in confusing or breaking down the boundaries between the body and the world and the body and technology. In bodybuilding, for example, the body itself is reconstructed to take on a new shape and identity, and this reconstruction entails high technology, employing elaborate machines and regimens of exercise and diet. The reconstructed body may then become the subject of presentations in popular media, such as film, television, and print advertising. As Anne Balsamo has argued, bodybuilding and its popular media representations acquire a special cultural charge when the bodybuilders are women and thus transgress the expectations about what women's bodies should look like (41–55). In cosmetic surgery too, the body, often a woman's body, is technologically reconstructed, although not in this case by the woman herself but often by a male surgeon (56–79). Balsamo shows how surgeons visualize the female body as an object for cosmetic reconstruction. Traditionally they used sketches to show the patient how treatment would improve her appearance; now they are relying on video and even computer graphics. Balsamo contends that "new visualization technologies transform the material body into a visual medium. In the process the body is fractured and fragmented so that isolated parts can be examined visually. . . . At the same time, the material body comes to embody the characteristics of technological images" (56).

In its character as a medium, the body both remediates and is remediated. The contemporary, technologically constructed body recalls and rivals earlier cultural versions of the body as a medium. The body as enhanced or distorted by medical and cosmetic technologies remediates the ostensibly less mediated bodies of earlier periods in Western culture. At the same time, the depiction of female bodybuilders on television and film, as well as the cosmetic surgeon's use of sketches, video, and computer graphics to refashion the body, are examples of the way in which one medium can be taken into another. The strategies of both transparent immediacy and hypermediacy are at work. As Balsamo points out, the remediations of the cosmetic surgeon often serve to reproduce signs of the cultural ideal of "natural beauty" (57ff.). Because prospective patients do not measure up to this ideal, the surgeon first uses graphics to remediate the patient's body visually and then employs the scalpel to bring this body into agreement with the visual remediation. It is a short step from the rhetoric of natural beauty to the rhetoric of the real and the immediate. The graphics and knife allow the surgeon to see and to cut through the patient's apparent deformities to a new visual reality that is supposed to be both ideal and natural. In doing so, the surgeon therefore realizes the ultimate male gaze, one that not only appropriates but also reconstructs. The desire for sexual as well as visual immediacy has led more than one cosmetic surgeon to marry a woman he has reconstructed or to reconstruct the woman he marries. (In Hitchcock's *Vertigo,* the paradigmatic Hollywood film about the desire for immediacy, Judy's body is remediated by Scottie as he dictates her clothes and even hair style and color in order to make her over into Madeleine. Cf. de Lauretis 1984, 153–155.)
▷ **p. 150**

Like the remediations of other medical specialties, the remediations of cosmetic surgery remain problematic. In pursuing the ideal of natural beauty, surgeons must fragment and isolate parts of the patient's body (Balsamo 1996, 56). Although cosmetic surgeons appeal to transparent immediacy, they end up pursuing a strategy of hypermediacy, which calls attention to the process of mediation. What better example could we find of the way in which the desire for immediacy passes into a fascination with the medium? The surgeon is compelled to examine with a clinical eye the video monitor or ultimately the patient's body as a medium for the least sign of the "unnatural," and in the course of this examination the patient is invited to become complicit in the male gaze. (Again in *Vertigo,* Judy also agrees to become complicit in Scottie's gaze, as he searches her appearance for flaws—ways in which she does not transparently reproduce Madeleine.)

The situation is rather different for female bodybuilders, who are in control of their own remediations and from the outset adopt a strategy of hypermediacy. In making their bodies hypermuscular, they transgress two traditional boundaries: they defy the cultural ideal of female beauty that women's bodies should be soft and feminine and defy the tacit cultural conviction that women's bodies are weak and frail in comparison with men's bodies. In challenging both conventions, they call attention to their bodies as media, as carriers of special cultural messages. At the same time, the popular magazines and films work their own remediation on these bodybuilders, often tacitly or explicitly criticizing them for their double "transgression."

Some performance artists, such as Orlan, Stelarc, and the transsexual Kate Bornstein, combine the cultural rhetorics of cosmetic surgery and bodybuilding in an astonishing determination to remediate their bodies. Orlan turns her cosmetic surgeries into performances, which she directs under local anesthetic (Dery 1996, 239–241; cf. Auslander 1997b, 126–140). Her surgeons are guided by digital composites made from faces of famous paintings. This procedure may or may not constitute a critique of Western notions of beauty, as Orlan claims, but it is certainly an act of double remediation, as she seeks to assimilate her body to the digital image, which is derived from classic paintings. She is reported to have said that she will stop her work only "when it is as close as possible to the computer composite" (Dery 1996, 240). In other words she is measuring her refashioning not against some "natural" ideal of beauty, but against a highly and overtly mediated representation.

Stelarc's challenge is similar, as he refashions himself into Haraway's cyborg. As Dery (1996) describes it, "His nearly naked body plastered with electrodes and trailing wires, the artist in performance bears a striking resemblance to a Borg, one of the implacable cyborg villains in *Star Trek: The Next Generation.* With his Amplified Body, Laser Eyes, Third Hand, Automatic Arm, and Video Shadow, he bodies forth the human-machine hybrid all of us are metaphorically becoming" (154). Stelarc explicitly sets out to embody McLuhan's noted assertion that media are extensions of the human senses (153–157). As Stelarc himself puts it, "It is no longer meaningful to see the body as a *site* for the psyche or the social but rather as a *structure* to be monitored and modified. The body not as a subject but as an object—NOT AS AN OBJECT OF DESIRE BUT AS AN OBJECT FOR DESIGNING" (cited by Dery 1996, 161). Finally, like Orlan and many other performance artists, Stelarc initiates or fosters elaborate media coverage of his acts of corporeal remediation.

New media are thus fully involved in the contemporary struggle to define the self as both embodied and mediated by the body. On the one hand, they contribute new strategies of transparency that would seem to reinforce the dissecting male gaze. In the case of cosmetic surgery, Balsamo (1996) describes the "process by which new imaging technologies [used by the surgeon] are articulated with traditional and ideological beliefs about gender—an articulation that keeps the female body positioned as a privileged object of a normative gaze" (57). On the other hand, through strategies of hypermediacy, new media refashion the normative gaze and its implied views of male and female identity, which is exactly what Orlan does by remediating her body as a new media display. Because transparency always passes into hypermediacy, these same new media can both enact and critique traditional beliefs about gender and self. Even virtual reality, which would seem to be the ultimate technology of the male gaze, can also undermine that gaze.

The Virtual Self

16

Cavell (1979) has argued that for the last two hundred years, we have been pursuing not only the presence of the world to the self, but also the presence the self to itself (22). Taking up this tradition, virtual reality and three-dimensional graphics in general are technologies for achieving self-presence through a newly mobilized point of view. ⊚ **p. 21** This freedom of movement becomes the defining quality of the virtual self.

THE FREEDOM OF THE VIRTUAL SELF

A principal cultural attraction of digital visual media is that they place point of view under the user's control, and this control can be understood in an operational sense. In a fully interactive graphic application, the viewer has what mathematicians characterize as six degrees of freedom, for there are six different ways in which she can alter her relationship to her visual surroundings: she can remain in one place and move her viewing angle up or down, left or right, or side to side, in each case changing her perspective without changing her location relative to the objects that she sees (fig. 16.1). She can also keep her viewing angle fixed and move her point of view in the three spatial dimensions: up or down, left or right, forward or back. Film possesses these same degrees of freedom, although in the Hollywood style, some shifts are less common than others. What makes interactive computer graphics unique is that the shifts can now take place at the viewer's will. Seated at a computer terminal, the viewer can work a mouse, keyboard, or joystick to roll, turn, and travel through graphic space. The whole genre of action computer games depends on this kind of navigation, through which the user occupies, explores, and traverses virtual space. In fully immersive

Figure 16.1 The three orientational degrees of freedom. Created by Sherry G. Strickland.

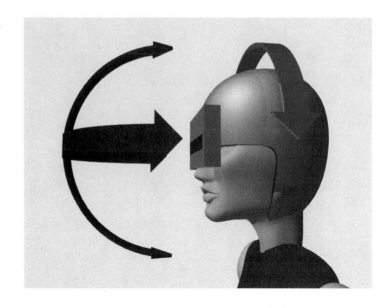

virtual reality, the whole interface is an expression of this freedom to move. (On mobility in virtual environments, see Manovich 1995–1996, 129–134.)

These operational degrees of freedom have metaphorical significance for our culture: they correspond to various attitudes about the role and value of the individual. By remaining in one place and pivoting in any of three dimensions, the viewer is changing her field of view without changing her own situation. When a digital medium offers us such changes in orientation, it is representing for us a kind of situated viewing, comparing our place to other places that we might possibly occupy. Situated viewing can be seen as corresponding to cultural relativism, an epistemological position that informs much contemporary multiculturalism. Meanwhile, the other three, translational degrees of freedom allow the viewer to occupy different station points. Translating one's position in space is a method of viewing that also has cultural significance. For example, since the Renaissance until perhaps the past few decades, Western culture has seen exploration as an unambiguously positive good: the traveler explores distant lands, the scientist explores and reveals the secrets of nature, and so on. Only recently have some theorists come to recognize that without situated viewing, such exploration easily becomes a vehicle for exploitation and domination of both nature and indigenous cultures. Nevertheless, the freedom to move through space has been and is still prized in an era of digital media. It is no mere coincidence that many of the enthusiasts for digital media are also enthusiastic about space exploration, which they often associate with a conservative and highly individualistic politics. They speak as if homesteading the asteroids were a possible or even likely scenario. Outer space becomes for these enthusiasts (many of them *Star Trek* fans) the "final frontier," just as the New World was a frontier for the European explorers and just as Western science has regarded nature itself as a frontier. On the other hand, because the freedom to move through embodied space or cyberspace can be the freedom to lay claim to physical and intellectual territory, postmodern and postcolonial writers often express justifiable suspicion about it.

Nonetheless, this same freedom can serve a more radical cultural purpose: to enable us to occupy the position, and therefore the point of view, of people or creatures different from ourselves. To occupy multiple points of view (serially if not simultaneously) becomes a new positive good and perhaps the major freedom that our culture can now offer. In part I, we quoted the interface designer and cyberspace enthusiast Meredith Bricken on virtual reality as a medium that can offer unmediated experience. ◨ **p. 22** We can now cite the whole quotation to see how point-of-view identification defines the self and gives the self its contemporary moral imperative:

You can be the mad hatter or you can be the teapot; you can move back and forth to the rhythm of a song. You can be a tiny droplet in the rain or in the river; you can be what you thought you ought to be all along. You can switch your point of view to an object or a process or another person's point of view in the other person's world.

Assuming multiple perspectives is a powerful capacity; only after young children are developmentally ready to understand that each person sees from a different perspective can they learn to relate to others in an empathetic way. (Benedikt 1991, 372)

Bricken is not alone in assuming that the path to empathy is the occupation of another's point of view. There is nothing new in praising the value of empathy and a shared point of view. We could trace this attitude back at least to the popularization of romanticism in the nineteenth century. But if in the nineteenth century the verbal or literary expression of point of view was as important as the visual, today virtual reality and computer graphics join with film and television to provide an insistently visual construction of point of view, and therefore a visual construction of empathy. And virtual reality surpasses film and television in convincing the user of the flexibility and the contingency of point of view.

In a virtual environment, the user learns by moving through a scene and sampling the available viewpoints. When the environment contains only buildings, rooms, and objects, the viewpoints are simply coordinates in space, but advocates of virtual reality imagine more elaborate scenarios in which several people or virtual animals may share the space. Examples of learning by occupying an empathetic point of view may be as predictable as the virtual day care center created by the programmers at Jaron Lanier's virtual reality company in the 1980s, in which the viewer can walk through the design for the proposed building at the eye level of an adult caregiver or can shrink herself to see everything from the perspective of one of the children. These alternatives are meant to ensure that the design will be suitable for both communities of users (Rheingold 1991, 166–168).

Virtual empathy can also be as radical as Lanier's suggestion that the user should learn about dinosaurs or even molecules by occupying their perspectives. Wearing a VR helmet, "You can visit the world of the dinosaur, then become a Tyrannosaurus. Not only can you see DNA, you can experience what it's like to be a molecule" (Ditlea 1989, 92). For Lanier, the immediacy of virtual reality makes possible a new kind of empathy. In the Virtual Gorilla environment developed by the Georgia Institute of Technology, the user assumes the point of view of an adolescent gorilla at the Atlanta Zoo and mimics the behavior of that animal in order to negotiate the territory with an adult male (fig. 16.2). Through empathy, the user is supposed to be able to learn "what it is like to be" a gorilla, a dinosaur, or a molecule. Furthermore, animals and even objects in virtual environments can be programmed to possess the same six degrees of freedom as the user. Indeed, in virtual environments that allow for multiple users, any other figure, animal or object, may also be the avatar of another user.

Empathy is so highly regarded today as a means of knowing presumably because empathy is everything that traditional, Enlightenment reason was not: immediate, embodied, emotional, and culturally determined. It is also a common narrative strategy, almost the *only* strategy, in the "dramas" on American television and in whole genres of popular film. In recent years there have been a number of films, such as *Back to the Future* (1985), *Big* (1988), and *Prelude to a Kiss* (1992), in

Figure 16.2 A virtual gorilla. Courtesy of Professor Larry Hodges, GVU Center, Georgia Institute of Technology.

which one character's ego occupies another body, in which two characters exchange bodies, or in which characters move ahead or back in time and so occupy their own bodies at a different stage of life. These plots all turn on the notion of empathetic occupation of another point of view. Virtual reality itself has been the subject of several recent films, and invariably in these films, a character casts his or her mind into the computer, usually to have it trapped there or to exchange or merge it with other minds. ▷ **p. 163** These virtual reality films take the process of empathetic learning dangerously far—dangerous, that is, for the characters, who may find it difficult to get their minds back into their original bodies. Ultimately, however, these films reaffirm the cultural importance of empathy. Furthermore, in both the dangerous and the apparently benign versions of empathetic learning, the integrity of the self is always compromised. The borders of the self dissolve, as it occupies the position and experiences the problems faced by other creatures.

In general, then, the freedom to be oneself is the freedom to become someone (or something) else. Because there is no single, privileged point of view, the self becomes a series of "other" points of view—the intersection of all the possible points of view that can be taken in a given space. The space of virtual reality—and insofar as virtual reality is a paradigm, the space of contemporary culture—redefines the ego in its traditional sense. On the one hand, there is nothing that drives character or self-definition: no romantic and no Freudian necessity. (There is, instead, a self akin to William James's "pure ego" that serves as the "brand" or "medium" that marks or holds together the various mediated empirical selves that make up the virtual self.) On the other hand, the virtual self seems to be defined precisely as a series of such empirical accessories that the individual puts on, just as she takes on characteristics in the game of Dungeons and Dragons, where a wizard may have sixteen charm points and only five strength points. Character is similarly parameterized in virtual reality and in many kinds of computer games, as well as in textual and visual MUDs and MOOs. Even "serious" computer interfaces, such as desktops and web browsers, treat identity as a matter of adjusting parameters. When computer interface designers talk about personalizing the interface, they mean adjusting the parameters in order to assimilate the interface to the person who uses it. The "adaptive interface" attempts to refashion itself automatically over a period of time to suit its user's tastes and habits. This characterization "by the numbers" would have made little cultural sense a hundred or perhaps even fifty years ago, yet it is how the self is defined today in digital space, with its six parameterized degrees of freedom.

THE DISSOLUTION OF THE CARTESIAN EGO

Virtual reality is a powerful expression of the desire for transparent immediacy and an enactment of the traditional male gaze that has been associated by Mulvey and others with the apparatus of the cinema.
◐ p. 79 Anne Balsamo (1996) has described virtual reality as a new staging of the filmic eye:

In most VR programs, a user experiences VR through a disembodied gaze—a floating moving "perspective"—that mimes the movement of a disembodied camera "eye." This is a familiar aspect of what may be called a filmic phenomenology where the camera simulates the movement of a perspective that rarely includes a self-referential visual inspection of the body as the vehicle of that perspective. (124–125)

Virtual reality offers a remediated definition of the self as a new kind of camera, for unlike traditional cinema, virtual reality enables the viewer to control the placement and duration of each "shot" and thus to manipulate her own perspective. If in hypertext the reader takes on some of the characteristics traditionally assigned to the author, in virtual reality the viewer becomes something like a film director, and this shift of control enables the viewer to explore the virtual space as she will. The ability to change perspective becomes the way to learn about the space, or, as Balsamo puts it, in virtual reality the filmic "perspective" becomes the locus of sense knowledge (125). In fact, perspective becomes the locus of *all* knowledge, because a virtual world is a simulacrum in which there is nothing to be known apart from the senses: there is nothing "behind" the images. Because the virtual traveler defines what she knows as what she can see and therefore "interact" with, knowledge *is* sense perception.

Martin Jay (1988) has pointed out that many postmodern theorists have come to regard the eye as the most abstract and abstracting of the senses. ◑ **p. 24** They associate Cartesian rationality with the Renaissance theory of linear perspective: Jay refers to "Cartesian perspectivalism" in which an "ahistorical, disinterested, disembodied subject" claims to know the world by gazing at it from afar (10). But this construction can be turned around. Vision can also be construed as involving the viewer in the world by reducing the abstract to the visible. For Descartes (as for Plato long before him), sight was ultimately tied to the body. In his *Meditations* Descartes considered the possibility that everything he saw (as well as heard or felt) was the product of an evil deceiver. To achieve real knowledge, he proposed to withdraw entirely from the realm of perception and concluded that sense perception itself was derivative from reason rather than the reverse. "I now know that even bodies are not strictly perceived by the sense or the faculty of imagination but by the intellect alone, and that this perception derives not from their being touched or seen but from their being understood; and in view of this I know plainly that I can achieve an easier and more evident perception of my own mind than of anything else" ("Second Meditation," 22). This and other passages indicate Descartes's profound ambivalence toward literal and metaphorical vision, as Dalia Judovitz (1988) has noted (72). After Kant's work, Descartes's attempt to disembody perception had few followers. And in the nineteenth century, as Jonathan Crary (1990) has pointed out, the investigation of afterimages and other optical illusions led to an increasing recognition of the role of the body in the production of visual experience (97–102).

Now, in the late twentieth century, no one in the virtual reality community can share Descartes's distrust of the senses. The virtual traveler sees and interacts with bodies, not minds, and she must be inclined to deny the traditional hierarchy in which we *are* minds and merely *have* bodies. Marcos Novak (1991), an architect and virtual reality enthusiast, writes:

The trajectory of Western thought has been one moving from the concrete to the abstract, from the body to the mind; recent thought, however, has been pressing upon us the frailty of that Cartesian distinction. The mind is the property of the body, and lives and dies with it. Everywhere we turn we see signs of this recognition, and cyberspace, in its literal placement of the body in spaces invented by the mind, is located directly upon this blurring boundary, this fault. (227)

Novak's rhetoric would seem to place virtual reality in the twentieth-century tradition of anti-Cartesianism that reaches from James to Wittgenstein, through Ryle and Rorty, to the poststructuralists and various postmodernists, all of whom have attacked the dichotomy of mind and body, as well as the rigid division of subject and object. It is hard to find a trend of twentieth-century thought that does not begin from a tacit or explicit denial of Cartesianism. N. Katherine Hayles (1993) has explained one important strategy for denial, when she describes what Bourdieu and many others advocate as "embodied knowledge":

To look at thought in this way [as Bourdieu does] is to turn Descartes upside down. The central premise is not that the cogitating mind can be certain only of its ability to be present to itself, but rather that the body exists in space and time and through its interaction with the environment defines the parameters within which the cogitating mind can arrive at its "certainties." . . . What counts as knowledge is also radically revised, for conscious thought becomes as it were the epiphenomenon corresponding to the phenomenal body the body provides. (160–161)

As Hayles points out, this strategy certainly does turn Descartes upside down. We have only to recall Descartes's famous rejection of the body to realize the gulf that separates him from his postmodern critics, who insist on the importance of the body for self-knowledge:

I will now shut my eyes, stop my ears, and withdraw all my senses. I will eliminate from my thoughts all images of bodily things, or rather, since this is hardly possible, I will regard all such images as vacuous, false and worthless. I will converse with myself and scrutinize myself more deeply; and in this way I will attempt to achieve, little by little, a more intimate knowledge of myself. ("Third Meditation," 24)

If the Cartesian rejection of images were the path to true knowledge, then true knowledge could certainly not be found in the lenses of a head-mounted display. As a technology for turning Descartes upside down, virtual reality's wandering filmic eye reduces all abstraction to a series of visual perspectives. What it offers in place of causal thinking is precisely that faculty of imagination (making images) that Descartes disparages. It is true that virtual reality depends on a mathematization of space that derives from Descartes and from technologies of representation like linear perspective. Virtual reality does in fact begin with the assumption that vision, like the self, is disembodied. Nonetheless, the goal of virtual reality is not rational certainty, but instead the ability of the individual to empathize through imagining. We already noted that when Jaron Lanier was asked to characterize this new technology, he pointed to new possibilities for emotional involvement: experiencing "what it's like" to be a dinosaur or even a DNA molecule. For Lanier, empathetic learning extends not only to other people, but also to objects or phenomena, so that even a molecule can be known through empathy rather than through the symbol systems of mathematics and physics.

Putting Novak, Lanier, and Bricken together, we can appreciate the notion of self that virtual reality and cyberspace promote. The key is to experience the world as others do, not to retire from the distractions of the world to discover oneself as a thinking agent. Instead of asserting its identity over against the world, the virtual self repeatedly denies its own identity, its separateness from others and from the world. It does not learn by scientific study in a subject-object relationship, but by "immersion," which produces empathy and identification. The technique of visual immersion distinguishes virtual reality from the classic transparent medium, linear-perspective painting. For Alberti, a painting in linear perspective is a window on to a world of representation; the viewer remains on one side of the window at a safe, analytical distance from the objects of representation. This separation is a key feature of Jay's Cartesian perspectivalism. In virtual reality, however, the user is immersed in the image, surrounded by the objects of representation.[1]

In all these ways, virtual reality seems to support the contemporary rejection of the Cartesian self. Yet Hayles (1993, 1994, 1995), and other postmodern and feminist critics remain suspicious. For them, the proper alternative to Descartes's decontextualized reason is an embodied knowledge that virtual reality cannot achieve. Virtual reality threatens to detach the user from her body—as, for example, Bricken seems to suggest above—and such detachment sounds dangerously Cartesian. Allucquère Rosanne Stone (1991) expresses this concern: "Cyberspace

1. For feminist film theorist Mary Ann Doane (1991), distance is also a key feature of the male gaze: women are excluded from spectatorship in film precisely because they are denied this critical distance (20–26). In this sense, at least, virtual reality would not seem to be a masculinist technology.

developers foresee a time when they will be able to forget about the body. But it is important to remember that virtual community originates in, and must return to, the physical. . . . Forgetting about the body is an old Cartesian trick" (113). For Simon Penny (1994), "VR reinforces Cartesian duality by replacing the body with a body image, a creation of mind (for all 'objects' in VR are a product of mind). As such it is a clear continuation of the rationalist dream of disembodied mind, part of the long Western tradition of the denial of the body" (243). Finally, for Balsamo (1996), virtual reality does not simply deny the body, but rather represses it: "What is of interest to me in my encounter with virtual reality is the way that the repression of the body is technologically naturalized" (126).

In psychoanalytic terms, what is repressed may reemerge as a symptom or a sublimation, and in fact a concern for the body does manage to reemerge in virtual environments. It is certainly true that the real-time computer graphics of virtual reality is not adequate to give the user a feeling of complete embodiment. On the other hand, embodiment remains the ultimate goal for some VR specialists, who have designed body suits that will allow the user to manipulate an image of her whole body, not merely her hand. There has also been serious work on "haptic feedback," so that a joystick or eventually a glove can simulate the resistance appropriate to the object that the user is trying to move in virtual space. Even the current visual systems can be embodied in the sense that they can be embedded in physical and social contexts: the virtual reality game arcades involve their players in physical action whenever possible. ▷ **p. 166** Although enthusiasts for virtual reality sometimes sound, as Bricken does above, as if they wanted to get rid of the body, nevertheless theirs is still a rhetoric of the senses and the body, for they do not have an alternative to offer. Randal Walser makes the following prediction about cyberspace that refers essentially to virtual reality:

More than any mechanism yet invented, {cyberspace} will change what humans perceive themselves to be, at a very fundamental and personal level. In cyberspace, there is no need to move about in a body like the one you possess in physical reality. You may feel more comfortable, at first, with a body like your "own" but as you conduct more of your life and affairs in cyberspace your conditioned notion of a unique and immutable body will give way to a far more liberated notion of "body" as something quite disposable and, generally, limited. You will find that some bodies work best in some situations while others work best in others. The ability to radically and compellingly change one's body-image is bound to have a deep psychological effect, calling into question just what you consider yourself to be. (cited by Rheingold 1991, 191)

Walser is no Cartesian; he is not denying the importance of the body in defining the self. For him, the importance of the body in defining the self is precisely the reason that virtual reality will have its great impact. Virtual reality will change our notion of self because we will now be dynamic or unstable bodies. The wandering perspective of virtual reality can define itself only in terms of visible bodies in visible space. Current virtual reality technology is the self envisioned, not fully embodied. Although the current technology is therefore open to the anti-ocularist critique of the phallic gaze, that critique does not show it to be Cartesian. It seems that any plausible definition of self must now deny Cartesian detachment and rely exclusively on knowledge obtained in context and through the senses; virtual reality proponents like Walser share that defining assumption. Yet perhaps media theorist Florian Rötzer (1995) is right in arguing that precisely because a sense of touch is hard to integrate into new digital media, it will be regarded as the privileged sensation: "With the audiovisual media, the sense of touch is becoming privileged, although there have been efforts to incorporate it into VR technology. It is not the eyes and the ears, not the forms, sounds and words, but the collision of bodies . . . that will become the primary indication of reality experience in the age of simulation" (124).

Virtual reality therefore contains the contradiction that it is both Cartesian and anti-Cartesian, abstract and sensual, centered and fragmented, perhaps even simultaneously masculinist and feminist in orientation—all because, like other transparent technologies, while seeking to enact the male gaze, it also leads to a fascination with the many viewing and viewed positions made possible by the mediated self (cf. Stone 1991). The user of virtual reality is constantly aware of the discrepancies between the virtual scene and the real world, and that awareness is an important part of her experience. Because she is aware that her body is not adequately represented in the virtual environment, she begins to explore the limits of the embodiment that the environment does afford—to manipulate her point of view in order to test what "feels" right and what does not. Whether consciously or not, the visitor to a virtual environment is participating in the remediation of the filmic tradition as she manipulates her point of view. What fascinates her about virtual reality is never that it is mistaken for the physical world, but precisely that it remediates both herself and other media as it seeks to represent the world. Virtual reality functions for its contemporary user as the so-called cinema of attractions did for filmgoers at the turn of the century. ▷ **p. 155**

Virtual reality defines the self through visible bodies, not through minds, which do not appear in virtual worlds. And we must remember that feminist theory recognizes the body as both a medium and an element in the interplay of contemporary media. ▷ **p. 236** The interaction of technology and the body today comes not exclusively or even principally through prostheses or breast implants but rather through the ways in which visual and verbal media present the body and participate in the definition of the self. We have argued throughout this book that media are as much a part of our contemporary world as physical objects; indeed they have physical manifestations. Those who insist that the body plays an undeniable part in the definition of the contemporary self should be prepared to recognize the mediations of the body that must also be part of that definition. Transparent technologies such as virtual reality do not simply repeat but in fact remediate the Cartesian self. They cannot succeed in denying the body; instead they can only remediate it.

The Networked Self

17

Even in the case of virtual reality, which tries to construct a purely transparent version of the digital self, there is a constant interplay between transparency and hypermediacy. ⊗ **p. 248** In other cases, the hypermediacy of the digital self is overt and acknowledged—for example, in multimedia applications in which the user is never allowed to forget the artifice that she is experiencing. In such cases, the self is expressed in the very multiplicity and fragmentation of the windowed style. In techno-rock videos and CDs such as the *Telecommunications Breakdown,* the fragmented self is reflected in the frenetic pace at which the windowed images appear and compete for our attention, and the very "theme" of the piece is that the unity of our selves is fractured by the televisual culture in which we live. ⊗ **p. 31** In place of the unity and consistency that we used to value, the "Electronic Behavior Control System" offers the momentarily unifying experience of watching the piece unfold. The self of windowed multimedia is the necessary inverse of the self of virtual reality. If applications like virtual reality offer the user one point of view after another, hypermediated applications like the "Electronic Behavior Control System" offer the viewer multiple, simultaneous points of view that cannot be reconciled. The hypermediated self is expressed in the tension of these competing viewpoints.[1]

In addition to the windowed style of multimedia CD-ROMs, the hypermediated self is expressed in the many forms of networked communication on the Internet. Newsgroups and email, MUDs and chatrooms all operate under the logic of hypermediacy, although until recently they have not supported multimedia at all, but have been limited to passing textual messages. They are hypermediated because they are hypertextual: they connect users in a web of interrelated textual

1. The hypermediated self recalls Kenneth Gergen's (1991) saturated self: "Emerging technologies saturate us with the voices of humankind—both harmonious and alien. . . . Social saturation furnishes us with a multiplicity of incoherent and unrelated languages of the self. For everything we 'know to be true' about ourselves, other voices within respond with doubt and even derision. This fragmentation of self-conceptions corresponds to a multiplicity of incoherent and disconnected relationships. These relationships pull us in myriad directions, inviting us to play such a variety of roles that the very concept of an 'authentic self' with knowable characteristics recedes from view. The fully saturated self becomes no self at all" (6–7). However, writing almost a decade ago, Gergen's emerging technologies are television and radio, not new media.

elements and compel users to acknowledge the medium as they communicate. A sense of presence of oneself to others and of the self to itself comes not through immediate visual perception, as it does in virtual reality, but through the feeling of being connected to others through the Internet. The self that does the connecting is, like the self of virtual reality, an active one; unlike the self of virtual reality, however, the self that is connected is defined and in a sense embodied through its participation in various media—whether synchronous or asynchronous, visual or textual, animated or still. While all of these applications support the feeling of connection that distinguishes the networked self from the self of virtual reality, the real-time applications such as chatrooms and MUDs (or MOOs—we need not bother with the distinction here) are more effective.

MUDs and the Self

MUDs and chatrooms seem to serve almost no other cultural function than the remediation of the self. Although computer specialists have tried for years to exploit them for practical communication (business conferencing or education), they have remained social environments, opportunities for (usually) young participants to conduct experiments in self-definition. A chatroom is a site for real-time dialogue, in which each user presents herself as a name and a set of typed expressions. A MUD is verbally more complex, because it consists of a set of texts describing rooms and objects, while the human participants themselves are figured as characters who visit and have conversations in these rooms. The MUD thus remediates the printed novel or romance (and in some ways the telegraphic network and telephone party line; cf. Marvin 1988). This remediation is apparent in the lineage of MUDs, which developed from the Dungeons and Dragons games played on both computers and gameboards, which in turn developed from the fantasy novels of J. R. R. Tolkien. Some MUDs are world structures explicitly based on novels, such as one deriving from the fantasy novels of Anne McCaffrey (http://www.yahoo.com/Entertainment/Science_Fiction__Fantasy__and_Horror/Organizations/Pern/ January 25, 1998). Others show their lineage by the ways in which characters name and style themselves: that is, the characters often act in ways that suggest the ritualized pseudomedieval world of contemporary fantasy literature.

That MUDs are "real-time" romances is not to say that they are sophisticated novels. In *Life on the Screen,* Sherry Turkle offers examples such as the following: a marriage of two players, Achilles and Winterlight, by the priest Tarniwoof in the Gargoyle MUD. For the wedding, Turkle informs us, Achilles had created "a sacred clearing in cyberspace, a niche carved out of rock, with fifty seats intricately carved with animal motifs" (195). During the ceremony, which was attended by guests signing in from Europe and North America, the following, "second-person" narrative appeared on the screen of the groom, Achilles:

Tarniwoof says, "At the engagement ceremony you gave one another an item which represents your love, respect and friendship for each other."
Tarniwoof turns to you.
Tarniwoof says, "Achilles, do you have any reason to give your item back to Winterlight?"
Winterlight attends your answer nervously.
Tarniwoof waits for the groom to answer.
You would not give up her gift for anything.
Tarniwoof smiles happily.
Winterlight smiles at you.
Tarniwoof turns to the beautiful bride.
Tarniwoof says, "Winterlight, is there any doubt in your heart about what your item represents?"
Winterlight looks straightly to Tarniwoof.
Winterlight would never return the thousand paper stars of Achilles.
Tarniwoof says, "Do you promise to take Silver Shimmering Winterlight as your mudly wedded wife, in sickness and in health, through timeouts and updates, for richer or poorer, until linkdeath do you part?"
You say, "I do."
Winterlight smiles happily at you. (Turkle 1995, 195–196)

This excerpt (from a transcript that continues for twelve pages) shows how immediacy can be pursued through the acknowledgment of the medium and the genre.[2] It is important to remember that the people engaged in this ceremony function only through their textual mediations. The solemnity presumably reflects the emotional seriousness of the participants, and yet it is a solemnity that is consciously literary. The text—and all each participant ever experiences is a text on his or her screen—is saturated with an awareness of contemporary fantasy-romance. The speech of Tarniwoof at the end would seem to endanger the illusion of immediacy with its references to MUDs, time-

2. Such contemporary weddings in MUDs have a remarkable parallel in the nineteenth century. Carolyn Marvin (1988) describes several examples of such ceremonies conducted by telegraph, including one in 1876 in which guests "attended" at telegraphic offices all along the line from Arizona to San Diego (94–95).

outs, and links, and yet to Tarniwoof's apparently inappropriate puns, Achilles says, "I do," and Winterlight smiles. Instead of challenging the authenticity of the experience, their collective acceptance of the medium reaffirms the experience. The participants seem to have no trouble explicitly admitting that they are communicating through a computer network and implicitly acknowledging that they are inhabiting a fantasy. Neither level of mediation seems to interfere with the immediacy that they desire. Traditional MUDs attempt to achieve immediacy through prose, just as authors are popularly believed to do in traditional printed novels. In MUDs the participants are quite clear about their own mediated status: by inserting themselves into a narrative, they are mediating themselves. In her book, whose subtitle is *Identity in the Age of the Internet,* Turkle (1995) offers numerous examples of the textual construction of identity in networked environments. The MUD participants she interviews are often young men and women who have difficulty establishing relationships in the real world, all of whom accept the mediated environment of the MUD as a site for authentic experience. Many regard their experiences in MUDs as more emotionally satisfying than their lives in the physical world.

It may be obvious why sex in chatrooms and MUDs is so common, or at least why it is so widely advertised and discussed, for these textually mediated encounters offer adventure within safe limits. But it is also worth noting that such sex is an extreme form of remediation. At least since the nineteenth century, sex has been represented in both visual and textual media (and also in music) as perfect immediacy. Sexual encounters in MUDs and chatrooms offer the challenge of achieving immediacy through first acknowledging and then trying to erase the medium. MUD sex is a chance to rewrite the pornographic novel, with the object of desire providing his or her own responses.

It is the desire for immediacy that makes such encounters controversial. In an infamous case in a MUD called LamdaMOO, one character forced others to perform sexual acts: that is, he programmed the MUD so that the prose descriptions of these characters' actions were no longer under their control, and they were described as having sex. These descriptions appeared on the screens of the characters themselves and anyone else in the room at the time. In the debate that followed, the question arose whether one could be raped in cyberspace (Dibbel 1996). In fact a rape occurred in exactly the same sense that rapes occur in films or novels: rape in a MUD can mean only that the participants became unwilling rather than willing remediators of the pornographic novel. The victims, however, experienced the rape as a serious and real violation of self precisely because their selves were constructed and maintained through the text that now betrayed them. A somewhat different violation in cyberspace was carried out by a male psychiatrist who posed in a chatroom as a disabled and disfigured woman (Turkle 1995, 228–229). His female persona apparently established friendly and sexual relationships with a number of other women, who then felt betrayed when they discovered the "true" identity of their companion. What was betrayed was the women's sense of the immediacy of their experience with the character that the psychiatrist had created, an immediacy that had emerged through and because of the hypermediacy of the Internet. When the psychiatrist's identity was revealed, his women correspondents were reminded of the layers of textual and electronic mediation that they had once acknowledged and then needed to forget.[3]

These encounters (wedding, rape, sex, and sexual deceit) all testify to the strength of the desire for immediacy in textual virtual environments. In these cases, the desire is not for the immediacy of the world, as it is manifested in linear-perspective painting and photography, in which objects of representation are supposed to become immediately available to the viewer. The desire is instead for the self: for oneself to be present to others or indeed to itself. This desire for the immediate self can be sublimated and can reemerge as a fascination with the intricacies of programming and inhabiting the MUD. Some participants that Turkle interviewed spent forty hours a week in a MUD; some of them built elaborate programming constructs. Turkle (1995) reports, for example, that "in the MUD universe, Kasha built a private planet whose construction took many weeks of programming. On the planet, Kasha built a mansion with flowers in every room. As a special gift to Robert, Kasha designed the most beautiful of these rooms as their bedroom" (206). Programming the MUD is an exercise in hypermediacy that a programmer like Kasha hoped would then lead to the sentimental immediacy of an electronic relationship with Robert. This construction of the self through a medium is nothing new. The complaint was, after all, leveled against the romance in the eighteenth century (e.g., Rousseau's controversial *Nouvelle Héloïse*) that it encouraged an artificial and yet dangerously immediate construction of the self among its young readers. From this historical perspective too, MUDs and chatrooms not only mediate but also remediate the construction of the self. The MUD is regarded as better than the romance or fantasy novel because the participants can insert themselves into the

3. Marvin (1988) describes similar violations of trust conducted through the telegraphic network of the late nineteenth century—for example, a confidence man who married a widow by wire, had her wire $3,000 to him, and then disappeared (93).

Figure 17.1 Identity and gender in the Palace. (*top*) "Are you really a woman?" (*bottom*) "Yes." © 1998, The Palace Inc. Used with permission.

that "male characters often expect sexual favors in return for technical assistance [given to female characters]. A male character once requested a kiss from me after answering a question. A gift always incurs an obligation" (444–445). In this way a traditional gender identity is simply reinscribed in a new networked environment. In other ways, however, gender is not only reinscribed but refashioned, as it is measured against constructions of gender in other verbal and visual technologies.

In a sexual encounter in a MUD, the primary appeal comes through the verbal description of the visual. The participants usually begin by describing their appearance and continue with a visual account of their actions. If MUD sex is the remediation of the (predominantly male and heterosexual) pornographic novel, it is also the remediation in prose of the male gaze as expressed in film and of the attendent desire for transparent immediacy. ⊘ **p. 78** But immediacy always passes into hypermediacy, and the simple male gaze—if it was ever simple even in film—is certainly complicated by our culture's fascination with the operation and texture of digital technologies. In particular, textual MUDs are complicated by our culture's difficulty construing text as a transparent medium. What undermines the male gaze in a textual MUD is that one can never be sure of the gender of one's partner. Participants can change their persona (names and descriptions) easily, and there can be no visual markers of embodied gender in textual environments.

Just as feminist theorists such as Judith Butler and Monique Wittig have sought to complicate the notion of gender for their readers, MUDs complicate that notion for their players. Gender for Butler is always a performance rather than an essential quality. Because one's identity is assembled through the staging of various gendered attributes, body habits, clothes, and so on, an individual can fluctuate between male and female identities, just as a MUD player can change avatars with a few keystrokes. MUDs thus give some feminist theoretical claims an operational significance. In a MUD, there is always the possibility that any relationship, from a casual conversation to some form of verbally mediated sex, is founded on such a gender confusion. This confusion constitutes the best example of the hypermediacy of MUDs, because it threatens the most culturally charged expression of the desire for immediacy. It is in such encounters that the user may care most strongly about the power and the limitations of the medium itself.

We may also wonder whether visual MUDs might facilitate the male gaze more straightforwardly than textual MUDs do. Yet this seems unlikely, because the visual MUDs provide their own forms of spoofing and gender swapping. In the Palace, for example, one can switch between male and female avatars in a matter of seconds. Even when the MUDs may have streaming video, so that players can "be themselves," it seems likely that players will also have the ability to refashion their own video images in ways that confuse or confound markers of gender. Players do this already in the Palace: they frequently create images that confuse or ignore gender, and some spend huge amounts of time programming and decorating their various personas. Players are so fascinated with the operational character of the Palace as a medium that they are simply not concerned to give a faithful or consistent representation of themselves. The hypermediacy of the digital self, never fully and finally repressed, seems to thrive in visual MUDs.

Conclusion

18

We close with two brief observations. The first concerns the endless crescendo of enthusiasm and expectations with which Western culture is greeting digital media. Each month seems to bring new evidence of the voracity with which new media are refashioning the established media and reinventing themselves in the quest for immediacy. Each new Hollywood blockbuster gives computer graphics artists and programmers the opportunity to claim that they are getting closer to transparency. More remarkable are those pageants of mediation and remediation that emerge as part of current events, such as elections, trials, and the deaths of famous people. In disseminating information about such events, the Internet is quickly taking shape as an established news medium alongside television, radio, and the press. The Internet is also now a full participant in the process of incorporating the media into the event itself.

The 1996 presidential and congressional contest was the first election covered widely and deeply on the World Wide Web. Partisan and nonpartisan web sites provided information throughout the campaign. On the evening of the election, news sites such as CNN Interactive were offering continuous streams of results from each congressional district. Their promise was that the viewer could bypass the television coverage, which while rapid was still rigidly linear, and get closer to the election itself. On television the viewer had to wait until the networks got around to displaying the results in her state or district; on the Net, the viewer could pass directly to particular elections that interested her. Furthermore, she could supposedly view the same election tallies on which the networks themselves made their projections, thus bypassing the middleman. The assumed immediacy of broadcast television was exposed as faulty, in that television could not be interactive and respond to the needs of each viewer. Unfortunately, the CNN Interactive web site was jammed with so many hits that most users could not get through at all. For these users, television was still a more efficient system for delivering information. Yet even this jamming was taken as evidence of the future of news delivery on the Web: it indicated that users clearly wanted an Internet-based news service.

When, in the summer of 1997, the Mars Surveyor spacecraft landed safely and released its Rover to photograph the surface, the Jet Propulsion Laboratory web site received millions of hits and became tantalizingly inaccessible. ⊳ **p. 205** Even more clearly than in the case of the 1996 election, the Mars landing was a mediated event in which media constituted the subject. The slow movement of the Rover, a special camera on wheels, was the only thing that was happening at the rocky desert landing site. The story was that this medium could itself provide an authentic and exciting viewing experience. Moreover, the photographs could now be refashioned into a web site, in addition to the customary presentations on television and in the print media. In covering the mission, each news medium made its own claim to immediacy, while both critiquing and emulating the coverage provided by the others.

Within two months, the Mars landing was eclipsed by the death of Princess Diana, an event that brought the mutual remediations among on-the-air and online media to a level of frenzy unprecedented in recent media history. The reality of media was demonstrated in a gruesome fashion, when the paparazzi pursued Diana's car and were blamed as at least the indirect cause of the accident. The story that the photographers may actually have interfered with those trying to help the victims showed again that media can intrude in the "real" world, with serious or fatal results. Even if it was not fully accurate, the story became an instant cultural obsession. The photographers, after all, seemed to be trying to achieve the ultimate immediacy by photographing death itself. Who can listen to the story of Diana without recalling Barthes's analysis of the immediacy of photography? ⊳ **p. 110** We may also think of Antonioni's *Blow-up* and of the computer game *Myst* that remediates the fatal stillness of Antonioni's films. ⊳ **p. 97** The picture of death taken by Antonioni's photographer was anything but transparent and immediate: each successive blow-up moved the image further along the scale toward hypermediacy. But in the case of

Diana's death, the photograph instantly took on such white-hot immediacy that it could not be published at all, although an apparent digital fake was made available briefly on the Internet and then removed. In that all the media joined the paparazzi in their pursuit of the immediacy of Diana's death, few could fail to see the irony that the press, television, and the Internet were condemning the photographers while themselves providing absurdly inquisitive and detailed coverage of a private tragedy. Yet even that irony was absorbed into the media coverage. The media even critiqued themselves as complicit in the death of Diana for having fed the public curiosity that led the paparazzi to pursue her in the first place. The news media thus expressed a fascination with media that they simultaneously condemned as morbid.

Meanwhile, television and the web were as always each promoting its own definition of immediacy: television through live coverage that went on for days and the Internet through web casting and the "participatory democracy" of the newsgroups, in which contributors could conduct their own grieving dialogue. Sometimes the emphasis in the television broadcasts passed from the live coverage to the authenticity of the emotional experience: the size of the crowds, its outpouring of grief, and so on. From there it was an easy move to hypermediacy. That movement became apparent, for example, in the broadcasts by CBS News. Because the funeral itself occurred for American audiences in the middle of the night, CBS decided to run a videotape of the whole ceremony later in the morning. At that time, however, the procession was still carrying Diana's body to its final resting place. The producers of the broadcast thus faced the problem of providing two image streams to their viewers. They decided not to switch the entire screen from one scene to the other, as they would undoubtedly have done five or ten years before. Instead, they periodically shrank the videotaped funeral to a window on the screen and slid in a second window carrying a shot of the continuing procession. The two windows would appear overlapping for some seconds or minutes. Above the one was the rubric "videotape" and above the other "live"—as if the live "shot" were any less mediated than the videotape. The producers chose the hypermediated windowed style, even though or perhaps because they wanted to elicit in their viewers feelings of authenticity and deep emotion. Because the two images (one videotaped and one live) were both available to the producers, both demanded their place on the screen. This crowding together of images, the insistence that everything that technology can present must be presented at one time—this is the logic of hypermediacy.

We can hardly imagine a better example of hypermediacy's claim to authenticity of experience. And yet other and perhaps better examples (both of hypermediacy and remediation) will no doubt appear, as each new event tops the previous ones in the excitement or the audacity of its claims to immediacy.

THE FUTURE OF REMEDIATION

Our second observation concerns our culture's insistence on the newness of new media. It is not surprising that enthusiasts should continue to make the claim of novelty, for they have inherited from modernism the assumption that a medium must be new in order to be significant. As Cavell (1979) has remarked, the task of the modern artist was always "one of creating not a new instance of his art, but a new medium in it" (104). In digital media today, as in modern art in the first half of the century, the medium must pretend to be utterly new in order to promote its claim of immediacy. It must constitute itself as a medium that (finally) provides the unmediated experience that all previous media sought, but failed to achieve. This is why each innovation on the World Wide Web must be represented by its promoters as a revolution. Streaming audio, streaming video, Java, VRML—each of these cannot merely improve what the Web offered before but must "reinvent" the Web. As we have shown, what is in fact new is the particular way in which each innovation rearranges and reconstitutes the meaning of earlier elements. What is new about new media is therefore also old and familiar: that they promise the new by remediating what has gone before.

The film *Strange Days*, with which we began our study, is not really a prediction about the future, but a description of our culture's current fascination with both transparent and hypermediated technologies of representation. Throughout this book, we too have tried to describe the present moment and to resist the urge, so tempting when writing about new media, to make predictions. We surely cannot predict how digital media will work their particular remediations in the coming years and decades. Today, virtual reality refashions film; the World Wide Web refashions television and everything else. However, as they develop, these technologies may change the focus of their remediations. Other digital hardware and software may be invented and deployed against the same targets (particularly television and film) or perhaps against others. Our one prediction is that any future media will also define their cultural meaning with reference to established technologies. They will isolate some features of those technologies (point of view, motion, interactivity, and so on) and refashion them to make a claim of greater immediacy.

The true novelty would be a new medium that did not refer for its meaning to other media at all. For our culture, such mediation without remediation seems to be impossible.

augmented reality   Any of a variety of computer systems that combines views of the physical world with computer-generated graphics. Wearing special glasses or a headset, the user can see the physical world, but additional graphical or textual information provided by the computer is also displayed on her eyepieces. The result is a hypermediated visual space.

camera lucida   A device that uses lenses or mirrors to enable an artist to create a perspective drawing of what he sees. Similar in purpose to the older camera obscura.

camera obscura   Any of a variety of devices from a box to an entire room, dating from the Renaissance to the nineteenth century: sunlight is focused through a pinhole or lens in one side or wall of the camera obscura and projected on the opposite side or wall. The viewer would see the projected image upside down in a linear perspective. The camera obscura becomes the modern photographic camera by placing photographic film at the focal point.

cyberspace   A term coined by cyberpunk novelist William Gibson to describe a future combination of networking and three-dimensional visualization. For Gibson, cyberspace encompasses all the computers and digitized data in the world. The term is now invoked broadly to describe any computerized medium, including the Internet, virtual reality, or even CD-ROM.

digital photography   The practice of altering, combining, and refashioning conventional photographic images by computer graphics techniques.

graphical user interface (GUI)   The current standard for interacting with a personal computer, in which the user views and manipulates text and images in windows on the screen. Files, directories, commands, and applications are represented by icons or menu items. The GUI works under the logic of hypermediacy.

html (Hypertext Markup Language)   The system of tags that control the appearance and behavior of text and images on World Wide Web pages.

hybrids   Media produced by heterogenous networks, such as computer graphics, digital photography, or the World Wide Web.

hypermedia   Computer applications that present multiple media (text, graphics, animation, video) using a hypertextual organization. Operates under the logic of hypermediacy.

hypermediacy   A style of visual representation whose goal is to remind the viewer of the medium. One of the two strategies of remediation; the other is (transparent) immediacy.

hypertext   A method of organizing and presenting text in the computer. Textual units of various sizes are presented to the reader in an order that is determined, at least in part, by electronic links that the reader chooses to follow. Hypertext is the remediation of the printed book.

icon   A small graphic used in a graphical user interface to represent files, directories, programs, and resources. Icons are part of the windowed style, which is an expression of hypermediacy.

immediacy (or transparent immediacy)   A style of visual representation whose goal is to make the viewer forget the presence of the medium (canvas, photographic film, cinema, and so on) and believe that he is in the presence of the objects of representation. One of the two strategies of remediation; the other is hypermediacy.

Java   A programming language used to create special applications that are downloaded from the World Wide Web and run inside a brower. Java enables the Web to go beyond its remediation of graphic design and refashion multimedia or computer programming in general.

linear perspective   A form of mathematical projection through which three-dimensional objects are represented on a two-dimensional surface. A key feature in the style of transparent immediacy pursued by western painting from the Renaissance until the late nineteenth century.

media   Plural of medium.

medium   The formal, social, and material network of practices that generates a logic by which additional instances are repeated or remediated, such as photography, film, or television.

MOO   A kind of MUD. Stands for MUD, object-oriented.

MUD   Multiuser dungeon. A programming system through which computer users in different physical locations can communicate in the same networked, virtual space. The background text of the MUD describes a world with rooms or other physical spaces. Users become characters in this world and participate in the creation of a collective narrative.

networks   A technical term to characterize the hardware and software that allow computers to exchange electronic information. We consider networks never to be purely technical but always to be made up of heterogeneous alliances and affiliations drawn from a variety of elements, including science, nature, language, media, society, culture, economics, and/or aesthetics.

photorealism   Computer photorealism is the practice of making computer graphic images resemble photographs; manual photorealism is a movement in contemporary art in which photographs serve as the basis of highly realistic paintings. Both of these photorealisms operate under the logic of transparent immediacy.

remediation   Defined by Paul Levenson as the "anthropotropic" process by which new media technologies improve upon or remedy prior technologies. We define the term differently, using it to mean the formal logic by which new media refashion prior media forms. Along with immediacy and hypermediacy, remediation is one of the three traits of our genealogy of new media.

repurposing   A term used in the entertainment industry to describe the practice of adapting a "property" for a number of different media venues, for example, Disney's creation of a soundtrack, a Broadway musical, a Saturday morning cartoon, and a complete line of children's products from *The Lion King*.

streaming audio/video   An Internet technology that delivers a continuous audio or video signal to the user's computer. Streaming permits the Internet and the World Wide Web to compete with and to refashion conventional radio and television.

ubiquitous computing   The use of electronic devices to refashion a physical environment, such as the classroom or the home. The devices are distributed throughout this environment and communicate with each other and with the user. Ubiquitous computing is in the spirit of hypermediacy and is the opposite of virtual reality.

virtual reality   Any of a variety of systems that immerse the user in computer-generated graphics. Wearing special glasses or a headset, the user sees only what the computer draws on the eyepieces. Virtual reality operates under the logic of transparent immeidacy and is the opposite of ubiquitous computing.

VRML   Virtual Reality Modeling Language. A code for describing three-dimensional objects and views to be displayed to the user in her World Wide Web browser.

webcam   A (usually stationary) video camera trained on some indoor or outdoor scene, whose image is automatically digitized, inserted into a web page, and made available over the World Wide Web. Because the image is updated at regular intervals (ranging from a few seconds to a few hours), a webcam seems to appropriate or rival the liveness of broadcast television.

web site   An interconnected set of pages that constitute a coherent offering for the World Wide Web.

World Wide Web   A service on the Internet. The Web consists of hundreds of thousands of web sites and can remediate any of a variety of earlier media.

Adams, Judith. 1991. *The American Amusement Park Industry: A History of Technology and Thrills.* Boston: G. K. Hall.

Alberti, Leon Battista. 1972. *On Painting and on Sculpture: The Latin Texts of De Pictura and De Statua.* Trans. and ed. Cecil Grayson. London: Phaidon.

Allen, Robert C., ed. 1992. *Channels of Discourse, Reassembled: Television and Contemporary Criticism.* 2d ed. Chapel Hill, N.C.: UNC Press.

Alpers, Svetlana. 1982. "Art History and Its Exclusions." In Norma Broode and Mary D. Garrard, eds., *Feminism and Art History: Questioning the Litany.* New York: Harper & Row.

Alpers, Svetlana. 1983. *The Art of Describing: Dutch Art in the Seventeenth Century.* Chicago: University of Chicago Press.

Anderson, Christopher. 1994. "Disneyland." In Horace Newcomb, ed., *Television, the Critical View.* 5th ed. New York: Oxford University Press.

Augé, Marc. 1995. *Non-Places: Introduction to an Anthropology of Supermodernity.* Trans. John Howe. London: Verso.

Auslander, Philip. 1997a. "Against Ontology: Making Distinctions Between the Live and the Mediatized." *Performance Research* 2,3 (Autumn): 50–55.

Auslander, Philip. 1997b. *From Acting to Performance: Essays in Modernism and Postmodernism.* London: Routledge.

Auslander, Philip. Forthcoming. *Liveness: Performance in a Mediatized Culture.* London: Routledge.

Balsamo, Anne. 1996. *Technologies of the Gendered Body: Reading Cyborg Women.* Durham, N.C.: Duke University Press.

Barthes, Roland. 1981. *Camera Lucida: Reflections on Photography.* Trans. Richard Howard. New York: Hill and Wang.

Battcock, Gregory, ed. 1973. *The New Art: A Critical Anthology.* New York: E. P. Dutton.

Baudrillard, Jean. 1983. *Simulations.* Trans. Paul Foss, Paul Patton, and Philip Beitchman. New York: Semiotext(e).

Bazin, André. 1980. "The Ontology of the Photographic Image." In Alan Trachtenberg, ed., *Classic Essays in Photography,* pp. 237–244. New Haven, Conn.: Leete's Island Books.

Benedikt, Michael, ed. 1991. *Cyberspace: First Steps.* Cambridge, Mass.: MIT Press.

Benjamin, Walter. 1969. "The Work of Art in the Age of Mechanical Reproduction." In Hannah Arendt, ed., *Illuminations,* pp. 217–252. Trans. Harry Zohn. New York: Schocken.

Bricken, Meredith. 1991. "Virtual Worlds: No Interface to Design." In Michael Benedikt, ed., *Cyberspace: First Steps,* pp. 363–382. Cambridge, Mass.: MIT Press.

Bruckman, Amy. 1996. "Gender Swapping on the Internet." In Victor J. Vitanza, ed., *CyberReader,* pp. 441–446. Needham Heights, Mass.: Allyn and Bacon.

References

Bryman, Alan. 1995. *Disney and His Worlds.* London: Routledge.

Bryson, Norman. 1981. *Word and Image: French Painting of the Ancien Régime.* Cambridge: Cambridge University Press.

Bryson, Norman. 1983. *Vision and Painting: The Logic of the Gaze.* New Haven: Yale University Press.

Bukatman, Scott. 1991. "There's Always Tomorrowland: Disney and the Hypercinematic Experience." *October* 57: 55–78.

Butler, Judith. 1990. *Gender Trouble: Feminism and the Subversion of Identity.* New York: Routledge.

Card, S. K., G. G. Robertson, and J. D. Macinlay. 1991. "The Information Visualizer: An Information Workspace." In *Proceedings of CHI '91,* pp. 181–188. New York: ACM.

Cavell, Stanley. 1979. *The World Viewed: Reflections on the Ontology of the Cinema.* Cambridge, Mass.: Harvard University Press.

Cavell, Stanley. 1986. "The Fact of Television." In John G. Hanhardt, ed., *Video Culture: A Critical Investigation.* Layton, Utah: G. M. Smith, Peregrine Smith Books.

Chase, Linda. 1988. *Ralph Goings: Essay/Interview by Linda Chase.* New York: Harry N. Abrams.

Clark, T. J. 1983. "Clement Greenberg's Theory of Art." In W. J. T. Mitchell, ed., *The Politics of Interpretation,* pp. 203–220. Chicago: University of Chicago Press.

Cotten, Bob, and Richard Oliver. 1993. *Understanding Hypermedia.* London: Phaidon Press.

Crary, Jonathan. 1990. *Techniques of the Observer: On Vision and Modernity in the Nineteenth Century.* Cambridge, Mass.: MIT Press.

de Lauretis, Teresa. 1984. *Alice Doesn't: Feminism, Semiotics, Cinema.* Bloomington: Indiana University Press.

Derrida, Jacques. 1976. *Of Grammatology.* Trans. Gayatri Chakravorty Spivak. Baltimore: Johns Hopkins University Press.

Derrida, Jacques. 1981. "Economimesis." *Diacritics* 11: 3–25.

Dery, Mark. 1996. *Escape Velocity: Cyberculture at the End of the Century.* New York: Grove Press.

Descartes, Réné. 1986. *Meditations on First Philosophy with Selections from Objections and Replies.* Trans. J. Cottingham. Cambridge: Cambridge University Press.

Dibbel, Julian. 1996. "A Rape in Cyberspace." In Victor J. Vitanza, ed., *CyberReader,* pp. 448–465. Needham Heights, Mass.: Allyn and Bacon.

Ditlea, Steve. 1989. "Another World: Inside Artificial Reality." *PC Computing* 2,11: 90–99, 112.

Doane, Mary Ann. 1991. *Femmes Fatales: Feminism, Film Theory, Psychoanalysis.* New York: Routledge.

Edgerton, Samuel Y., Jr. 1975. *The Renaissance Rediscovery of Linear Perspective.* New York: Basic Books.

Elkins, James. 1994. *The Poetics of Perspective.* Ithaca, N.Y.: Cornell University Press.

Emergency Broadcast Network. 1995. *Telecommunications Breakdown.* CD-ROM. New York: TVT Records.

Feuer, Jane. 1983. "The Concept of Live TV." In E. Ann Kaplan, ed., *Regarding Television: Critical Approaches—An Anthology,* pp. 12–22. Frederick, Md.: University Publications of America.

Fisher, Philip. 1991. *Making and Effacing Art: Modern American Art in a Culture of Museums.* New York: Oxford University Press.

Fiske, John. 1987. *Television Culture.* London: Routledge.

Flitterman-Lewis, Sandy. 1992. "Psychoanalysis, Film, and Television." In Robert C. Allen, ed., *Channels of Discourse, Reassembled: Television and Contemporary Criticism,* pp. 203–246. Chapel Hill, N.C.: UNC Press.

Foley, James D., et al. 1996. *Computer Graphics: Principles and Practice.* Reading, Mass.: Addison-Wesley.

Foster, Hugh. 1997. "Get in the Game." *ComputerLife* 4,7 (July): 83–84, 89–93.

Foucault, Michel. 1971. *The Order of Things: An Archaeology of the Human Sciences.* New York: Vintage Press.

Foucault, Michel. 1977. "Nietzsche, Genealogy, History." In Donald F. Bouchard, ed., *Language, Counter-Memory, Practice: Selected Essays and Interviews.* Trans. Donald F. Bouchard and Sherry Simon. Ithaca, N.Y.: Cornell University Press.

Fried, Michael. 1983. "How Modernism Works: A Response to T. J. Clark." In W. J. T. Mitchell, ed., *The Politics of Interpretation,* pp. 221–238. Chicago: University of Chicago Press.

Friedberg, Anne. 1995. "Cinema and the Postmodern Condition." In Linda Williams, ed., *Viewing Positions: Ways of Seeing Film,* pp. 59–83. New Brunswick, N.J.: Rutgers University Press.

Fry, Tony, ed. 1993. *RUA/TV? Heidegger and the Televisual.* Sydney: Power Institute of Fine Arts.

Gamman, Lorraine. 1989. "Watching the Detectives: The Enigma of the Female Gaze." In Lorraine Gamman and Margaret Marshment, eds., *The Female Gaze: Women as Viewers of Popular Culture,* pp. 8–26. Seattle: The Real Comet Press.

Gergen, Kenneth J. 1991. *The Saturated Self: Dilemmas of Identity in Contemporary Life.* New York: Basic Books.

Gibson, William. 1986. *Neuromancer.* New York: Ace Books.

Gombrich, E. H. 1982. *The Image and the Eye.* Oxford: Phaidon Press.

Goodman, Nelson. 1968. *Languages of Art: An Approach to a Theory of Symbols.* Indianapolis: Bobbs-Merrill.

Greenberg, Clement. 1965. "Collage." In *Art and Culture: Critical Essays,* pp. 70–83. Boston: Beacon Press.

Greenberg, Clement. 1973. "Modernist Painting." In Gregory Battcock, ed., *The New Art: A Critical Anthology,* pp. 66–77. New York: E. P. Dutton.

Greenberg, Clement. 1986. "Towards a Newer Laocoon." In John O'Brien, ed., *Clement Greenberg: The Collected Essays and Criticism,* vol. 1, pp. 23–38. Chicago: University of Chicago Press.

Grossberg, Larry. 1987. "The In-Difference of Television." *Screen* 28,2:28–45.

Gunning, Tom. 1995. "An Aesthetic of Astonishment." In Linda Williams, ed., *Viewing Positions: Ways of Seeing Film,* pp. 114–133. New Brunswick, N.J.: Rutgers University Press.

Hafner, Katie, and Matthew Lyon. 1996. *Where Wizards Stay Up Late: The Origins of the Internet.* New York: Simon & Schuster.

Hagen, Margaret A., ed. 1980. *The Perception of Pictures.* Vol 1: *Alberti's Window: The Projective Model of Pictorial Information.* Vol 2: *Dürer's Devices: Beyond the Projective Model of Pictures.* New York: Academic Press.

Hagen, Margaret A. 1986. *Varieties of Realism.* Cambridge: Cambridge University Press.

Haraway, Donna J. 1991. *Simians, Cyborgs and Women: The Reinvention of Nature.* New York: Routledge.

Haraway, Donna J. 1997. *Modest Witness@Second Millennium. FemaleMan© Meets OncoMouse™: Feminism and Technoscience.* New York: Routledge.

Harpold, Terry. 1998. "The Misfortunes of the Digital Text." In Stephanie B. Gibson and Ollie Oviedo, eds., *The Emerging CyberCulture: Literacy, Paradigm, and Paradox.* Creskill N.J.: Hampton Press.

Hayles, N. Katherine. 1993. "The Materiality of Informatics." *Configurations* 1: 147–170.

Hayles, N. Katherine. 1994. "Boundary Disputes: Homeostasis, Reflexivity, and the Foundations of Cybernetics." *Configurations* 2: 441–467.

Hayles, N. Katherine. 1995. "Embodied Virtuality, Or How to Put Bodies Back into the Picture." In Diana Augaitis, Douglas MacLeod, and Mary Anne Moser, eds., *Immersed in Technology: Art and Virtual Environments.* Cambridge, Mass.: MIT Press.

Heim, Michael. 1991. "The Erotic Ontology of Cyberspace." In Michael Benedikt, ed., *Cyberspace: First Steps,* pp. 59–80. Cambridge, Mass.: MIT Press.

Herz, J. C. 1997. *Joystick Nation: How Videogames Ate Our Quarters, Won Our Hearts, and Rewired Our Minds.* Boston: Little, Brown.

Hodges, Larry F., Barbara Olasov Rothbaum, Rob Kooper, Dan Opdyke, James Williford, and Thomas C. Meyer. 1994. *Presence as the Defining Factor in a VR Application.* GVU Technical Report 94–06. Atlanta: Graphics Visualization and Usability Center.

Holtzman, Steven. 1997. *Digital Mosaics: The Aesthetics of Cyberspace.* New York: Simon & Schuster.

Huhtamo, Erkki. 1995. "Encapsulated Bodies in Motion: Simulators and the Quest for Total Immersion." In Simon Penny, ed., *Critical Issues in Electronic Media,* pp. 159–186. Albany, N.Y.: State University of New York Press.

Hunter, Ian W., Tilemachos D. Doukoglou, Serge R. Lafontaine, Paul G. Charette, Lynette A. Jones, Mark A. Sagar, Gordon D. Mallinson, and Peter J. Hunter. 1993. "A Teleoperated Microsurgical Robot and Associated Virtual Environment for Eye Surgery." *Presence* 2, 4 (Fall): 265–280.

Ivins, William M. 1973. *On the Rationalization of Sight.* New York: Da Capo Press.

James, William. 1950. *The Principles of Psychology.* 1890. Reprint ed., New York: Dover.

Jameson, Fredric. 1991. *Postmodernism: Or the Cultural Logic of Late Capitalism.* Durham, N.C.: Duke University Press.

Jay, Martin. 1988. "Scopic Regimes of Modernity." In Hal Foster, ed., *Vision and Visuality,* pp. 3–23. Seattle: Bay Press.

Jay, Martin. 1993. *Downcast Eyes: The Denigration of Vision in Twentieth-Century French Thought.* Berkeley: University of California Press.

Jeffords, Susan, and Lauren Rabinovitz. 1994. *Seeing Through the Media: The Persian Gulf War.* New Brunswick, N.J.: Rutgers University Press.

Johnson, Stephen. 1997. *Interface Culture: How New Technology Transforms the Way We Create and Communicate.* San Francisco: HarperEdge.

Joyce, Michael. 1995. *Of Two Minds: Hypertext Pedagogy and Poetics.* Ann Arbor: University of Michigan Press.

Judovitz, Dalia. 1988. *Subjectivity and Representation in Descartes: The Origins of Modernity.* Cambridge: Cambridge University Press.

Jussim, Estelle. 1983. *Visual Communication and the Graphic Arts: Photographic Technologies in the Nineteenth Century.* New York: R. R. Bowker Co.

Kasson, John F. 1978. *Amusing the Million: Coney Island at the Turn of the Century.* New York: Hill and Wang.

Keller, Evelyn Fox, and Christine R. Grontkowski. 1996. "The Mind's Eye." In Evelyn Fox Keller and Helen E. Longino, eds., *Feminism and Science.* Oxford: Oxford University Press.

Kellner, Douglas. 1995. *Media Culture: Cultural Studies, Identity and Politics Between the Modern and the Postmodern.* London: Routledge.

Kellogg, Wendy A., John M. Carroll, and John T. Richards. 1991. "Making Reality a Cyberspace." In Michael Benedikt, ed., *Cyberspace: First Steps,* pp. 411–433. Cambridge, Mass.: MIT Press.

Kelly, Kevin, and Gary Wolf. 1997. "Kill Your Browser." *Wired* 5,3 (March): 12–23.

Kemp, Martin. 1990. *The Science of Art: Optical Themes in Western Art from Brunelleschi to Seurat.* New Haven: Yale University Press.

Kozloff, Sarah. "Narrative Theory and Television." In Robert C. Allen, ed., *Channels of Discourse, Reassembled: Television and Contemporary Criticism*, pp. 67–100. 2d ed. Chapel Hill, N.C.: UNC Press.

Kubovy, Michael. 1986. *The Psychology of Perspective and Renaissance Art.* Cambridge: Cambridge University Press.

Lanham, Richard. 1993. *The Electronic Word: Democracy, Technology, and the Arts.* Chicago: University of Chicago Press.

Latour, Bruno. 1987. *Science in Action: How to Follow Scientists and Engineers Through Society.* Cambridge, Mass.: Harvard University Press.

Latour, Bruno. 1990. "Drawing Things Together." In Michael Lynch and Steve Woolgar, eds., *Representation in Scientific Practice*, pp. 19–68. Cambridge, Mass.: MIT Press.

Latour, Bruno. 1992. "Where Are the Missing Masses? The Sociology of a Few Mundane Artifacts." In W. E. Bijker and J. Law, eds., *Shaping Technology/Building Society: Studies in Sociotechnical Change*, pp. 225–258. Cambridge, Mass.: MIT Press.

Latour, Bruno. 1993. *We Have Never Been Modern.* Trans. Catherine Porter. Cambridge, Mass.: Harvard University Press.

Levinson, Paul. 1997. *The Soft Edge: A Natural History and Future of the Information Revolution.* London: Routledge.

Manovich, Lev. 1995–1996. "Eine Archäologie des Computerbildschirms." *Kunstforum* 132 (November–January): 124–135.

Manovich, Lev. 1997. "Was ist ein Digitaler Film?" *Telepolis* 2 (June): 42–57.

Marvin, Carolyn. 1988. *When Old Technologies Were New: Thinking About Electric Communication in the Late Nineteenth Century.* New York: Oxford University Press.

McLuhan, Marshall. 1964. *Understanding Media: The Extensions of Man.* New York: New American Library, Times Mirror.

Mechner, Jordan. 1997. *The Last Express.* CD-ROM. Novato, Calif.: Broderbund.

Meisel, Louis K. 1993. *Photorealism Since 1980.* New York: Harry N. Abrams.

Messaris, Paul. 1994. *Visual Literacy: Image, Mind, and Reality.* Boulder, Colo.: Westview Press.

Metz, Christian. 1977. *The Imaginary Signifier: Psychoanalysis and the Cinema.* Bloomington: Indiana University Press.

Meyer, Pedro. 1995. *Truths and Fictions: A Journey from Documentary to Digital Photography.* CD-ROM. Los Angeles: Voyager Company.

Mitchell, W. J. T. 1986. *Iconology: Image, Text, Ideology.* Chicago: University of Chicago Press.

Mitchell, W. J. T. 1994. *Picture Theory.* Chicago: University of Chicago Press.

Mitchell, William J. 1994. *The Reconfigured Eye: Visual Truth in the Post-Photographic Era.* Cambridge, Mass.: MIT Press.

Mitchell, William J. 1995. *The City of Bits: Space, Place, and the Infobahn.* Cambridge, Mass.: MIT Press.

Modlesky, Tania. 1988. *The Women Who Knew Too Much: Hitchcock and Feminist Theory.* New York: Methuen.

Mulvey, Laura. 1989. *Visual and Other Pleasures.* Bloomington: Indiana University Press.

Myst. 1993. CD-ROM. Novato, Calif.: Broderbund.

Nash, Jim. 1997. "Wiring the Jet Set." *Wired* 5,10 (October): 128–135.

Novak, Marcos. 1991. "Liquid Architectures in Cyberspace." In Michael Benedikt, eds., *Cyberspace: First Steps,* pp. 225–254. Cambridge, Mass.: MIT Press.

Panofsky, Erwin. 1991. *Perspective as Symbolic Form.* Trans. Christopher S. Wood. New York: Zone Books.

Penny, Simon. 1994. "Virtual Reality as the Completion of the Enlightenment Project." In Gretchen Bender and Timothy Druckrey, eds., *Cultures on the Brink: Ideologies of Technology,* pp. 231–248. Seattle: Bay Press.

Penny, Simon, ed. 1995. *Critical Issues in Electronic Media.* Albany, N.Y.: State University of New York Press, 1995.

Rath, Claus-Dieter. 1989. "Live Television and Its Audiences: Challenges of Media Reality." In Ellen Seiter et al., eds., *Remote Control: Television, Audiences, and Cultural Power,* pp. 79–95. London: Routledge.

Reeves, Byron, and Clifford Nass. 1996. *The Media Equation: How People Treat Computers, Televisions, and New Media Like Real People and Places.* Stanford, Calif.: CSLI Publications; New York: Cambridge University Press.

Reid, Robert H. 1997. "Real Revolution." *Wired* 5,10 (October): 122–127, 174–188.

Rheingold, Howard. 1994. *The Virtual Community: Homesteading on the Electronic Frontier.* New York: HarperCollins.

Rheingold, Howard. 1991. *Virtual Reality.* New York: Simon & Schuster.

Riven. 1997. CD-ROM. Novato, Calif.: Broderbund.

Rogge, Jan-Uwe. 1989. "The Media in Everyday Life: Some Biographical and Typological Aspects." In Ellen Seiter et al., eds. *Remote Control: Television, Audiences, and Cultural Power,* pp. 168–179. London: Routledge.

Rokeby, David. 1995. "Transforming Mirrors: Subjectivity and Control in Interactive Media." In Simon Penny, ed., *Critical Issues in Electronic Media,* pp. 133–158. Albany: State University of New York Press.

Rose, Al. 1974. *Storyville, New Orleans: Being an Authentic, Illustrated Account of the Notorious Red-Light District.* University, Ala.: University of Alabama Press.

Rötzer, Florian. 1995. "Virtual Worlds: Fascinations and Reactions." In Simon Penny, ed., *Critical Issues in Electronic Media,* pp. 119–131. Albany: State University of New York Press.

Satava, Richard, and Richard A. Robb. 1997. "Virtual Endoscopy: Applications of 3D Visualization to Medical Diagnosis." *Presence* 6,2 (April): 179–197.

Schwartz, Vanessa. 1995. "Cinematic Spectatorship Before the Apparatus: The Public Taste for Reality in Fin-de-Siècle Paris." In Linda Williams, ed., *Viewing Positions: Ways of Seeing Film,* pp. 87–113. New Brunswick, N.J.: Rutgers University Press.

Seiter, Ellen, Hans Borchers, Gabriele Kreutzner, and Eva-Marie Warth. 1989. *Remote Control: Television, Audiences, and Cultural Power.* London: Routledge.

Sérullaz, Maurice. 1978. *Phaidon Encyclopedia of Impressionism.* Trans. E. M. A. Graham. Oxford: Phaidon Press.

Smith, Gregory M. Forthcoming. "Navigating Myst-y Landscapes: Utopian Discourses and Hybrid Media." In Henry Jenkins, Jane Shattuc, and Tara McPherson, eds., *Hop on Pop: The Pleasures and Politics of Popular Culture.* Durham, N.C.: Duke University Press.

Sorkin, Michael. 1992. "Introduction: Variations on a Theme Park." In Michael Sorkin, ed., *Variations on a Theme Park: The New American City and the End of Public Space.* New York: Hill and Wang.

Stafford, Barbara. 1996. *Good Looking.* Cambridge, Mass.: MIT Press.

Steinberg, S. H. 1959. *Five Hundred Years of Printing.* New York: Criterion.

Stone, Allucquère Rosanne. 1991. "Will the Real Body Please Stand Up?" In Michael Benedikt, ed., *Cyberspace: First Steps,* pp. 81–118. Cambridge, Mass.: MIT Press.

Strickland, Dorothy, Larry Hodges, Max North, and Suzanne Weghorst. 1997. "Overcoming Phobias by Virtual Exposure." *Communications of the ACM* 40,8 (August): 34–39.

Tagg, John. 1993. *The Burden of Representation: Essays on Photographies and Histories.* Minneapolis: University of Minnesota Press.

Talbot, William Henry Fox. 1969. *The Pencil of Nature.* New York: Da Capo Press. [Reprint of the 1844–46 ed.]

Talbot, William Henry Fox. 1980. "A Brief Historical Sketch of the Invention of the Art." In Alan Trachtenberg, ed., *Classic Essays in Photography,* pp. 27–36. New Haven, Conn.: Leete's Island Books.

Telotte, J. P. 1989. *Voices in the Dark: The Narrative Patterns of Film Noir.* Urbana: University of Illinois Press.

Tiffin, John, and Lalita Rajasingham. 1995. *In Search of the Virtual Classroom.* London: Routledge.

Tomas, David. 1991. "Old Rituals for New Space." In Michael Benedikt, ed., *Cyberspace: First Steps,* pp. 31–47. Cambridge, Mass.: MIT Press.

Trachtenberg, Alan, ed. 1980. *Classic Essays in Photography.* New Haven, Conn.: Leete's Islands Books.

Turing, A. M. 1963. "Computing Machinery and Intelligence." In E. A. Feigenbaum and Julian Feldman, eds., *Computers and Thought.* New York: McGraw-Hill.

Turkle, Sherry. 1984. *The Second Self: Computers and the Human Spirit.* New York: Simon & Shuster.

Turkle, Sherry. 1995. *Life on the Screen: Identity in the Age of the Internet.* New York: Simon & Shuster.

Ulmer, Gregory. 1989. *Teletheory: Grammatology in the Age of Video.* New York: Routledge.

Want, Roy, Bill N. Schilit, Norman I. Adams, Rich Gold, Karin Petersen, David Goldberg, John R. Ellis, and Mark Weiser. 1995. "An Overview of the ParcTab Ubiquitous Computing Experiment." *IEEE Personal Communications.* (December): 28–43.

White, Mimi. 1992. "Ideological Analysis and Television." In Robert C. Allen, ed., *Channels of Discourse, Reassembled: Television and Contemporary Criticism,* pp. 161–202. 2d ed. Chapel Hill, N.C.: UNC Press.

Williams, Linda, ed. 1995. *Viewing Positions: Ways of Seeing Film.* New Brunswick, N.J.: Rutgers University Press.

Williams, Raymond. 1975. *Television: Technology and Cultural Form.* New York: Schocken Books.

Wright, Richard. 1995. "Technology is the People's Friend: Computers, Class, and the New Cultural Politics." In Simon Penny, ed., *Critical Issues in Electronic Media,* pp. 75–104. Albany, N.Y.: State University Press of New York.

Young, Paul. 1998. "Virtual Fantasies, Public Realities: American Cinema and the Rival Media, 1895–1995." Ph.D. dissertation, University of Chicago.

Žižek, Slavoj. 1993. *Tarrying with the Negative: Kant, Hegel, and the Critique of Ideology.* Durham, N.C.: Duke University Press.